LOOKING BACK

Editors' Selections from

50 Years

of

STUDIES

in Art Education

Kerry Freedman, Editor

NATIONAL ART EDUCATION ASSOCIATION

The reprinted articles here, which date from the 1960s, are published as they originally appeared in *Studies in Art Education*, with formatting and editorial style intact, but without abstracts. The full reference for each reprinted article is found on the first page of the chapter that introduces that article.

Table of Contents

Celebrating *Studies*

Kerry Freedman

Senior Editor, 2003-2005

This volume is a commemoration of the 50th anniversary of *Studies in Art Education*, the journal of research and issues of the National Art Education Association. In it are articles from the journal selected by Senior Editors of the journal.

Studies in Art Education is the most widely distributed research journal in our field. It is read throughout the United States and in other countries in the world where art education is studied. Having worked in over 25 countries, I have seen the positive influences of this journal on the research and teaching of preservice and in-service teachers, graduate students, and higher education colleagues. *Studies in Art Education* has long been one of the most important contributors to the international growth of art education.

The 50th anniversary of *Studies* is remarkable because of this influence on research and teaching ideas and practices—but it is also important as a symbol of professionalization in the field. When *Studies* first began, art education was at a pivotal time. The first doctoral programs in art education were developing and conducting research was becoming a defining characteristic of our work, as in other academic fields. The establishment of *Studies* indicated that the field took intellectual work seriously and that our professional organization was committed to recognizing its intellectual foundations.

The journal began in 1959 resulting from the work of the original NAEA Research Committee, chaired by Manuel Barkan (Ohio State University), and made up of Reid Hastie (University of Minnesota), Edith Henry (Denver school district art supervisor), Jerome Hausman (Ohio State University), and Vincent Lanier (University of Southern California). The Research Committee first produced a series of three research yearbooks, starting in 1954. However, members of the Committee sought a venue that would have "a continuing presence" (Hausman, personal communication) and

Kerry Freedman is a Professor of Art and Education at Northern Illinois University. Professor Freedman began her career as a K-12 art teacher. Her research focuses on questions concerning the relationship of curriculum to art, culture, and technology. Dr. Freedman has published numerous books, articles, and book chapters in art education and in interdisciplinary venues. Her work has included over 200 presentations in international contexts. As well as having been a Fulbright Scholar, she has received several national and international awards, including national Higher Education Art Educator of the Year. She is a Distinguished Fellow of the NAEA.

could be published more often in order to keep up-to-date with the developing research agenda of the field and to enable greater participation. Jerry Hausman became the first editor of the journal and initiated the idea of a short-term elected editor's position so that the journal would be 'owned' by the field at-large. A 4-year term was established so that each editor could serve 2 years as an associate editor before serving 2 years as Senior Editor. The journal began with several issues of invited articles, but is now refereed by an elected review board.

This book seeks to reveal the influence of *Studies in Art Education*. Art education is so complex that no single volume could adequately represent such influence; however, this book is made up of articles that have influenced Senior Editors of *Studies* or are overviews of work that has influenced the field. All of the living Past-Senior Editors were invited to participate in the project. Each of the Past-Senior Editors who agreed to participate was asked to select an article or two from an assigned decade of *Studies* issues for reprinting in the book and to write a short explanation of their reasons for selection as an introduction to their selection(s). Each editor's introduction reflects their perspective of the selected article and reveals, to some extent, their perspective of art education.

Senior Editors of *Studies* are elected to that post because they are leading scholars in the field. To serve as an editor of this journal is a monumental task as well as one requiring dedication to the development of research and theory in art education. Through their scholarship, as well as by virtue of being an editor of this journal, each editor has had their own, great influence on the field.

When I was invited to edit this volume, my first consideration was to explain why these historical articles are pertinent today. First, *Studies in Art Education* documents the character of the field. Several of the articles in this book are overviews of conditions of art education that help us to theorize what it means to teach and learn about the visual arts. These articles, in a sense, report on the state of the field, and reveal the ways in which the profession has grown through the decades. They illustrate, for example, that scholarly critiques of art education have become more sophisticated and that the research methods used to study the field have increased in complexity.

Second, journal authors critique the field and theorize reform, thereby making large-scale change possible. Although educational change can only happen quickly on a small scale, theorizing can enable people to envision change and open our minds to new ideas about practice. The idea of educational reform is a keystone of education in the United States; the notion of change reflects the cultural optimism of the country and is tied to other mainstream cultural ideals, such as radical individualism, a science able to solve social problems, and decentralized curriculum. Some of the articles reprinted here address issues of reform by providing a systematic critique of educational practice to broaden or otherwise change established perimeters and challenge taken-for-granted assumptions.

Third, *Studies in Art Education* focuses on teaching and learning about the visual arts and some of the articles here illustrate or recommend best practices. Interestingly, few of the articles selected are based on empirical or historical research; however, several of them discuss new ideas in their time that have become part of mainstream discourse. Like all retrospectives, this book illustrates what is valued now as well as in the past through the selection of articles about issues and topics which have become important, such as multicultural perspectives, newer technologies, and interdisciplinarity. These issues have persisted over time, in part, because they are complex and may require decades of discussion and debate.

Before becoming a Senior Editor of *Studies*, I acted as Guest Editor for an issue in 1994. That issue of *Studies* included papers by Doug Blandy, Laurie Hicks, Wanda May, Patricia Stuhr, and myself from a Super Session on the social reconstruction of art education held at the 1993 NAEA National Convention. The session was to usher in a transformation of theory and practice in art education. The roots of this change have been part of the field for a long time, as the article selections in this volume illustrate. But, a contribution of the consciousness of the 1990s was the idea that large-scale change could be shaped shaped by grassroots sociocultural critique. I asked Elliot Eisner to be the respondent to the Super Session papers, in part, because he had summarized some historical and pervasive ideas in art education that he called "myths" in a 1973-74 *Studies* article (which is reprinted following this introduction). That article led me to delineate what I saw as contemporary "myths" of art education a generation later (Freedman, 1994).

Eisner (1973-74) discussed the mythological character of seven beliefs that contributed to an emphasis on therapeutic self-expression in art education. These myths were: a) children should be left on their own to work with art materials; b) the purpose of art instruction is to develop children's general "creativity;" c) artistic process, not product, is important; (d) children perceive the world more clearly than adults; e) children's art should not and cannot be evaluated; f) teachers should not talk about art because talk ruins the effect of art; g) good art education for young children should provide the widest range of materials and studio activities possible. Eisner argued that these myths should be challenged through the development of art curriculum based on what is valued and can be known about art.

Consistent with Eisner's aims, educators shifted toward a greater emphasis on looking at and talking about art in school. However, in the process, new myths—or taken-for-granted assumptions—emerged, which I discussed in the 1994 editorial: a) art has inherent value; b) art is a universal language; c) art can be studied effectively without studying the context of production and appreciation; d) hard and fast distinctions exist between fine art and other forms of visual culture; e) the interpretation of art is the domain of art experts; f) all art can be understood through certain analytical (Western) aesthetic models; and g) art education should always start with the object. Since writing the editorial that questioned these assumptions, much has changed in response to these myths, which is illustrated by the work published in *Studies in Art Education* since that time.

Distinctions among knowledge, myth, and belief are not so clear as either Eisner or I may have suggested. And, good reasons exist for maintaining certain myths; for example, myths connect us to our past through threads of human psychology and sociology. But, the challenge facing art education is to maintain practice that aids students in their pathways to learning as we review and revise what we do for the future. That is what past articles in *Studies in Art Education* can help us to do.

The articles here chart major changes in research and theory in art education during the life of the journal from an emphasis on therapeutic self-expression, through discipline-based art education, to visual/material culture perspectives of art education. Readers of the volume will find much to reflect on. Congratulations to all involved in the publication of *Studies in Art Education.*

References

Eisner, E. (1973-74). Myths of art education. *Studies in Art Education, 15*(3), 7-16.

Freedman, K. (1994). Editorial, *Studies in Art Education, 35*(3), 131-135.

Hausman, J. (2008). Personal communication.

Examining Some Myths in Art Education

Elliot Eisner

Vol. 15, No. 3, 1973-1974

No one should underestimate the power of myths, beliefs, or convictions in shaping one's view of the world and one's treatment of new evidence. Most of us have a set of core values or beliefs that colors what we perceive, indeed, profoundly influences what we perceive. Ideas that do not fit into our existing cognitive field cause discomfort. We can deal with such discomfort in several ways. We can leave the arena in which those ideas are at play, we can transform these ideas so that they are sufficiently altered to fit into our own existing cognitive field, or we can actively appraise the ideas we encounter and reject them on good grounds, or if acceptable, alter our own field as a result of them. Indeed, an entire psychological theory called dissonance theory has been developed by Festinger (1962)[9] which explains how people cope with what Festinger calls "cognitive dissonance."

There are seven myths that seem to pervade a good deal of thought about art education. In this paper I will identify each of these seven myths, try to state their rationale as forcefully and as clearly as I can and then proceed to examine each critically. Finally I will indicate what I think a rejection of these myths implies for educational practice in the field of art education. In examining these myths, indeed even in identifying them, I am of course employing my own values and beliefs concerning the field of art education. These values and beliefs, too, are susceptible to examination. It is through tough minded analysis of existing beliefs, including one's own, that we are able to increase our clarity concerning what we are up to professionally.

The first myth can be stated as follows: "Children develop best in art if left to their own resources provided they have plenty of art materials and emotional support from the teacher." This belief stems from the concern that many art educators have that adults too often interfere with the child's natural development in art. Many art teachers have encountered cases in which children are afraid to draw or to paint and believe that these attitudes are inculcated by parents who interfere with their children in art and who do not provide the proper emotional support for their efforts. The belief is also related to a conception of human development that analogizes the child to a budding flower. The child is believed to possess a potential to become a certain kind of person and the teacher's task like that of a good gardener; it is to provide the conditions that will allow the child's potential to come to fruition.

This belief is related to a conception of child development which sees such development occurring primarily from the inside out, rather than from the outside in. In this view the goal of education in general, and of art education in particular, is to enable the potential the child possesses to actualize. This is best realized when the teacher functions not so much as a teacher as a person who sets up a rich environment and allows the child to proceed.

I know there were, and there probably exist today, many places in which such a view would serve as a needed remedy for art education programs that are authoritarian, mechanical, and insensitive to children as people. Where such programs exist such a view can be defended on instrumental grounds; it is defensible because it is needed to counteract practices in school which are too often miseducational in nature. Yet the utility of such a belief for instrumental purposes should not be confused with its long range validity. Because one recognizes that there have been situations in which children's interests and confidence in art have been stifled because programs were rigidly structured is no reason for assuming that the opposite extreme provides the optimal conditions for their development in art. The teacher who subscribes to the myth that children develop best in art if left to their own resources is reduced to being a dispenser of materials and a fountain of emotional support. But neither love nor materials are enough. Of course children's feelings and personal imagery should be considered and respected, but these conditions are starting points for educational practice not their ends. Once these conditions are provided, and I hope they would be provided in every classroom, the teacher of art can do much more than merely provide encouragement and material. What I think some people fail to realize is that the ability to perceive is learned ability. We are not born with "sight," we acquire it through experience and through trial and error. To see something is to have intellectually constructed a perceptual realization.

This proposition can be supported by a variety of studies that have been done on perception. What these studies show among other things is that the infant slowly begins to coordinate his vision and gradually begins to learn how to focus, to track moving objects, and to anticipate the visual probabilities of the environment. Later he begins to associate the noises we call words with visual forms and can eventually use those words as substitutes for those forms. When this occurs the perceptual processes tend to be put in the service of concept formation. Once an object has been labeled the label is most frequently used for purposes of recognition. (1934)[4] And when recognition is the driving motive the enrichment of perception through visual exploration is diminished. Art teachers have an enormous contribution to make to the growing child by helping him to keep his visual explorations going. In schools, with their great emphases on reading skills and the recognition of words, there is a tendency to underplay the education of perception. In such schools, concept replaces percept as rapidly as possible.

Similarly the ability to use one's percepts as sources for art, whether those percepts be those that are secured from the external environment or from the eidetic imagery all of us have, requires an ability to create visual struc-tures that will carry those images and the feelings pervading them forward. This usually means the ability to take some material and to be able to use it as a medium of expression. Without the skills necessary for making such a transformation, the material never achieves the status of a medium and the ideas, images, and feelings the child has remain locked within the psyche, unable to take shape as a public form.

Now it should be clear especially to those who have worked long and hard on the problems encountered in painting, sculpture, graphics and the like, that the skills needed for artistic expression are not acquired simply by getting older. Artistic development is not an automatic consequence of maturation. On the contrary, many of the skills art teachers and artists possess were taught by people more competent at the time. Many of the skills were acquired through self instruction: by ruining some expensive sheets of water color paper, by having a clay sculpture crack in the kiln, by seeing a pot collapse on the wheel. It was from these kinds of experiences as well as the experiences secured by seeing really competent and inspired work that learning occurred.

Why should it be assumed that children need so much less?

I must confess that I am always puzzled by the insistence of so many nursery and infant school teachers that children need to use upright easels to be able to express themselves in art. Those easels are generally set up at an 80 degree angle, a sheet of newsprint is clipped on at the top, thin tempera paint is provided and finally camel hairbrushes which usually have little or no resiliency are handed out. No experienced painter would consider working in such a situation but five year olds, it seems, must cope with running paint on a sheet of paper not intended for paint in the first place; while he uses brushes that cannot be managed or controlled, all in the name of "free expression." The point here is that the ability to use visual form as a vehicle for expression is in large measure a learned ability and that the teacher has a much more complex task than simply providing materials and encouragement. Positive teaching does not have to be insensitive or mechanical. Without such teaching, students I fear will continue to come out of the schools with a conviction that develops at about age nine or ten: that they have neither ability nor a keen sense of satisfaction from the visual arts.

A second myth in art education is one that holds that, "The major function of art education is to develop the child's general creativity through art." The argument for this belief goes something like this: art is intimately related to the creative process since without the exer-cise of creativity there can be no art. Since the vast majority of children will not become professional artists it would be foolish to try to use their creativity as an instrument for producing art. The other way around is better. Art can be used to develop their general creativity. Furthermore, since all children possess creative potential and since that potential is not likely to be realized if the constraints of logic and rule weigh too heavily upon the child, a freer, more permissive alternative seems in order. It seems reasonable to assume that art is a perfect vehicle since it not only is nonverbal and alogical but also pre-verbal. Art activities can tap feelings and creative resources that are not likely to be reached by the more academic disciplines. Art in the schools, therefore, has its greatest contribution to make when it unlocks and nurtures the creative potential that each child possesses. An American writing in a recent issue of *INSCAPE* the Journal of the British Association of Art Therapists (1971)[11] says:

Today there is an obstruction to the true growth and development of students at all age levels by the continuous imposition of verbal knowledge and techniques by educators of most academic subjects. Even the concern of art educators with the correct use of art materials and the development by their students of acceptable art products is often over-emphasized at the sacrifice of the originality and uniqueness of each student's personality and development. Any detailed discussion of the methods of training art educators to release spontaneous art expression from the unconscious has, because of the required brevity of this paper, been postponed for the discussion period. During the discussion I would like to go into the matter of specialized art training of art educators as a means of helping them release the repressed and unconscious emotions of students into spontaneous verbalization and free art productions. [p.21-22]

Thus the idea that art teachers should be part therapist and part mid-wife in the service of mental health and creativity has been salient in the literature of art education. Art education, the belief holds, makes its greatest contribution when it unlocks the child's creativity.

Well, what's wrong with such a belief.

Creativity is a good thing, isn't it? Of course creativity is a good thing (except in spelling, perhaps). But art educators have no special monopoly on the development of creativity. Any field well taught can in principle develop the child's creative ability in that field. Why should art educators make their claim to educational time and money by resting their case on a contribution that a wide range of other fields can also claim to make?

Now I happen to believe that the formulation of objectives for any educational program in any field of study requires not only an understanding of the characteristics of the field, but an understanding of the pupils and the society in which they are living. What is educationally valuable depends in significant measure on whom something is intended for. Furthermore while one might agree that something is good for someone or some group, educational decisions always require that some consideration be given to the issue of priorities. Something might be considered quite valuable, but not more valuable than other things. Thus one cannot prescribe a single goal for art programs for all children for all times. Responsible educational planning requires diagnosis of the situation and a formation of priorities.[10] Yet, in general, for pupils in an "abstract" sense, I would argue that art educators have not only something valuable to offer to the young; but something unique as well. What is it that art teachers can contribute that no other member of the school's staff is likely to provide? Surely it is not the development of creativity. What competent teacher of science would not claim that the development of the child's creativity in science was not an important objective in his field? And if art educators respond by saying, "We are concerned not merely with developing creativity in art but with developing the general creative ability of students," I can only point out that there is precious little evidence that this can in fact be done. The range of transfer of creative ability may be narrower than we might like to believe.

I said that art educators have distinctive contributions to make. What are those contributions? I would identify three. First, I believe that art educators can develop and refine perception so that the world can be encountered and experienced as aesthetic form. A biology teacher can help students see a tree, for example, as a species of living things, a historian as a legacy of another age, a chemist as a collection of molecules in motion; but only an art teacher is likely to help children to see it as an expressive visual form. Certainly biology, history, and chemistry teachers can also marvel at the expressive qualities of trees and even help children see such qualities; but when they do this they teach not biology, history, or chemistry, they teach art. It will pay us in the field of art education not to con-fuse their roles with ours, nor our roles with theirs. Second, art teachers can help children transform their ideas, images, and feelings into some public visual form. No other member of the staff is professionally responsible or trained to do this. Third, art teachers can help children appreciate the relationship between works of art, large and small, and the culture in which they were made. Understanding this interaction is one of the conditions of liberal education.

These contributions, I believe, are not marginal niceties in educational programs but values whose priorities ought to be very high indeed in most educational hierarchies. Learning to see the expressive power of visual form is an ability usefully satisfying throughout life. Being able to utilize expressive modalities other than the linguistic ones that now saturate schools provides options that expand human freedom, and the appreciation of art's relationship to culture illuminates man's nature in ways different from those that sociology and philosophy provide. Creativity is important but I do not believe its development is our major mission.

A third myth in art education is the belief that what's important in art education is process not product. I cannot count the times I have heard this little slogan uttered as though it were a profound philosophic insight. This myth, related to the one on creativity, argues that what is educationally significant for children is the process they undergo while making something, not what it is that they make. It is argued further that when attention is devoted to the product rather than to the process the child's growth is likely to be hampered; one would be, so to speak, keeping one's eye on the wrong target. It's not what a child makes but how he makes it that is important.

I will not take the tack that just the opposite is true. I will not argue that the product is what's important, not the process. I won't do this because I believe that dichotomizing process and product is wrongheaded to begin with. In the first place, there can be no product without some type of process. The processes we use at whatever level of skill shapes the qualities of the product that will be realized, whether that product is ideational or material. Similarly the product or end-in-view that we aspire to create shapes the means we employ and provides a criterion against which choices in the present are made. Further unless some of us here are mind readers we will never be able to see the processes the child is undergoing. What we see are the manifestations of those processes: what they produce. It is from these products that we are able to make certain inferences about process. To disregard what the child produces puts us into an absolutely feckless position for making inferences about those processes. In addition without attention to what is produced we have no basis for making any type of judgment regarding the educational value of the activity in which the child is engaged. Process and product therefore cannot be dichotomized. They are like two sides of a coin. Processes can be improved by attending to the product and products improved by making inferences about the processes. To neglect one in favor of the other is to be pedagogically naive.

A fourth myth in art education is the belief that children see the world more clearly than adults. The argument goes that children's perception is not jaded as is adults'. They have not acquired the habits that keep the eyes from seeing and the heart from feeling. Because of their youth they can see freshly, noticing those things that are oblivious to adults because of the perceptual ruts into which most adults have fallen.

Because of this belief some art educators have urged that adult visions of reality should not be imposed upon the young which in practice has meant that adult art should not be shown to children lest it influences them. I am told, by a person who as a child studied in Franz Czicek's classes in Austria that he disallowed adult art in the studio. His objective, like the objectives of other art educators was to keep the child's painting and drawings naive and spontaneous. The presence of naivete and spontaneity testified to the fact that the teacher had not intervened and that the child's view of the world remained child-like. The childlike vision of reality and his depiction of it is a value that adult artists seek to achieve in their own work. The tragedy, the argument goes, is that this freshness and spontaneity in both perception and production is stifled as children go through school. By the time children are eight or nine, rigormortis has already set in; by adolescence the corpse has begun to smell.

It is curious that such a belief should be subscribed to in the face of so much evidence that indicates that the refinement of perception is a gradual achievement and that highly refined perception often requires years of intensive work. Gestalt theorists such as Rudolf Arnheim (1964)[2] have pointed out that perceptual development is not due to the perception of atomistic units which eventually constitute a whole, but due to the gradual differentiation of previously undifferentiated wholes. Our earliest perceptions as infants are of differences between light and darkness. As we get older we learn to see more and more in the things we thought once to be simple. Perhaps this is the truth in the sage's comment to an impatient questioner when he said, "Ask the young, they always know." Perhaps this is also the reason why experts tend to see a wide spectrum of grays in the situations they study. Black and white answers to complex issues generally reveal both poor insight and poor eyesight.

One serious argument to support the belief that children's perception is more compre-hensive than that of adults has been developed by Anton Ehrenzweig in his very inter-esting book, *THE HIDDEN ORDER OF ART.* (1967)[6] Ehrenzweig argues that until children are about eight years of age their perception of the world is syncretistic, a type of seeing in which the child scans wholes and identifies telling cues which allows him to see rela-tionships that analytic vision does not see. Analytic vision, which Ehrenzweig says begins about eight and which tends to dominate adult perception, is a type of perception which is highly focused and controlled by logic and discursive reason. Analytic vision does not scan rapidly but builds up element by element. Although I believe that Ehrenzweig's efforts to explain children's perception is both serious and imaginative, I think much of it is theoretically faulty and at times contradictory. For example in one chapter he says,

The child's more primitive syncretistic vision does not, as the adult does, differentiate abstract details. The child does not break down the shape of some concrete objects into smaller abstract elements and then match the element of his drawing one by one. His vision is still global and takes in the entire whole which remains undifferentiated as to its component elements. [p. 6][7]

So far, so good. This assertion is consistent with Gestalt theory. But later in the same chapter Ehrenzweig says:

A young baby will smile at a terrifying crude mask if only it has certain minimum cues suggesting the mother's face, but will show signs of fear if the cues are missing. This recognition of objects from cues rather than from the analysis of abstract detail is the beginning of syncretistic vision. [p. 15][8]

What is curious here and contradictory is that the perception of cues from a whole requires an act of differentiation, an analytic feat; yet this is precisely what Ehrenzweig says does not happen in describing syncretistic vision earlier in the chapter.

There is no question that perceptual habits such as the perceptual constancies that we experience, those arising from expectation and those that are a function of "einstellung" or set, do impede the perception of certain features of the visual field. Art education can help people overcome these habits in those situations where they are a hindrance, but one need not include that because such habits are not as strong for young children therefore they see more than adults. Children's more global perceptual tendencies frequently have two important consequences; they lead them to neglect what is detailed in a later pattern and they lead them to miss seeing what is qualitatively subtle. I consider it to be one of art education's major functions to foster the type of perceptual learning that will make vivid what has been overlooked or neglected. This type of perceptual achievement results from learning how to see, both analytically and synthetically. The art teacher can play a critical role in helping students acquire the tools which make the analysis and synthesis of visual qualities possible.

A fifth myth in art education is that teachers should not attempt to evaluate work in art since the child's mind is qualitatively different from an adult's. This belief is not only related to the notion that adults cannot see the world as children and vice versa; but also that art, unlike spelling and history, is an individual and personal thing and should not be evaluated by someone other than its creator. The argument proceeds that the imposition of external criteria are not only inappropriate to the nature of artistic activity but that they generate anxieties in children that block the pathways that must remain open for creative activity to result. After all, why should a child of seven, nine, or even eleven years of age be evaluated in art? Isn't this one of the few places in the en-tire curriculum where children should be unfettered, free of artificial or conventional standards and rules. What is being sought in art is a personal and authentic response not the production of prede-termined forms to be measured and graded like eggs or cheese.

The fact that people who argue that children's art should not be evaluated, are among the first to exclaim their outrage when they see work that they consider tight does not seem to pose a problem for them. The fact of the matter is that evaluation, even for those who claim not to do it, is being done all the time. I would go even further and say that not to evaluate children's art, even if this were possible, is to be educationally irresponsible. Education is a value oriented activity. As teachers we are concerned not simply with bringing about change; but with bringing about *desirable* change, improvement if you will. If a teacher does not evaluate what children do, how can he determine if what he is doing is contributing to or hampering their growth in art? Of course imposition, interference, and insensitive appraisal can hamper the child's development in art; but anything can be done badly.

The recognition that insensitive teaching can be miseducational is not an argument against teaching, it is an argument against a certain kind of teaching. The same holds true in the area of educational evaluation. In addition the constant approval of what children produce, regardless of its quality or the effort that went into the work, may backfire as far as the student is concerned. If anything he does, regardless of how trivial, is met with "that's fine, won't you tell me about it," he is likely to conclude that there can't be anything important about what he's doing. Children respect thoughtful evaluation and criticism because it testifies to them that their teachers are taking them and their work seriously.

There are a variety of things that can be evaluated in the teaching of art. With respect to the product that the child produces one can appraise its creativity or ingenuity, one can evaluate its technical competency, and one can assess its aesthetic quality. With respect to the child, one can appraise his apparent satisfaction with his work, his engagement in it, and the insight revealed by his comments about his own work and the work of others. In this latter area, Brent Wilson (1966)[13] has done some very interesting and useful work in classifying what children see and what they say about visual form. Far from functioning as an ostrich and putting one's head in the sand, art teachers should, I would argue, carefully evaluate their student's work and behavior not only because such an appraisal can be helpful to the student directly; but because it provides the data necessary for responsible improvement of curriculum and teaching. The data secured through evaluation tell us as much about the wisdom of the decisions we have made as teachers as it does about the performance of our students.[12]

A sixth myth in art education is the belief that teachers should not attempt to talk about art since verbalization usually kills art. The argument for this belief is that art is after all a non-verbal activity that yields a non-discursive form. The best way to appreciate such forms is through direct visual experience, not through verbal analysis. Such analysis, because it requires the application of verbal categories, is inappropriate and alien to art. It pulls the work apart into the categories that constitute verbal language and thus eviscerates any sense of organic unity that the work might have possessed. Furthermore schools are at present over saturated with verbalization. There is nothing so characteristic of schools as their bookishness. Why should a nonverbal area like art be made to suffer the slings and arrows of words in an institution that already is drowning in language and whose rewards are too narrowly confined to those with verbal skills.

I would be among the first to agree that words cannot adequately replace the work of visual art as a source of aesthetic experience and insight. If works of visual art could be duplicated by discourse the uniqueness of and need for visual modes of expression and communication would evaporate. But there are words and there are words. Verbalization can interfere, even block, any aesthetic experience a student might have had with a visual work or it can provide the cues many people used for having such experience in the first place. Critics, the people whose professional responsibility it is to talk about art, should aim at vivifying one's perception of the work of art. Criticism, Dewey wrote, has as its end the re-education of the perception of the work of art. (1934)[5] When this end is attained it is because the critic has functioned as an aesthetic mid-wife whose language has enabled the individual with less experience than he to have a live birth. The language used by the critic is not intended as a surrogate for the work but as a set of pointers that illuminate aspects of the work that are likely to be missed. Such a function is as important in helping an American appreciate the finer points of English soccer as it is in helping an Englishman appreciate the nuances of an end run from a split T on an American football field. Verbalization kills art when the talk is incompetent or inappropriate for the level at which the student is, not because it is talk. The teacher of art can do much more than stand in mute silence before a work of visual art, whether it's the work of his students or those found in the great museums of the world. Learning to talk about art insightfully, poetically, and sensitively is one of the great educational needs in the preparation of art teachers. It is, alas, one of the areas most neglected in teacher education.

Finally, a seventh myth in art education that I will identify is the belief that "the best curriculum in art for primary school children is one that provides the widest variety of materials with which they can work". The argument for this belief is based upon the conviction that it is good for children to have an opportunity to explore different materials because it helps sensitize them to a variety of textures and problems and provides new avenues for self expression. Each new material has particular tactile and tensile characteristics. What better way to help children expand their awareness of these characteristics than to have an opportunity to work with them in the classroom? Diversity of materials expands the child's experience and the expansion of experience is clearly one of the major aims of education. The late Manuel Barkan (1962), one of the most perceptive students of art education in America, writes of this belief:

> Any careful reading of the current literature in art education, both in books and in periodicals, would lead to the inescapable conclusion that virtually all art educators believe in using a variety of art media. Indeed, I don't think that I am overstating the case by saying that a great many art teachers judge the effectiveness of their teaching in terms of the number of different media they include. The more media they provide, the better they think they are teaching; the more varieties of media their children experience, the better they assume the learning to be. Talk to a great many art teachers and by all means, talk to most undergraduate students who are

preparing to become art teachers, and ask them to tell you something about a good art education program. Almost all will place experience with a wide variety of media uppermost on their list of values. Most of them are on a perpetual hunt not only for media but also for new ones. [p.15]

Now the expansion of human experience through schooling is a laudable goal. Insofar as the experience is positive and contributes to growth who could argue against it? But there is a confusion Manny Barkan pointed out in equating width and depth of experience with the number of art materials or types of art projects one encounters in school. Brief excursions into new materials and projects so characteristic of primary school art education in the United States often limits rather than expands experience, since by moving from one project to another on a week to week basis the child seldom has the time to acquire the skills necessary for using the material as a medium of expression. Most often the youngster is so preoccupied with managing the material that little is left over for attention to expressive or aesthetic considerations. What we often forget is that because each new material makes new demands upon the child, he needs to have the time to become sufficiently acquainted with it to be able to use it as an extension of his self. The hustling of children from one material or problem to another on a weekly or bi-weekly basis is one of the best ways I know of to insure triviality in an art program. Expression in art is not to be equated with merely pushing around paint or clay; but using it, controlling it, and knowing when and how to take advantage of the happy accidents that occur during the course of one's work. Expression is the conversion of a material into a medium. That conversion is not likely to occur if the development of skill is aborted by skittering from one material to another.

Now the reason that so many primary school art programs are calendar-governed and project-saturated is not simply because teachers believe children should work with a variety of materials. It also is because many teachers do not know what they are after in art education and focus therefore on activities or projects. It is also because so many teachers run out of steam after a project is introduced. Since they do not know how to help the child move the project forward or how to build upon it, they do the next best thing: they introduce a new activity or a new project. This pedagogical tactic is reasonable in view of their abilities but is a stop-gap measure at best. Too often it is legitimized on theoretical grounds, even when those grounds will not withstand analysis. Although as a general rule I would not endorse it, I believe a richer art program can be provided by basing a curriculum on drawing alone than by introducing children to a new project or new material each week.

These then are some of the myths in art education that I have encountered over the past decade. Each has, I believe, influenced the teaching of art. I do not believe that this field can grow either theoretically or practically if we do not examine our beliefs with all the clarity we can muster.

Endnotes

[1] The original version of this paper was prepared for delivery at the School of Art Education, Birmingham Polytechnic, Birmingham, England.

[2] Arnheim, Rudolf. *Art and visual perception.* Berkeley & Los Angeles: University of California Press, 1964.

[3] Barkan, Manuel Transition in art education. *Art Education,* 1962, 15(7), 15.

[4] Dewey, John. *Art as experience,* New York: Minton, Balch & Co., 1934. (Especially

[5] Chapter I II for an elaboration of the distinction between perception and recognition.)

[6] *Ibid.* Especially Chapter XIIL

[7] Ehrenzweig, Anton. *The Hidden order of art.* London: Weidenfeld and Nicholson, 1967.

[8] *Ibid.* 6.

[9] *Ibid.* 15.

[10] Festinger, Leon. *A Theory of cognitive dissonance.* London: 1962.

[11] In the United States this process has come to be known as "needs assessment."

[12] Naumberg, Margaret. *The need for a deeper psychological awareness for art teachers. INSCAPE Journal of the British Association of Art Therapists,* 1971, 3, 21-22.

[13] This is a basic notion in the field of curriculum. For too long educators have considered examination scores simply as indices of pupil performance. They are, one can argue, significant indicators of the effectiveness of the school.

[14] Wilson, Brent. An experimental study designed to alter fifth and sixth grade students perception of paintings. *Studies in Art Education,* 1966, 8(1), 33-42.

Selections
from the
1960s
1970s
1980s
1990s
2000s

STUDIES
in Art Education

Jerome Hausman

Editor, 1959-1961

ARTICLE SELECTION

Embler, W. (1960). Frescoes for September. *Studies in Art Education, 1*(2), 5-9.

Like many in the field of art education, I am drawn to present-day discussions seeking to expand our field so that we can accommodate the fantastic and far-reaching changes in our visual world. New media and techniques as well as changing social and environmental circumstances are forcing a reappraisal of how and what we are teaching. I find myself drawn to a continuing interest in the dynamics of how we see and respond to objects and events in our lives.

A book that I have found fascinating is T. J. Clark's (2006), *The Sight of Death: An Experiment in Art Writing*. In January 2000, Clark served a "six-month stint" at the Getty Research Institute. His project was most interesting and involved maintaining a diary of descriptive notes and reflections on two Nicolas Poussin paintings *(Landscape with a Calm* and *Landscape with a Man Killed by a Snake)*. His daily journal entries became the content for the book. Changing circumstances in encountering the works, observations and reflections about the paintings' details, comparisons and discoveries with the passage of time all combined with sustained looking to lead to an unfolding of different thoughts and ideas. It is this kind of attention that has all but disappeared in a world of instant messaging and fleeting imagery.

This is the reason I am calling attention to Weller Embler's "Frescoes for September." As he put it: "If we are wise we shall revisit the world. And while we are there, we shall try to keep a nice balance between the inner and the outer, between thought and fact, between our fondness for the world and knowledge of ourselves" (p. 6).

Jerome Hausman, the first editor of *Studies in Art Education,* was Director of the School of Art, Ohio State University. He was Professor at New York University and Consultant to the JDR3rd Fund's Arts in Education Program from 1968 to 1975. Between 1975 and 1982, he was the President of the Minneapolis College of Art and Design. Hausman edited numerous NAEA publications: *The Journal of the NAEA; NAEA Yearbook* (1959), *Research in Art Education; Report of the Commission on Art Education* (1965), and the *Report on the Conference on Art Criticism and Art Education* (1970) with D. Ecker and I. Sandler.

Technological advances have brought about changes in what we do and how we think. Technologies have become extensions of humans. Most important we should recognize that we are being changed by our technologies. A recurring theme in literature is the "robotization" of human beings. This is what makes it more essential that distinctively human sensitivities be recognized and utilized as a balance in the dynamics of our thoughts and actions. As Embler concludes:

to exist is to touch with our minds the reality of the world. To exist is to hear the dead leaves tremble as they fall softly in the September afternoon, tender farewells whispered across the gentle air ... to exist is to name the objects of the world, to shape the unshaped, to make substantial the unsubstantial. To exist is to know the reality of the not-me objects, that they are the varied forms taken by divine spirit, the divine influence which is permanent and inexhaustible, which is concealed in the thing but is also found out in the thing, released into the knowing which is our knowing and our knowledge. (p. 8-9

Reference

Clark, T. J. (2006). *The sight of death: An experiment in art writing.* New Haven: Yale University Press.

Frescoes for September

Weller Embler

Sometimes in the journey through life we become suddenly aware that we have lost touch with reality—with that out-thereness which is not ourselves, which we have abandoned in favor of our own inner person. The world ceases to exist for us. It is a blur of things. The world outside is a dark wood laid with many traps and snares. We devote ourselves to our inner being, dallying and playing with it, musing and meditating upon it. We thought we could understand the world if we looked within to see what is going on inside ourselves, only to discover that we have lost contact with reality and that a consuming loneliness has descended upon us.

The sense of reality, of otherness, is necessary to human health. Childlike wonder about the world which is not myself, an out-going preoccupation with the world and its contents is resurgent; it comes and goes in the history of peoples and places. It is, for instance, the spirit of classicism, and "Classicism is health," said Goethe. If we are wise we shall revisit the world. And while we are there, we shall try to keep a nice balance between the inner and the outer, between thought and fact, between our fondness for the world and knowledge of ourselves.

And yet, reality! What is the real? In order to repossess the world, its dimensions, its continuity, its not-me objects, I walk often in the Park, and the world for me is composed of the river, the trees, the fields of the Park and its walks, the autumn sky like a baroque ceiling, the apartment buildings of the Drive in a variety of styles facing the Park and the river, the elm-lined promenade, men and women sauntering, idling, children running, playing, dressed in many colors, always returning somewhere, like a fugue, the dilletant strolling, taking in the genius of the place, the boy and girl hand in hand, the student reading, mothers gossiping. A low parapet of granite lines the promenade, and over it vistas of the river and the shore beyond appear through the white ash and buttonwood trees. The birds hold congress overhead among the branches of the tulip trees, and the pigeons are at home on the grass and walks of the Park. Self-possessed boats pursue the highway of the river, and automobiles hurry along the drives and parkways. The leaves of the trees, of the elms and the oaks, the sweet gum and black locusts cast shadows in park-like pattern. Iron fences mark the path I often walk, street lamps, shrubbery—the privet and the hawthorn—compose themselves in pictures before me as I sit on the park bench watching the pageant—the trees, the sky, the river, the bridge, the people, the boats; and all the shapes and outlines of the various world stretch with spacious intent to the north, to the bridge, and to the south to the open mysterious expanse of water that I know is somewhere beyond. All this, I say to myself, is the world, and I am in it, a part of it. The scenes of the park are not the same twice over. I like them best by night when they are sometimes soft and misty sketches, vague poetic outlines melting, if one is in the mood, into some picture which suggests the possibility of an essence in the composition, some Olympian design meant to charm the eye and agitate the mind, an essence arising out of this arrangement of world shapes. The thought is probably absurd. We tend to make too much of what is quite simple enough for our daily purposes. The picture pleases? Very well, then. Why twitch at the curtain and peek behind the scene? Nevertheless, when the tableau of night presents itself framed in purple velvet, the lustre of street lamps like chains of necklaces embracing the city, I am irresistibly moved to reflection, and I ask why this should be so evocative, I ask the meaning of this little drama of appearance so delightful to the inner as well as to the outer eye.

By day the sights seem more real. Light is our natural element.

I see the young oak for what it is. All objects are clear in the noonday sun. I see them easily and directly, the granite walls, the river, and the tower of the Church lofty above the September foliage. Let us be perfectly serious. These things are clear to me and so, curiously, is the idea of them. Their essence, by a careful attention of my mind, is known to me. They are ideal things—ideal in themselves, the beautiful objects of the world, traceable to my sight, tangible to my touch, knowable to my mind. Yet there lingers a question in the trembling air, a question like hovering smoke or lucent sounds dropping in the noonday sun. How shall I see these objects. What is their secret, the secret of myself, the secret of the locust tree; for surely, as I live, there is a silence of the hidden which like a magnet draws my mind toward it but will not yield its mystery.

Sometimes I see the scenes of the Park as painters have taught me to see them—bold, forceful masses of color, strong shapes asserting themselves, a dashing world; sometimes I see them as soft still shapes shimmering in the violet air, on the brink, as it were, of a revelation; sometimes the scenes are reticent pen and ink drawings; sometimes I see only a colorful poetic effusion, sometimes the tension of powerful structures built mass upon mass. But mostly, on the mall, by day or night, the trees arrange themselves along the walk just as I have seen them in Seurat's famous painting, indubitably objects of the world mingling with the people promenading, telling the story of their existence in their way, the right way (or so it seems to me when I am in this mood), the only way for them, being what they are. And yet I am not satisfied. The pictures fade into the light of common day, and the mystery and the silences remain.

Sometimes the sights from the granite ramparts surprise in me memories of music, of tinted chords hanging over the river, the trees, the lamplit promenade. By day I listen to sunny sounds, blithe and debonaire, a nimbus of music around the gay aimless walkers, the children with their mothers or their nursemaids, strolling, capering, taking in the sights, happy in the sunshine. At night I hear notes melting into one another as the yellow streetlights across the river melt into the night and into the dark waters of the river. Melodies and tender sounds hang in the night air.

At times I hear plangent echoes and metallic phrases in the rhythm of the traffic lights, dots here and there of red and green and yellow in a dancing pattern. And sometimes the night is ripped by violence, as though the screams of dying things were crowded along the walks and alleys, through the fields and upon and down the river.

September poses many questions, philosophical problems. But the world is cunning and plays with me as a knowing man would play with an unknowing child. (On a crisp November day, for instance, when the sun is a bright disk, when the leaves are gone and the trees stand like sticks stuck here and there in the ground—silent sleeping trees without life enough to dream, with no secret, having given their secret to the earth for safe winter keeping—all the philosophical questions dissolve as though they had never been, as though if they did exist, it was I who had made them up, ideas with which I played like a child. Only the river and the cloudless sky and the bare locust trees and the granite ramparts exist in the certainty of the sun, sleeping a winter sleep.)

In the quiet of the September evening when I sit in the city Park musing on the scenes before me, I know there is a perfection in them. They speak brightly of it and daily show it forth. The band of blue night stretching across the sky, the black shapes of trees against the twilit horizon, and the expanse of the dark river streaked with silver tell me that the sign is also the thing it stands for. The river scene is as it is and that is its idea. There is no secret, no silence. But there is that which is concealed and which can be found out and expressed—in music, in painting, in architecture, in words. It is not perhaps that words stand for something else, or that a painting stands for that which it depicts, or that the black locust stands for the perfect and ideal tree as that these things are perfect in being perfectly what they are. They are themselves the revelation of that which was hidden until they came into being through some creative act of the universe.

Why do we stand astonished before a work of man's hands and his imagination if not because it has shaped that which was not heretofore in existence, had not yet been created out of the fruitful nothingness. There is always perfection; we have but to make it shine in a creation, though it be no more than the creation of a city park with its myriad scenes of charm and beauty, though it be no more than the rain-drenched locust alive in the world, its spirit transformed into the thing itself. May not the same be said, then, of the spirit, that it exists in all its perfection and that we may know it creatively and give it life in the world through our own expression of it, as in a beautiful act, as in human love, as in a work of art, as in a profound thought? The spirit is real, as the locust is real. The universe is spirit, and its epiphany is in that which is, in the 'stone, in all living things, in the locust tree, in the painting by Seurat, in the bridge, in the poem. To exist is to touch with our minds the reality of the world. To exist is to hear the dead leaves tremble as they fall softly in the September afternoon, tender farewells whispered across the gentle air. To exist is to read the mystery of the blue, lamplit band of night that stretches between dark pillars of oaks and weeping beech trees. To exist is to name the objects of the world, to shape the unshaped, to make substantial the insubstantial. To exist is to know the reality of the not-me objects, that they are the varied forms taken by divine spirit, the divine influence which is permanent and inexhaustible, which is concealed in the thing but is also found out in the thing, released into the knowing which is our knowing and our knowledge.

D. Jack Davis

Senior Editor, 1975-1977

ARTICLE SELECTION

Lowenfeld, V. (1960). Creative Intelligence. *Studies in Art Education, 1*(2), 22-25.

The first decade of the publication of *Studies in Art Education* (Autumn 1959–Spring 1969) represented a landmark in the field of art education, providing a scholarly venue that was devoted exclusively to issues and research in the field. One hundred thirty-six (136) articles plus editorials, comments on articles, bibliographies, research reviews, project abstracts, and book reviews were published in the first ten volumes. These covered a broad range of topics and included both issue articles and research reports. Among them were the nature of the discipline of art education; research and research needs of the field; how art related to a variety of human characteristics and personality traits; the nature of art at various levels of education and for various types of individuals; investigations of teaching methodologies; the various ways that individuals learn, solve problems and visually express themselves; art history and aesthetics; and international art education. The dominant methodologies used in the research reported were quantitative ones. A few historical studies were included; however, there was a noticeable absence of research studies that used qualitative methodologies, in contrast to current research published in *Studies*.

Given the breadth of topics and the roster of authors, which includes legendary figures in the field, selecting one contribution from the first ten years of publication for inclusion in this book was a daunting task. The selection of "Creative Intelligence" by Viktor Lowenfeld was guided by the current rebirth of interest in the topic of creativity,

D. Jack Davis is Professor of Art and Director of the North Texas Institute for Educators on the Visual Arts at the University of North Texas (UNT). During his 38-year tenure at UNT he has served as Vice Provost of the University and as Dean of the School of Visual Arts. He has authored more than 40 publications and presented more than 70 papers at professional meetings. A lifetime member of NAEA, he has served on many committees for the organization. He currently chairs the Trustees of the National Art Education Foundation.

the seeming lack of acknowledgment that there is a rich history of activity in this area in the field of art education, and the frequent occurrence of the concept in the articles published in the first decade of *Studies* (26). This article clearly meets two of the selection criteria for articles to be published in this book: (a) the author is highly regarded, and (b) it establishes an idea in the field. Viktor Lowenfeld is widely acknowledged as the most influential art educator of the 20th century (Chapman, 1982). Because of his influence, this article, no doubt, has had an enormous impact on the work of many others. It also establishes the beginning of an idea that has become prevalent in the field—multiple intelligences. In the article, Lowenfeld recognized the need for a change in direction in approaching the study of creativity, noting that "mere observation and experience had to be replaced by controlled research" (Lowenfeld, p. 22). Recognizing that individuals like Torrance, Getzels, Jackson and others "have given us evidence that creativity and intelligence, as measured by our common tests, are different traits" (Lowenfeld, p. 22), Lowenfeld concludes that creative intelligence may well be one of the unique contributions of art education to general education.

This brief article was the only one that Lowenfeld published in *Studies in Art Education,* as his untimely death occurred in the same year that it was published. Had he lived, it goes without question that he would have been a frequent contributor to *Studies.*

References

Chapman, L. (1982). Foreword by Laura H. Chapman. In J.A. Michael (Ed.) *The Lowenfeld lectures* (pp. ix-xiii). University Park & London: The Pennsylvania State University Press.

Creative Intelligence

Viktor Lowenfeld

Time and again in this Sputnik inspired era of creativity supposedly new discoveries have been made in regard to the creative mind which for the teacher in the arts have long been common knowledge. That our I.Q. tests do not assess the creative mind is not surprising to the art teacher for all along he knew that Johnny may have an excellent scholastic record—"a good mind"—without ever having the urge to express himself creatively. He also knows that some of his most creative pupils are not necessarily the outstanding ones in their intellectual pursuit for knowledge. All along we have also been conscious of the fact that the quality of the work of the artist does not depend on his intellectual sophistication. We have witnessed that both, naive and great minds have given us great works of art. In short, we knew that, at least in the visual arts, creativity and intellect are not necessarily related.

In this creativity and research conscious era, however, mere observation and experience had to be replaced by controlled research. Studies by Getzels,[1] Jackson, Torrance,[2] Burkhart,[3] Taylor[4] and others have given us evidence that creativity and intelligence, as measured by our common tests, are different traits. Taylor[4] in a recent presentation made "a sharp distinction" between "the gifted" and "the creative." In his opinion the word "gifted" has been tied too much to high academic performance "whereas with some exceptions, most school-like activities are not creative in nature." It is, indeed, not new that intelligence tests measure only a small segment of the human mind, completely neglecting the creative aspects of it. What is new is that this fact has been confirmed by research and that educators and psychologists are giving it increasing attention. It is also relatively new that attempts have been made to find criteria which more closely define the creative mind and which may lead to a better understanding of the unfolding process of the creative potentials in individuals. Any breaking down of generalities into their detailed components not only create greater sensitivities but help to raise the level of understanding from a mere intuitive, accidental, to one of a more controlled nature. A clearer distinction between academic intelligence and creativity then has helped greatly to better understand the contribution of both for human growth.

While such a distinction appears to be necessary, for matters of clarification, it seems to me important to stress not only the differences but also the similarities and especially to clarify some aspects which may be misleading particularly to educators. I am referring here to the misunderstanding that academic intelligence may be an achievement of the mind and that creativity may "merely" be part of the intuitive unconscious faculties, somehow on a "lower level" of human activity. This is far from being so.

In fact, both activities, although different in nature, are to various degrees activities of the human mind. Intelligence as well as creativity are essential to human growth. In the same way as we can differentiate between potential and functional intelligence, we can distinguish between potential and functional creativity. In both instances, we presume that there are greater potential abilities in every individual than those which actually are available to him for usage, that is those which function. Education, in both instances, tries to unfold the potential abilities in man in order that he may use them. Thus, it is one of the foremost tasks of education to develop all potential abilities in man and make them function. This should be true not only for the intellect but also for the unfolding of man's creative potentialities.

It seems to me essential for the understanding of both to know that intelligence, at least in its academic interpretation, is based on the assessment and use of facts while creativity greatly depends on the use and application of sensitivities. In the same manner as the nature of the intellect may be naive or sophisticated or any mixture of it, also the nature of creativity may be naive or sophisticated or both in an infinite variety of degrees. In German there is a word for the naive wisdom of the "uneducated." It is referred to "Bauernschlauheit," the shrewdness of the peasant, or also to "Mutterwitz," the wit which is obtained by living, through mother as it were, and not acquired through education. Creativity on a naive level is best seen in primitive and folk art and also in the art of children. Its use and application differentiates itself mainly from the sophisticated in its uncontrolled and uncritical application. It is interesting to note that in both instances our common available measurements would fail to assess the naive mind, for in intelligence as well as in creativity most of our tests are based on an average "educated" population, or better on "academically educated" individuals. Yet in all instances, we deal with activities of the mind even if the emphasis in intelligence may be more on assessing facts *objectively* while in creativity the weight may be on the *subjective use* of sensitivities and their flexible and fluent application. Even intuition, an important part of creativity, is a complex and involved activity of the mind, consisting of such factors as the ability to take advantage of continuously changing situations.[5]

It is needless to say that also in purely intellectual activities sensitivities are used. However, these sensitivities are quite different from those applied in creative activities, especially in the arts. Usually we define *intellectual sensitivity* as the ability to distinguish from a bulk of knowledge what is essential from what is non-essential for its understanding and communication. What is essential indeed changes from problem to problem. However, on all levels of intellectual sophistication it can be objectified. It can be measured. Many mathematicians when confronted with an equation will have to arrive at the same result in regard to what is essential and what is non-essential for the solution of the problem. Although their approaches may differ, their final results will be the same. What is essential for the expression of the aesthetic experience, however, changes not only from individual to individual, from medium to medium, from one stage of growth to the other, but also from experience to experience. A six year old who was guided by his father across the street felt the big hand of his Dad when it held his little hand. He felt it almost disappearing in the "big hand" of Dad. Essential for his expression (although unconscious in nature at this stage of naive expression) was a big shape representing his individual concept of the "big hand" of Dad and a tiny shape in it representing his own "hand." It is needless to say that what is essential for the expression of aesthetic experience refers not only to the kind of expression but also to the medium with which it is expressed. Thus, the ability to differentiate the essential from the non-essential in creative activity, especially in the arts, is highly subjective and in as much as it changes for each individual expression, it is most difficult to assess. It is then this highly differentiated form of activity, the ability to relate expression and medium so intimately and uniquely to each other that they are so essential to each other that none can be replaced, which constitutes, creative intelligence. That in this continuous search for such unique relationships, the creative individual becomes completely involved in his search for "subjective truth," or as Barron[6] reports, that he has an "intense aesthetic and moral commitment to his work," is self evident. However, what is surprising is the neglect of recognition of the meaning which creative intelligence has for education and society in general. It is indeed important for learning to assess facts objectively. But is it not equally important for education to emphasize what is essential for one's own individual expression? Does not life to a great extent consist of the eternal search for "what is essential to me?" And is it not equally important for our democratic thinking not to neglect the sagacity, the wisdom of the naive, as well as the creativity of the unsophisticated? We have preached individual differences, and have too often served conformity. Creative intelligence as the sensitivity which is necessary for the differentiation of what is essential from what is unessential for the individual's own mode of expression may well be one of the unique contributions of art education to general education, for creative intelligence is essential for the creative expression during all stages of growth of the naive as well as the sophisticated.

Endnotes

[1] Getzels, J.W. and Jackson, P.W. "The Meaning of "Giftedness"—An Examination of an Expanding Concept," *The Phi Delta Kappan.* Vol. XXXX No.2, 1958.

[2] Torrance, Paul E. "The Social Strategy of the Highly Creative Child," *Creativity Conference.* University of Minnesota, 1959.

[3] Burkhart, Robert C. An Analysis of Individuality of Art Expression at the Senior High School Level. *Research in Art Education.* 9th NAEA Yearbook, 1959. Washington, DC.

[4] Taylor, Calvin W. "Identification of the Creative Individual," *Creativity Conference.* University of Minnesota, 1959.

[5] Lowenfeld, Viktor. "Creativity and Art Education," *School Arts,* October 1959.

[6] Barron, Frank. "The Disposition Toward Originality," The 1955 University of Utah Research Conference on The Identification of Creative Scientific Talent. Brighton, 1955.

ARTICLE SELECTION
Ecker, D. (1963). Some Inadequate
Doctrines in Art Education and
Proposed Resolution. *Studies in
Art Education*, 5(1), 71-81.

Jerome Hausman

Editor, 1959-1961

How many times have we heard it said: "it's all a matter of timing"? Each of us has seen instances when an individual is "carried forward" by the tides of circumstance. George Kubler (1962) observed:

good or bad entrances are more than matters of position in the sequence. They also depend upon the union of temperamental endowments with specific positions. Every position is keyed, as it were, to the action of a certain range of temperaments. When a specific temperament interlocks with a favorable position, the fortunate individual can extract from the situation a wealth of previously unimagined consequences. (p. 7)

My "entrance" to the field of art education, more than 50 years ago, was one in which I encountered prevailing doctrines as identified by David Ecker: (a) we believed in developing the full potentials of the child; (b) we believed in educating the whole child; (c) we believed the art teacher understands and meets the needs of the child; (d) we believed in teaching according to developmental levels; and (e) we believed in promoting creativity through art. At the time, I thrived on these beliefs. However, Ecker's article begins by pointing out that these relatively unquestioned assumptions have at least one feature in common: "they confuse facts and values."

With the passage of time, we can see clearly that intervening factors have radically altered the context in which 'art' is being created, experienced by others, and taught. The larger context of art education is in flux. The very notion of 'art' is now seen as an essentially contested concept. New media and technologies have made possible radically different forms. Our social, cultural, and economic circumstances have made possible new and expanded roles for artists in community settings.

Such circumstances and events exert forces that alter our notions of art and art education. We need to continually examine prevailing doctrines for teaching of art. Ecker's article illustrates this by shifting emphasis from Lowenfeldian doctrine to the idea of

Jerome Hausman, the first editor of *Studies in Art Education*, was Director of the School of Art, Ohio State University. He was Professor at New York University and Consultant to the JDR3rd Fund's Arts in Education Program from 1968 to 1975. Between 1975 and 1982, he was the President of the Minneapolis College of Art and Design. Hausman edited numerous NAEA publications: *The Journal of the NAEA; NAEA Yearbook* (1959), *Research in Art Education; Report of the Commission on Art Education* (1965), and the *Report on the Conference on Art Criticism and Art Education* (1970) with D. Ecker and I. Sandler.

"qualitative intelligence." He points out that "qualitative ordering is not confined to painting, sculpture, and drawing activities." The "doors of possibility" are open to many forms and eventualities. Of course, art teachers will continue to instruct in methods, materials, and techniques, but the end-in-view is not limited to particular outcomes. As Ecker stated, we seek "general formulations as prescriptions for directing qualitative intelligence." The outcomes resulting from such instruction will be as varied as the people and contexts involved. After all, quality can be manifested in many ways. As art educators, we should welcome the possibilities afforded by diverse media and ideas. Ecker's conclusion is straightforward and open-ended: "We believe art education ought to play a major role in the development of that qualitative intelligence which is engaged in refining itself, even as it extends its bounty for the refinement of others."

Reference

Kubler, G. (1962). *The shape of time: Remarks on the history of things*. New Haven: Yale University Press.

Some Inadequate Doctrines in Art Education and a Proposed Resolution

David W. Ecker

EDITOR'S NOTE: An address given to the Annual Convention of the Indiana Art Teachers Association, April 19, 1963, Bloomington, Indiana.

> *Man is the only animal that laughs and weeps; for he is the only animal that is struck by the difference between what things are and what they ought to be.*

In this discerning observation of human nature, William Hazlitt, the great Romantic English literary critic and art connoisseur, captures the essence of what I have to say. My charge is that our central doctrines of art education have failed to account for the difference between "what things are and what they ought to be." These doctrines have failed to distinguish between the "is" and the "ought," between fact and value, between means and ends. This intellectual fallacy results in a failure to give art teachers *direction*, a sense of purpose at the present crucial period in the history of art education. If Hazlitt's turn of phrase gives the essence of my resolution of this inadequacy, my task is to provide its substance. To extrapolate from Hazlitt, *art teachers* are not laughing or weeping nearly enough.

My strategy is as follows: First, I shall try to persuade you that our central beliefs, our basic premises, our relatively unquestioned assumptions about the teaching of art, have at least one feature in common-they confuse facts with values. I shall argue that these doctrines are inadequate primarily because of this confusion. Secondly, I shall briefly review the major alternative approaches to a conception of the relationships between facts and values. Finally, I shall outline a new proposal for art education, a new doctrine if you wish, that I believe *will* provide direction for teachers of art.

I

Art education doctrines, like all doctrines, are not merely matters of fact to be checked out against the evidence, although they may rest on factual information. Doctrines arise because of some human need or problem; and, ideally, they function to give purpose and direction to human endeavors. They provide a focus, a rallying point, for organized group efforts in a particular area of shared experience. Thus, in my effort to persuade you of the inadequacy of our doctrines, I shall not cite facts, nor report on experiments, nor quote authorities—not many of them anyway. My initial critique will center upon inherent contradictions, false analogies, equivocations—in short, upon the logical fallacies contained in these doctrines. Of course, the optimistic assumption underlying all of my arguments is that any normal, sane, rational person would not willingly harbor fallacies in his thinking once they are exposed; he would be persuaded to reject them.

Since the notion of logical contradiction will carry a heavy burden in the discussion, it would be well to review it briefly. We recall that the Principle of Noncontradiction states that no statement can be both true and false. For example, a person is either brave or not brave. No degrees of braveness will change the law. That is, once we decide on the meaning of "brave," and fix conditions of time and place, we cannot argue both that a person is brave and not brave.

Which leads us to the first doctrine: *We believe in developing the full potentials of the child.* Almost in the same breath art teachers add, "and his aesthetic potential is developed in the art room." This doctrine, I'm sure, goes back to Aristotle and his acorn. The acorn does have a potential, if by potential we mean: *If* an acorn is provided certain nutriments—soil, water, air—it will *then* become an oak tree. However, the analogy between the acorn and a child begins to break down when we note that, unlike acorns, children have grown up and will probably continue to "grow" into quite diverse "species" of adults. Thus, when educators persist in drawing this false analogy, the genuinely alternative human products issuing from various kinds of schooling are slurred over. We fail to see that there is a *choice* in potentials: the child can be taught to be dishonest and deceitful, *or* he can be taught to be honest and straightforward. Each is a potential, but the realization of one precludes the attainment of the other. To affirm statements of educational goals that include both possibilities is to harbor a contradiction. It is therefore *logically* incorrect to assert that we should develop the *full* potentials of the child; the teacher must encourage some potentials at the expense of others. Indeed, she must suppress certain potentials. If an advocate of this doctrine were to reply, "Oh, but no one could justify the teaching of dishonesty," this would be begging the question. Or, rather, *another* question concerns the respective *values* to be placed on contradictory, competing, or alternative educational goals or potentials; e.g., the justification of an art education for children. Our first doctrine fails us at precisely this point.

One may plead that the preceding argument is built solely around the ambiguity of the word "full" in the expression, "full potentials." So let us examine a closely related doctrine which has been fully elaborated upon in educational literature. It is: *We believe in educating the whole child.* Viktor Lowenfeld states this fundamental theme early in his book *Creative and Mental Growth:*

> Because every creative process involves the whole child and not only a single segment of him, art education may well become the catalyst for a child-centered education in which the individual and his creative potentialities are placed above subject matter; in which his inner equilibrium may be considered as important as his scientific achievements. Later, Lowenfeld declares that an educator's aim should be to achieve an "integration" of the seven "segments" of the child; the "intellectual," "emotive," "social," "perceptual," "physical," "aesthetic," and "creative."

Lowenfeld's basic injunction for art teachers is, of course, one of the most insistent claims to be found in education circles: the necessity of teaching "the whole child." The "whole child" has become some mystical, non-empirical entity to whom educators are forever offering invocations; often in order to justify the inclusion of that subject in the curriculum in which they have a special interest. It has long been believed that art in the public schools is justified in precisely this manner. Yet what is this "whole child"?[1] Can it be the addition of his intellectual, emotive, perceptual components; or his weight, height, pulse rate, metabolism, and the electronic impulses in his central nervous system? There are disciplines which provide scientific knowledge about these matters. But can the stuff of this data be considered as *components* of the human to be taught? Do they add up to a single and unified organization which it merely pleases educators to name the "whole child"? And can it be said that, when available knowledge from these disciplines is added up, a scientific conception of "the human" is the result? *What science can be said to do this?*

There is the possible claim that science can only *approach* the whole, in which case we have a judgment about science that is itself exempt from scientific canons; that is, the judgment is offered as a true statement of the relationship between science and something called "whole," but whose truth or falsity as a statement is incapable of being determined. While it is commonly accepted that the educational undertaking is primarily the modification, alteration, or directed change of what is called the "human," or the "child," educational theory has yet to define scientifically its unique subject matter. The terms "whole child" and "human" taken from ordinary language function as ritualistic slogans, rather than conveyors of scientific meanings. But since ordinary language contains much terminology that is scientifically meaningless, vague, or ambiguous, it fails to provide explicit and commonly understood directives for the profession. Under the rubric "educate the whole child," *any* activity the child is able to participate in—swimming, stone throwing, hopscotch, or swearing—is as much justified as is art activity. Again, facts are confused with values; what the child *can do* is mistaken for what he *ought to do.*

A further difficulty is to be found in Lowenfeld's conception of the role of the art teacher, although almost any textbook in art education would illustrate the third doctrine as well. It is: *We believe the professional art teacher understands and meets the needs of the child.* Now, does the teacher actually have a choice either to meet the "creative needs" of the child wherever they may lead, or to teach him according to adult objectives? Is not the notion of "creative needs" an adult notion?[2] Lowenfeld claims that, "The student has to be guided *in the direction* of *his* thinking," (Lowenfeld's emphasis) and that, "In evaluating a product of art, it is the teacher's task to find out whether the child or youth has reached *his own standard.* This is not always easy."[3] (Emphasis added.) The confusion is established further by a proposal for *adult standards:* "In evaluating the organization of a child's creative work we shall consider three major points: (1) How meaningful to the child are the areas of the picture? (2) Did the child follow a mode of expression consistently? (3) Is the work a coherent whole?"[4] Scattered throughout the book are evaluation charts, lists, and tables for the use of adults. My point here is that teachers logically cannot abscond from their responsibility for determining the nature and direction of the learner. The effort to be morally neutral is expressed in the statement that art teachers must not "impose their wills on the child." However, this injunction is simply another proposed way of influencing the child, and when affirmed it is an adult standard. Whatever may be the facts about children's needs, artistic or otherwise, the art teacher still has the *moral* problem of deciding which ones to cultivate and which to deny.[5]

Closely allied with the "needs" doctrine is a fourth and perhaps the strongest doctrine of all, coming as it does from educational psychology:

We believe in teaching according to developmental levels. Since Lowenfeld has probably done more to promote this doctrine in art education than anyone else, I again turn to his form of the principle. Lowenfeld claims there are ascending "mental levels" of "Scribbling Stage," 2 to 4 years; "Preschematic Stage," 4 to 7 years; "Schematic Stage," 7 to 9 years; "The Gang Age," 9 to 11 years; and "The Stage of Reasoning," 11 to 13 years. The hierarchy of developing mental stages continues in "The Period of Decision: The Crisis of Adolescence as Seen in Creative Activity." In this latter stage there is "The Psychological Change in the Imaginative Concept," and throughout all the stages there develop two distinctive types of children: the "visual" and the "haptic."[6]

Now, as to the question of whether there are, in fact, "visual" and "haptic" types, or whether there are "mental levels" is a matter for *empirical* confirmation. My quarrel centers on the *logical* error of presenting certain preselected facts of child growth and development as criteria to guide the teacher's evaluation of child growth and development. My point is that the so-called descriptive categories to be found in "growth" charts already reflect hidden values; the kinds of facts presented in each category have already been prescribed. Here is another case of an uncritical "ought" being converted to an alleged scientific "is." Because values are thus disguised as scientific facts, they avoid critical examination and are readily accepted by art teachers. On the other hand, even if it *were* possible to describe all the facts of child development, we would still be left with the job of deciding which kinds of development we should promote. Remember that Fagin and Bill Sikes were two excellent teachers of the fine arts of pickpocketing and housebreaking, respectively. They well understood that Oliver Twist was precisely at that developmental stage which included such features as nimbleness, small body, capacity for stealth, sufficient motor coordination—all facts which they highly valued for the performance of their art forms. Why aren't pickpocketing skills included in our "growth" charts?

Since these skills are *not* selected for inclusion in charts, scales, and guides for art teachers, we must restrict our examination to those behaviors that *are*. This inevitably leads us to a fifth doctrine, the one receiving the most attention today: *We believe in promoting creativity through art.* Now, the current uses of the word "creativity" are notoriously misleading because of their ambiguity; the word is typically employed in such a manner that it can be taken to have one or another of several possible meanings, ranging from the artistic to the theological. Here I am concerned with only one ambiguous usage: where the so-called "facts" of creativity in art are described or illustrated in charts that are then used to distinguish the "creative" from the "noncreative" child-a rigorous form of value judgment. The most well-known art educator who claims his criteria are based on scientific evidence is, of course, Lowenfeld. So I again turn for an example to his use of the doctrine.

Lowenfeld's basic confusion rests, I believe, in his confounding of aesthetic with psychological categories: he confounds the *art styles* to be found in the art work of children-styles which he claims can clearly be called abstract, realistic, etc.,—with the "subjective feelings" of his two psychological types of children—the "haptic" and the "visual." Throughout his charts Lowenfeld tends to place a higher value on *less representational styles* by including in his checklist such words as "inclusion of self," "free lines and brush strokes," "free from inhibitions," "self identification," "sensitiveness," "independence," "originality," "creativeness," "imaginative," "intensity of experience," "subjective color," and "absence of schemata." For the *more representational art styles* he reserves words with negative connotations: "stereotyped," "mere objective reports," "stiffness," "rigid," "schematic," and so on. This prompts the challenge: does the "visual" child stop having "subjective feelings" when he paints realistically, or are his feelings just naturally inferior to those of the "haptic" child who paints abstractly? I suspect that the trouble lies not so much with the children as with the charts.

Make no mistake, I am not suggesting that we should solicit more realistic artwork from children. (Personally, I prefer their nonobjective work.) What I am trying to indicate is that the words in these charts are neither primarily descriptive of children's art work, nor descriptive of their "subjective feelings." Rather, they are preferential; they guide the value judgments of art teachers. But the value judgments of teachers are being structured by words in charts which reflect values that are not themselves the consequence of ethical inquiry. The categories dividing up children's artwork are *not* the results of critical examination of the alternative values that have been or could be placed upon the facts about ways children paint, draw, or sculpt. These categories merely represent implicit values or attitudes held toward children's work. To say of Johnny that he is creative is, under normal conditions, to *praise* his artistic behavior, not merely to *describe* it. However, creativity is not just naturally good; Willy Sutton was certainly a creative bank robber, as the Boston police well knew. The point is that social values must be brought into play to determine what *forms* of creativity ought to be encouraged-and which forms discouraged-in education and society. Thus, for teachers to say that they "promote creativity" is inadequate justification for the practice of art education; for again ethical problems are buried under the apparent facts of creativity.

II

For the sake of clarity, we cannot delay any longer an examination of the distinction underlying my analysis of each of these five doctrines: the difference, as Hazlitt put it, between "what things are and what they ought to be." By way of a warning, however, I must remind you that there are other ways of distinguishing "fact" from "value"—ways alternative to my own—which offer impressive credentials. These approaches characteristically take the form of a dichotomy which, once accepted, presents an unbridgeable gulf between fact and value. Some of these are: "physical· mental," "tangible-intangible," "objective-subjective," "logical-psychological," and "material-spiritual." By definition they deny the possibility of human mediation between facts and values.

The motives for proposing these dichotomous categories are varied.

The Idealist tradition supports the notion that ultimate values are "non-natural" and somehow *revealed* to man; they come from an intuitive or transcendental source. These values (allegedly justified by nonscientific methods) are thought, thereby, to be protected from scientific assessment. On the other hand, the philosophy of Scientific Realism tends to argue that values are *discovered* in nature, thereby identifying values with natural "goods," or with the facts of human desires. The underlying motive here, apparently, is to preserve the notion that human preferences are expressions of the inner reality of humans and, hence, by definition, these preferences are certified by "nature."

The distinction I propose, while accepting a naturalistic account of the relationship between facts and values, is located in the Experimentalist philosophical orientation, which holds that values are *created* by men in order to meet their problems and needs. I support the major value premise that ultimate moral authority ought to rest with humans striving to solve their problems through shared inquiry. My factual premise is that there is no warrant for *any* values outside of human intelligence, including those values employed as bases by opposing philosophies to give sanction to their own points of view. Indeed, the opposing philosophies are in the curious position of having built *with their intelligence* a structure of ideas which, while warranting their own value schemes, at the same moment asserts the impossibility that such a structure can be built by mere human intelligence.

For the remainder of this article, I shall incorporate the Experimentalist meanings for "value" and "fact," rather than their classical meanings; thus, I will attempt to show continuities between *ends* and *means,* while yet functionally distinguishing between them. My motive or purpose is to point to a new direction for teachers of art.

III

One of the traditional aims of education has been to develop, unfold, or release human intelligence. In this historic view, intelligence is generally conceived as consisting of the rational or reasoning powers of man. The conception of intelligence, which is equated with cognitive activity, is usually joined with the idea that reasoning at its best is a means by which man can get to know reality, the nature of the good, higher truths, or God. This "absolute knowledge," valued as the most worthy of human goals or ends, is to be achieved by dialectical, deductive or *a priori* methods of discursive thought. But whatever spiritual values are obtained by this kind of thought are more than offset by the notorious failure of these dialectical methods to solve the insistent and demanding problems of men-the problems of survival in the face of the vicissitudes of nature, as well as the problems of associative living. In striking contrast are the enormous successes of the empirical method and procedures of modern science in solving many of the problems of this world, among them the control of disease, maintenance of a food supply and adequate shelter—even the problem of national defense, where the most abstract of the physical sciences have practical bearings on human affairs. Thus, scientific knowledge is instrumental; it is valued as a *means* rather than as an ultimate end. If an "ultimate" *end* be sought, perhaps a plausible candidate would be human intelligence itself. The success of science has persuaded some contemporary educators that the method of science is the method of intelligence. Indeed, Dewey argues that the method of science originates from the practical affair of living; it is the method of experience made explicit and more refined for the purpose of gaining more control over the means and ends of experience.

What is to be noted about the alternative values placed upon intelligence in the history of education is that formal schooling has traditionally directed human intelligence toward the "oughts" and the "ultimate" goods of life—sometimes, as of yore, to the rewards of a "life hereafter"—typically separating these ends from the practical, daily means of existence. The first is spiritual; the second is corporeal. The rejection of this dualism which sets ends apart from means stems from the practice and conclusions of science. A scientific alternative to dualism holds that goals are obtainable only as we have hypotheses that direct us to perform those operations which conceivably secure the ends sought. Thus, means and ends are not to be taken as dichotomous, but rather as functionally related items to be identified in inquiry. *Intelligence, as here conceived, is the procedure of ordering means to ends; it involves purpose and control.* Intelligence is always an affair of experience; it is a dynamic process which arises from past experience; it acts significantly to modify the context of present experience; and it is assessed in terms of its consequences in future experience. It is, then, a reconstructive, creative activity whereby present materials (alternative means) are selected and rejected on the basis of whether they will secure anticipated futures (selected ends).

The question arises as to how, or in what sense, can the past and future be available in a given present. What is the material mediated? The answer given by some investigators is that the materials of intelligence, or purposeful thought, are *symbols*. That is, the past and possible futures are *represented* in the present. Materials in the present signify either events already taken place or imagined future events.

If intelligence can be fairly described as the relating of means to ends, is it also fair to hold, as traditionalists often do, that intelligence is exhausted by and limited to rationality, to the manipulating of linguistic symbols—words or numbers? It would seem that such human activities as sports, games, hunting, the fine arts, and warfare contain examples of both purposes and controls which *do not* primarily involve linguistic materials. Yet materials *are* manipulated; means *are* related to anticipated ends. For example, a spear fisherman assembles his diving gear—a mask, compressed· air gun, flippers, aqua-lung (he rejects a rod, reel, and net)—as appropriate means for his anticipated ends; his quarry, a deep sea bass (not seaweed, coral, or plankton). Other means employed are the techniques of submerging, swimming, and breathing, while stealth and attentiveness characterize his actions. Were he able to speak as he acts, he could probably describe his intentions, doubts, fears, and choices among possible maneuvers. Yet, while he may think the words "bass," "undertow," "riptide," "shark," "danger," when the referents for these words are not present, he may also think or "picture" the non- present referents themselves. This is *prima-facie* evidence in support of the claim that means- ends orderings that are not linguistic are present in experience. Apparently, purposive behavior or activity is not limited to overt linguistic behavior, or even to unspoken verbal thoughts, but includes imaginative, pictorial, or other orderables. "Planning-seeking-spearing fish" behavior, since it is not random, but a case where means and ends are selected and rejected, is also a mode of intelligence.

A host of problems now present themselves. If logic is the normative science which yields controls or regulations for valid reasoning-the kind of thought which consists in the manipulation of propositions—then what is it that acts to regulate or control such nonverbal, purposive behavior as I've described? If there are other than the controls for knowing, are they symbolic? If there is more to intelligence than knowing, what is the significance of this idea for art educators? Can the controls over *artistic* means—ends orderings be located?

I think they can and have been located.[7] There is abundant evidence in art history that artists do order lines, textures, volumes, and colors as qualitative *means* to achieve their qualitative ends-objects that we call examples of "Impressionist," "Constructivist," and "International" styles of painting, sculpture, and architecture, respectively. We can pin these labels on art because critics have provided us with these theoretical symbols, each of which refers to a pervasive quality characterizing a series of art works. However, the critic's naming activity comes *after* the creation of what is named; e.g., the label "Cubism" appeared on the scene subsequent to the appearance of the quality pervading the paintings of Picasso, Braque, and Gris in the first decade of this century. I am suggesting here that the availability of labels for styles—or titles for individual works—is not a necessary condition for one's being able to locate the artist's nontheoretical control; the controlling quality is already empirically available. Further, I am claiming that the pervasive quality acts as a *qualitative criterion* by which the artist selects, rejects, and relates qualitative means, from among available qualities, to achieve his qualitative end-in-view. His criterion and his method are as one.

Now, qualities to be considered as *symbols* must be shown to act in a representing or mediating capacity. At the same time, they must be distinguished from cognitive or "theoretical" representation and mediation. In support of the idea of "qualitative symbol," we may profitably consider the possible intention behind this amusing and paradoxical statement:

"If everything we perceived were white, there would be no white." "White" as a term, here, would be meaningless; since it apparently refers to everything, it thereby refers to nothing. We see that a quality is distinguishable only as there is a relationship or contrast noted, say, a white figure on a blue ground. However, to *distinguish* a color is not necessarily to *name* it. In fact, we do not have enough color-words in the English language to name even a small part of the colors artists have created, discriminated, and ordered in their work. The labels on paint tubes do not assist in the artist's qualitative task. So I think we have a qualitative symbol when a quality represents the relationship which would present it, the relation which established it as a distinguishable characteristic in the world. This triadic relation generates quality as symbol. While a theoretical symbol represents anything *other than* itself, a qualitative symbol represents a system of relations in which itself is included, i.e., the qualitative symbol presents itself and represents the relation of contrast. Hence, artistic ordering may be properly viewed as an example of *qualitative intelligence.*[8]

To generalize these findings, in both linguistic and qualitative ordering, the distinctive feature of human conduct is its symbolic structure; the ends-in-view, objectives, or intended futures are represented in present conduct through the office of symbols, which are in some sense an outgrowth of past experience. Our task is not only to describe the controls actually at work in art, but also to propose reconstructions of those controls which are to be used for the purpose of future orderings. Moreover, it is essential to realize that qualitative ordering is not confined to painting, sculpture, and drawing activities. It is going on in the classroom, in the playground, and in life, but does so, for the most part, unattended. That is, qualitative orderings have not received systematic attention from educators, schoolmen, or art teachers; this mode of intelligence has been neglected in educational theory and generally ignored in practice. It is because education is essentially a *moral* undertaking that the kind of reconstructive activity I have proposed is so vital-one in which art teachers should be engaged. The consequences to be expected of this kind of inquiry are general formulations as prescriptions for directing qualitative intelligence. It is precisely this kind of inquiry that has been so lacking in the central doctrines of art education.

If we are struck by the contrast between the present state of affairs in art education as compared with a vision of what ought to be, then, according to Hazlitt, we should be weeping. Better, we should be seeking to reconstruct the means and ends of our field. To sum up the range of ideas I have presented here, I offer to art teachers the following credo:

We believe art education *ought* to play a major role in the development of that qualitative intelligence which is engaged in refining itself, even as it extends its bounty for the refinement of others.

Endnotes

[1] Lowenfeld, Viktor. *Creative and Mental Growth.* Third edition. New York: The Macmillan Company, 1957. p. 11. The importance of Lowenfeld's contribution to art education is so great that any criticisms I may bring to bear on his ideas can only serve to honor his service and memory.

[2] *Ibid.,* pp. 62-3.

[3] *Ibid.,* p. 63.

[4] *Ibid.,* p. 64.

[5] See Childs, John L. *Education and Morals.* New York: Appleton-Century-Crofts, Inc., 1950. Chapters I, II, and IX.

[6] Lowenfeld, *op. cit.* The quoted material is sub-chapter and section headings.

[7] One may find in John Dewey's essay, "Qualitative Thought," perhaps the earliest original source of ideas in the English language relevant to the task of building a methodological conception of artistic control; *i.e.,* its means-ends and method. The range of ideas in this document focuses on his central theme that " ... the immediate existence of quality, and of dominant and pervasive quality, is the background, the point of departure, and the regulative principle of all thinking." Further, he states, "Construction that is artistic is as much a case of genuine thought as that expressed in scientific and philosophical matters, and so is all genuine aesthetic appreciation of art, since the latter must in some way, to be vital, retrace the course of the creative process." (*Philosophy and Civilization.* New York: Minton, Balch & Company, 1931. p. 116.)
Dewey's suggestions and methodological analyses of controlled production in the arts, found scattered throughout his writings, have since been so revised and critically extended as to have yielded certain fundamental changes in the Deweyan formulation of the philosophy of experimentalism. This work was initiated by F. T. Villemain in "The Qualitative Character of Intelligence," and continued by N. L. Champlin in "Controls in Qualitative Thought," both unpublished dissertations, Columbia University, 1952. See also their article, "Frontiers for an Experimentalist Philosophy of Education," *The Antioch Review,* 19: 345-359; 1959. Of further interest is "John Dewey Centennial:
A Special Section," co-edited by Villemain and Champlin, *Saturday Review,* November 21, 1959, pp. 16-26. This manifesto draws the broad implications of the notion of qualitative intelligence for American education, as does Villemain's article, "Democracy, Education and Art," *Educational Theory* Vol. XIII, No. 4, Fall 1963. For a technical and analytical statement, see Villemain's "Methodological Inquiry into Aesthetic Subject Matter," *Proceedings of the Seventeenth Annual Meeting of the Philosophy of Education Society,* Detroit, Michigan, March 26-29, 1961, pp. 151-167.

[8] Qualitative intelligence understood as qualitative symbolic mediation is, of course, derived from the above sources and has provided the specific motivation and direction for the writer's own work in "Toward a Methodological Conception of Problem and Control in Art Education," unpublished dissertation, Wayne State University, 1962, and other papers; e.g., "The Artistic Process as Qualitative Problem Solving," *The Journal of Aesthetics and Art Criticism,* 21: 283-90; Spring 1963.

Selections from the

1960s
1970s
1980s
1990s
2000s

STUDIES
in Art Education

ARTICLE SELECTION

Efland, A. (1976). The School Art Style: A Functional Analysis. *Studies in Art Education*, 17(2), 37-44.

Laura H. Chapman

Senior Editor, 1977-1979

Arthur Efland's article on the school art style appeared in a special issue of *Studies* for which Brent Wilson served as guest editor. The whole issue offers new perspectives on child art created in and out of school, but Efland's article became a landmark. It is still cited in efforts to make art education more responsive to the lives of students and more relevant to practices in the multiple art worlds beyond school.

Efland draws on concepts from cultural anthropology and sociology in order to disclose how the culture of schooling sustains differences between the manifest aims of education (e.g., cognitive development, participation in a democratic society) and the latent function of schools (socializing the young to accept authority). His analysis of school art shows that schools impose many more rules on students and teachers than are typically acknowledged in rhetoric about creativity and self-expression.

Efland succeeds in positioning school art as inauthentic, insular, self-replicating, and distant from the lives of students and contemporary practices in art. By implication, reforming art education in schools would entail more flexible scheduling, freedom of choice in media and thematic content, wide reaching studies in art history (including contemporary art), and critically informed perspectives on art beyond formalism. Some of these ideas were evident in Barkan's (1966) concept of discipline-centered art education where, in theory, professionals in the art world would serve as exemplary sources for rethinking curricula and instruction.

Laura H. Chapman, a consultant and writer on arts education, is based in Cincinnati, Ohio. Her teaching experience ranges from preschool to adults in a variety of settings including Indiana University, The Ohio State University, University of Illinois, and University of Cincinnati. She has been a consultant for the National Endowment for the Arts, Educational Testing Service, National Instructional Television, and The J. Paul Getty Trust. In 2000, a national panel selected her *Instant Art, Instant Culture: The Unspoken Policy for American Schools* (1982) as a "Book of the Century in Education." She is a Distinguished Fellow of NAEA.

More fundamentally, Efland questions whether the hierarchical structures embedded in schooling can ever be hospitable for art education. In this respect, his scholarship serves the interests of those who wish to see local artists and arts agencies enter schools as provocateurs of arts-centered "whole school" reform (e.g., Eisner, 2002; Rabkin & Redmond, 2006). The issue of authenticity is also at the center of claims that de-schooling art education, making it a voluntary pursuit, may be wise and encourage diverse communities of practice, unencumbered by theory associated with schooling (e.g.,Anderson & Milbrandt, 1998; Blandy, Bolin & Congdon, 2001).

The continuing citation of Efland's analysis of the school art style is evidence of its enduring value, even in international contexts (e.g. Hardy, 2006). His article highlights two central and still debated issues: (a) what counts as "authentic" art education in and beyond schools, and (b) who gets to decide.

References

Anderson, T. & Milbrandt, M. (1998). Authentic instruction in art: Why and how to dump the school art style. *Visual Arts Research,* 24(1), 13-20.

Barkan, M. 1966. Curriculum problems in art education. In *A Seminar in Art Education for Research and Curriculum Development,* (240-255), Edward L. Mattil, Ed., U.S. Office of Education Cooperative Research Project No. V-002. University Park: Pennsylvania State University.

Blandy, D., Bolin, P., & Congdon, K. G. (2001). *Histories of community-based art education.* Reston, VA: National Art Education Association.

Eisner, E. (2002). *The arts and the creation of mind.* Chapter 4, What the arts teach and how it shows (70-92). New Haven, CT: Yale University Press.

Hardy, T. (2006). *Art education in a postmodern world: Collected essays.* Bristol, England: Intellect.

Rabkin, N., & Redmond, R. (2006). The arts make a difference. *Educational Leadership,* 63(5), 60-64.

The School Art Style: A Functional Analysis

Arthur Efland

It's Thursday, and the fourth grade class is happily marching to the art room. The children are glad, because for a whole hour they can forget about reading and mathematics and take up with the enticements of colored construction paper, papier-mache, paint, and clay. The teacher greets the art teacher with a cheery "Hi, Mona. Am I glad you have them now. They are higher than kites". Then she says halfway apologetically, "I hope you won't mind, but Johnny has remained in the room to finish his reading. He was out a lot with flu, and he's fallen behind." The art teacher really does mind, but she has been on friendly terms with this teacher for a long time, so she lets it go.

In this fictional account a phenomenon that recurs with great regularity in the life of an elementary art teacher was depicted. The art teacher is the recipient of a double message. On the one hand she is valued as a member of the school staff by students and professional peers; yet, she also is told that her subject, art, is not as important as are other subjects. In the example above she and the classroom teacher acted as though they believed this to be true. Even so, her services are valued. Time spent in art provides students with needed release. The teacher is relieved from the duties of maintaining control over a large, slightly unruly class, and hence is free to provide remedial reading to a youngster that had fallen behind.

That art is not regarded as the most valued of school subjects is driven home with repeated regularity in hundreds of thousands of incidents like the one above.

If art is less valued than reading, why does the school try to find time for art? Why is it missed when it is not in the curriculum? What I want to focus upon, then, is the phenomenon of school art, what it is, and what it does.

School art is first of all a form of art that is produced in the school by children under the guidance and influence of a teacher. The teacher usually is not an art teacher but an elementary classroom teacher (NEA, 1963, pp. 24-26). Though student work done with art teachers differs in artistic complexity from that done with classroom teachers, the definition that I'm advancing includes both. School art is not the same thing as child art. Child art is a spontaneous, unsupervised form of graphic expression usually done outside of school by children for their own satisfaction or in response to a need felt in an environment other than the school. Wilson (1974) identified the characteristics of child art. He says:

> This art has seldom been allowed into our highly controlled art classes. It is the spontaneous *play art* of young people … It has little of the polished lushness of art classroom art, but once one learns to look at tatty little drawings done in ballpoint on lined paper, a whole world of excitement unfolds. From play art we can learn why young people make art in the first place and why some keep on making it while others stop. (p. 3) Wilson's paper focuses attention on child art as a phenomenon through the study of a single practitioner in the work of an eleven-year-old boy named J .C.

Holz. Historically, teachers like Franz Cizek of Austria thought they were bringing child art into fuller development by their teaching, but actually they created a new style, the school art style. Wilson describes school art with terms such as game-like, conventional, ritualistic, and ruled-governed. "Conventional themes and materials are fed to children which result in school art with the proper expected look" (Wilson, 1974, pp. 5-6). While Wilson characterizes the school art style, he leaves open the question of why there is need to invent a style that has little or no counterpart either in the personal spontaneous expression of children or in the culture outside of the school. What is so amazing about school art is that it doesn't exist anywhere else except in schools, and it exists in schools around the world. The school art style is international in scope (Asihene, 1974; Glover, 1974; Suleiman, 1974).

The three studies referred to above document the fact that African schooling practices, for example, tend to resemble the curriculum provided by former colonial overlords, in these cases the art curriculum of England. Ghanian children, in one instance, were seen illustrating English nursery rhymes like *Little Bo Peep*. These writers interpret such manifestations as evidence of Western influence upon their respective countries, but the persistent presence of such alien influences in their educational institutions, some fifteen years after independence, calls for another explanation—one that takes into account the fact that the school as an institution has a latent tendency to assert its autonomy and authority. It does so in these cases by retaining the alien influences. Any educational material would have sufficed, provided that it was sufficiently obscure or irrelevant to the population surrounding the school.

Most of us are familiar with the products, themes, and media given play in the school art style. The products range from tempera paintings on newsprint applied with large brushes to string paintings; string printing; dried-pea-mosaics; tissue collages; fish-mobiles; and masks of every size, shape and description. Themes range from topics like "Playing in the School Yard" (Lansing, 1972, p. 446), "Picking Apples" (Viola, 1949, p. 134; Lowenfeld, 1952, pp. 116, 125), and "I am at the Dentist". (Lowenfeld, 1952, p. 94). Halloween, Thanksgiving, Christmas, and Valentine's Day are observed with products in the form of cultural symbols.

School art is an institutional art style in its own right. It is not the first such style. There is a church art and a corporate art, and there is a museum art. All of these art styles deal with different subjects and themes, have different social functions, and involve different people. Church art is perhaps best understood in the context of how it enhances the act of worship. Corporate art is best understood in the context of its merchandizing function, while museum art is best understood in the context of curators, connoisseurs, and art lovers and what they do in the presence of the art in the museum collection. School art presumably should be art that is understood in the context of its educative function. Institutions like schools can be and have been treated by anthropologists and sociologists in their own right (Dalke, 1958). These institutions develop internal social structures (Merton, 1968), channels of communication, and the people involved in these cultures behave in certain ways that are mediated by the use of symbolic forms. Hence we can say that these institutions frequently develop symbolic artifacts to facilitate these activities. These artifacts are sometimes called art.

Now I am getting into a problem!

The school presumably exists to transmit a cultural heritage including the knowledge, beliefs, values, and patterns of behavior that are prized by the society that established the school. Part of this heritage is the art of the culture. Why, then, does the school develop a new and different art style that is only marginally related to the heritage? Why does the school, which is the agency providing the transmission, proceed to invent a new and different style of its own? My perplexity is compounded by the fact that the school art style does not seem to be a pedagogical tool for teaching children about art in the world beyond the school, though this is its manifest function, to be sure.

When mathematics is taught in the school, there is some correspondence between what is taught as mathematics and the mathematical understandings at large in the minds of men and women in the world outside of the school. This is less so with art, where there is little resemblance or relation between what professional artists do and what children are asked to do. To answer the riddle I am going to rely on some anthropological assumptions. First, all art as an artifact originating within particular cultures or subcultures tells us something about those cultures within which they originate. Fischer (1971) cited evidence that there is a correspondence between the social structure of a given society and certain formal attributes of its art styles. The products of the school art style as artifacts of a school culture should be able to tell us something about that culture that may, on first look, not be obvious. Thus, the social structure or religion of a vanished people can sometimes be reconstructed from small fragments of physical remains such as potshards or carved bone. Art forms are made in response to a constellation of situations that arise within a culture, and hence these can be read as evidence about the culture itself. The products of the school art style, no less than the style of ancient Egypt, can be interpreted as evidence to support claims we might wish to make about that culture. If a culture is egalitarian or hierarchical in its social structure, these facts might show up either in some aspect of a product's form, or are explained by the social circumstances for which the particular work was made or by the social conditions under which it was to be perceived—when and by whom. If this is true, then it should follow that the school art style is like any other style in that it expresses the culture within which it originates. Let us turn the statement around and ask it as a question. Can the existence, indeed the apparent need for a school art style, be explained by the structure of social relations or the structure of beliefs that operate within the school? Do the forms that school art takes express these cultural components? If this is so, then art teachers need to face the fact that what is frequently taken to be the content of the art that is made in school isn't about art as it exists beyond the school; it may be more a function of the school life-style itself. This is not to say that school art is bad or mistaken in its objectives. Rather, it is an attempt to explain the facts as many professional art educators have observed and decried them with repeated regularity over the last fifteen years. One is the fact that art education remains a peripheral concern within general education (Eisner, 1972, p. 1). It is one of the last subjects to be added to the curriculum and the first to go when funds are short.

Another perennial fact is the continuing pre-dominance of studio art instruction in both elementary and secondary schools (Barkan, 1962). This exists in spite of the fact that the profession has gone on record supporting critical and historical study (NAEA, 1968).

We have in the past attempted to explain these facts by alluding to anti-aesthetic tendencies in American culture going back to the Puritan fathers, and we have attributed the reluctance to engage students in critical and historical approaches to study in the arts to an incipient anti-intellectualism among rank and file art teachers. Placing the blame within these sources has the effect of getting the profession off the hook. Blaming it on the culture is like blaming it on providence, leaving the fate of art education in the lap of the gods beyond the ken of human volition. This is a fatalism that says that nothing can be done—a position I am not willing to accept. Blaming it on the anti-intellectual traits of art teachers is a little like blaming the crime on the victim.

The Hidden Curriculum Problem

There exists a literature that is written and spoken by school officials, teachers, and school board members. It is a collective attempt to define the school's purposes—what it attempts to accomplish for the individual and society. The literature attempts to state the ideology or philosophy of the school with statements about the worth of the individual, the democratic process, equality before the law, fair play, respect for law and order, scholarship, free enterprise, individual initiative, and the like. The school's rhetoric of service is usually stated in the form of goals accomplishing these general aims. These statements express the manifest functions of the school, i.e., those which the persons involved in the school recognize and accept as the right ones. Schools have *latent* functions (Merton, 1968) which go unrecognized even by those who carry out these functions. Thus, Illich (1971) described the fact that most people think that a school's manifest function is the cognitive development of the students, but, in his view, its latent function involves socializing the individual into accepting the authority of the school as a prelude for accepting the authority of other institutions. Once he accepts the authority of the school, he is able to accept the authority of the corporation, the military, and the welfare bureaucracy. The school's rhetoric of service seems, sometimes, to obscure these latent functions which go unrecognized. For this reason we can use this rhetoric as a benchmark for purposes of analysis.

In my view the presence of the school art style can be explained as a result of the conflicts that arise between a rhetoric articulating the manifest functions and the latent functions which go unstated. In art education our manifest functions have to do with helping students become more human through art (Feldman, 1970) by having them value art as an important aspect of their lives. The typical art program operates in a school where students are regimented into social roles required by society. If the school's latent functions are repressive in character, what effect does this have on the art program? It's my speculation that the art program's manifest functions are subverted by these pressures. As the repression builds, art comes to be regarded as "time off for good behavior" or as "therapy."

Illich's views were stated with extreme passion and vituperation which sometimes outstripped his facts, but in a critique sympathetic to Illich, Gintis (1973) cited some historical studies that lend corroboration to the Illich thesis. For example, one study traced the organization of the American school and that of the American corporation as both evolved their hierarchial forms of social organization. One conclusion made by Gintis was that the school's structure was patterned after the corporation rather than the society as a whole. In essence then, the social relations of the American school are described as democratic in their service rhetoric though in actuality they more closely approximate the hierarchic organization of the modern corporation.

Because the school is compulsory there are no genuine democratic options, i.e., children do not have the option of not attending school. In that sense it is more obligatory than military conscription where at least one can refuse service on grounds of conscience. In that light, Cass (1974) noted that the teaching profession was the third most authoritarian profession now being practiced, succeeded only by the police and the armed services.

Functions of the School Art Style

1. Making the service rhetoric credible.

One of the functions of the school art style is to provide behaviors and products that have the look of humanis-tic learning. I don't know if humanism involves the use of a given look, but I would wager that in the popular view art products that would be deemed humanistic would be those having an "unregimented," "irregular," "individual" look. School art activity would have to be designed to produce such products, yet within a predetermined range. A class where everyone draws the same view of the same leaf (see Gombrich, 1960, p. 148, Illustration #106) would not be tolerated as an accepted practice today. Teachers know in advance the look of the products they want and what they don't want. Usually they do not want pictures with a copied look or comic stereotypes. Abstract, free form or scribble designs would be sanctioned within their expectations as monsters would be. As long as the art program seems to be producing products that have a free and creative look, school persons can say that life in school is not just a cognitive matter. Man does not live by bread alone. Thus, while mouthing these homilies and even believing them, the school with characteristic alacrity is free to pursue its hidden curriculum of socialization.

The self-same creative activities may not be as free as they look. Children are after all required to take art. They cannot copy or imitate which is an option that a free individual may wish to exercise; they must use the media provided them, and they must experiment with it in certain ways to produce the look that their teachers will reinforce. Some of the qualities involve filling the space, using clean colors, spontaneous brush strokes, looseness as opposed to tightness, etc. The art that is produced is suggested by the teacher who commissions it and motivates the students to accept the commission. The teacher is also the client-patron for the products produced and is the dispenser of rewards for commissions completed within specifications. In other words the teacher is in charge of the game, and it is not so very different from the other games that are ordinarily played within the school. Art teachers, like all teachers, assert the authority of the institution;

and if, in the eyes of the system, they are good teachers they will be able to turn on the creativity and turn it off again in time to clean up and get the children back to math and reading.

2. The Morale Function.

Art is supposed to be easy and fun.

Though most art teachers find such talk perjorative, the fact of the matter is that art is one of the areas that is used to vivify school life and break up the deadening routine. Much art production is associated with school holidays such as Halloween, Christmas, and Valentine's Day. The evaluators for the Arts IMPACT Program in the Columbus public schools, for example, noted that there is a statistically significant increase in pupil attendance on days when the program occurs over days when it is not present (Arts Impact Evaluation Team,[1]).

The school uses art as therapy, minimizing the psychological cost of institutional repression. This assertion may help explain why it is that when art teachers try to make their subject more rigorous or intellectually challenging, such efforts meet with resistance. The last thing that many art teachers feel they can do is to make art another academic discipline. This latent social role may well explain why art teachers have difficulty introducing art criticism or history into their programs. The expectations that children, classroom teachers, and administrators have built up through the years disallow any weakening of the therapeutic functions of art.

Formal Requirements of the School Art Style

Because art has acquired some of the latent functions described above, the question that now must be answered is:

Why are these hidden functions furthered by the particular school art style that we see? Asked in the reverse way, the question is: Does the presence of these hidden functions of school art help explain its stylistic attributes? I will answer the question by writing a prescription for an art style that would serve these latent functions. (a) The style would need to be one that is relatively free of cognitive strain. It needs a lot of manual activity rather than one that involves the use of the head. The avant-garde styles like conceptual art certainly would not be desirable. (b) The products have to have a range of identifiable differences which the client-patrons of the style can detect. No look-alike art is acceptable here. The products should be ones that can be made in a short time. The range of allowable variations in differences should not tax the decorum of the school. (c) The media should be resilient, easily manipulated and controlled so that they yield a wide range of products with a low order of skill and dexterity. They should be perceptually inviting, i.e., colors bright, interesting textures, etc. The media should be non-toxic and easily cleaned, since clean-up presumably is an essential part of the art learning experience. (d) While some stylistic influences creep in from the comics, from illustrations in children's books, and from the more sophisticated art styles of professional artists, all of these should be kept to an absolute minimum. All forms of such influence are seen as destructive to the child's in-dividual creativity. That artists like Duchamp, Warhol, Lichtenstein, Picasso, and Cezanne have on occasion copied without undue damage to their creativity is not a relevant matter. What the child may have on his mind for his expression may be the Snoopy symbol in Peanuts, but such manifestations need to be discouraged by the teacher who alone knows what the art of children should look like and, what's more, knows how to get it to look like that. These prescriptions are required to bring into being a style which squares with the school's service rhetoric in some important ways. The prohibition against copied forms and outside influences functions to keep the art looking child-like, a look that is accepted by parents and classroom teachers as evidence of the school's humane intentions of helping to advance creativity and individuality. The media that are used cannot help but produce a range of products that cannot possibly be alike. Competence in school art is condoned, but it is usually ascribed to parental pushing and, hence, is possibly regarded as a source of harm (Lowenfeld, 1954).

As it happened, history played right into our hands, because such a style was invented for school use around the turn of the century. It was the style that Cizek invented when he thought he found a method to further child art. He identified all the components: easy materials like colored paper and paints, a range of subjects and themes to remind the children of what they are supposed to do, a prohibition against copying, or even looking at other art. It struck America between the wars when schools moved for a time into a child centered orientation. The style became associated with what was to become accepted as a liberal stance in education. Previous school art was regimented and authoritarian in its form and content. The new style, by contrast, was a more vivid and freer expression. Cizek changed the game plan; and, hence, the school art style changed. In some ways, however, it serves the same functions that it always had.

Another important reason why the style was readily adopted was simply the fact that it made few professional demands on the teacher. Teachers did not have to know much art to teach it! They had only to follow Cizek when he said of his method "All I do is take the lid off, when most teachers clamp it on" (McDonald, 1971). The fact that artistic competence seemed not to be a prerequisite enhanced the popularity of the method, because the school could have a liberal, humane, and creative art program without adequately trained teachers. The school could look good while its fundamental commitments are based in a curriculum with a hidden agenda of repression.

Conclusions

Vincent Lanier (1972) made the observation that teaching practices in the school have remained static for the last several decades. The goals change from time to time so that we justify our practices by alluding to the importance of creativity in one year only to be followed by some other rationale in another. Yet the school art style has remained essentially the same for the last forty-five to fifty years. To be sure, some of the flavor of contemporary art finds its way into the classroom, harboring the illusion that the curriculum is changing. Society outside of the school changes, too. Children rarely have the chance to go to grandma's to pick apples, and the snow that they roll into snowmen is polluted with the exhaust fumes of 80 million automobiles. In the face of these perplexities one would expect to see something else happen in the art programs of the school. What I suspect is that the school art style tells us a lot more about schools and less about students and what's on their minds. If this is so, then maybe we have been fooling ourselves all along. We have been trying to change school art when we should have been trying to change the school!

References

Asihene, E.V. Art education development and curriculum planning for national development in Ghana (Doctoral dissertation, The Ohio State University, 1973). *Dissertation Abstracts International.* 1973, 34, 683-A. (University Microfilms No. 73-18,861)

Barkan, M. Transition in art education. *Art Education.* 1962, 15(7), 12-18; 27-28.

Cass, J. An environment for creative teachers. *Saturday Review World.* April 6, 1974, p. 51.

Dalke, H. O. *Values in culture and classroom.* New York: Harpers, 1958.

Eisner, E. *Educating artistic vision.* New York: Macmillan, 1972.

Feldman, E. *Becoming human through art.* Englewood Cliffs, N.J.: Prentice Hall, 1970.

Fischer, J. L. Art styles as cultural cognitive maps. In C.F. Jopling (Ed.), *Art and aesthetics in primitive societies.* New York: E.P. Dutton & Co., Inc., 1971.

Gintis, H. Toward a political economy of education: A radical critique of Ivan Illich's *Deschooling Society.* In A. Gartner, C. Greer & F. Riessman (Eds.), *After Deschooling, What?* New York: Harper & Row, 1973.

Glover, E.A. Rationale for radical innovation in the Ghanian educational system in general and art education in particular (Doctoral dissertation, The Ohio State University, 1974). *Dissertation Abstracts International,* 1975, 35, 5237A-5238A. (University Microfilms No. 75- 3073).

Gombrich, E.R. *Art and illusion.* New York: Pantheon Press, 1960.

Illich, I. *Deschooling society.* New York: Harper & Row, 1971.

Lanier, V. Objectives of teaching art. *Art Education,* 1972, 25(3), 15-19.

Lansing, K. *Art. artists and art education.* New York: Macmillan, 1972.

Lowenfeld, V. *Creative and mental growth* (2nd ed.). New York: Macmillan, 1952. Lowenfeld, V. *Your child and his art.* New York: Macmillan, 1954.

Merton, R. K. *Social theory and social structure.* New York: The Free Press, 1968.

National Art Education Association. *The essentials of a quality art program.* Washington, DC: Author, 1968.

National Education Association. *Music and art in the public schools* (Research Monograph 1963-M 31). Washington, DC: Author, 1963.

Suleiman, S. The roles and relevance of art in educational development in the developing Nigeria (Doctoral dissertation, The Ohio State University, 1974). *Dissertation Abstracts International,* 1975, 35, 4880A. (University Microfilms No. 75-3207)

Viola, W. *Child art* (2nd ed.). Peoria, Illinois: Charles A. Bennett Co., 1949.

Wilson, B. The superheroes of J.e. Holz plus an outline of a theory of child art. *Art Education,* 1974, 27(8), 2-9.

Endnotes

[1] Arts Impact Evaluation Team. *Arts impact: A curriculum for change: A summary report.* University Park, Penn.: The Pennsylvania State University, March 1973.

ARTICLE SELECTION
Lanier, V. (1977). The Five Faces
of Art Education. *Studies in Art
Education*, 18(3), 7-21.

Graeme Chalmers

Senior Editor, 1997-1999

Vincent Lanier provides a provocative map for understanding the various facets or positions held by those who wrote about art education 30 years ago. He does this with the flair, panache, and style of the raconteur that he was, opting for what he calls "a colorful way" to identify positions "associated with the people who most vividly exemplify them." He characterizes the writers in our field as magicians, mechanics, merchants, muckrakers, or mosaicists. Lanier's images and metaphors help us to understand a maturing field. As Lanier states, the images represent a cast of characters who have moved, and perhaps still move, across art education's stage. Within our own histories of art education we can ask ourselves if we "performed" any of these characters?

But Lanier's article does not need to be seen as primarily "historical." There are some questions that we can ask as we engage with contemporary literature, and attend conference presentations:

- Do magicians, mechanics, merchants, muckrakers, and mosaicists still represent discrete clusters of attitudes, or have these characters been upstaged by others?
- Are today's characters even more complex and less single minded?
- What other provocative "M" (or other) words can be used to describe those who contribute to the literature of our field?

His cast of characters is drawn only from those who write and publish and Lanier cautions that we also need to consider the views of a much larger group, who teach but do not publish. For this reason I have often had my students read this article in conjunction with Efland's (1976) seminal paper, published a year earlier: "The school art style," and readers of this anthology may wish to consider the two papers together.

As *Studies in Art Education* is, and has been, a journal concerned with research *and issues* in art education, one reason for suggesting that this article be included in the

Graeme Chalmers is Professor Emeritus of Art Education at the University of British Columbia, Vancouver, Canada, where he also held the David Lam Chair in Multicultural Education and was named a Distinguished University Scholar. He is known for his research and publications in history of art education (particularly the 19th century), and art education in arenas that acknowledge diversity and address issues of social justice. He is a former Chief Examiner in Visual Art for the International Baccalaureate Organization. His work has resulted in many awards both in Canada and internationally.

anthology has to do with Lanier's journalistic "style." I was fortunate enough to have been taught by this captivating "center-stage" personality, to have him serve on my doctoral committee, and to spend a post-doctoral year teaching with him at the University of Oregon. Among his many personas, Vincent was a man of ideas, he was *concerned with issues,* he was most certainly a muckraker; he was an activist. In a comment about another's reaction to Lanier's article, Dubinsky (1981) views "muckraker" as a word that often conjures up political scandal, of the type often associated with hard-hitting journalism. In this important article, and in his other work, Vincent Lanier was a journalist and a "hard-hitter" who sought to get beneath surface appearance, and expose the political currents.

References

Dubinsky, L. (1981). These "m's" and the realities of art education: A comment on Geoffrey Hodder, *Canadian Journal of Education,* 6(1), 73-76.

Efland, A. (1976). The school art style: A functional analysis. *Studies in Art Education,* 17(2), 37-44.

The Five Faces of Art Education

Vincent Lanier

As is likely to be the case with all human enterprise, the study of the teaching of art has many facets. One might with reasonable accuracy design a chronological or geographical "map" of art education, locating for example, an idea such as creative self-expression in its most characteristic time, the 1920s, or place, Vienna. Such an effort would probably be entertaining, of some use for students as a learning game and even, perhaps, productive of some insights about the development of the ideas which provide structure for the field.

However, a more colorful way to identify positions relative to art teaching might be to associate varieties of stance with the people who most vividly exemplify them. Undoubtedly, any reader with even the most rudimentary acquaintance with art education, will quickly relate the haptic-visual dichotomy with Lowenfeld or art as a humanistic study with Feldman, to name the obvious. Thus, instead of a map, we might construct a cast of characters who move across the stage of art education, illustrating, like the actors in a morality play, a spectrum of postures. Obviously overlap of characterization will be more prevalent than singularity of role. Most of our players are complex rather than singleminded, showing a multiplicity of ideas, many of them interwoven with the ideas of their colleagues. Nonetheless, a number of instantly recognizable identifications might be selected, since each of our players is best known for one or two major positions.

Unfortunately, this cast of characters must of necessity be chosen from among those who write and publish in the literature of the field. This is not, of course, to say that those who do not do so have less or lesser ideas. Those who teach but do not publish are simply less visible to the field in general and thus cannot easily serve as models for various conceptions of art teaching. One might wish that this, in a sense, invisible group—far larger in number than the authors—might be heard more often. Such exposure might be especially valuable since this group more authentically represents those who have direct contact with the pupils in the classrooms, the essential and ultimate target of all of our conceptualizing.

Whatever our views of the ideas or positions articulated by art education and the people who embody these positions, it would be safe to suggest that one can describe them as discrete clusters of attitudes. Thus, for example, one group of attitudes places central emphasis on artistic creation as the paradigm for art teaching. This cluster of ideas usually includes suspicion of, if not active disdain for, empirical research as a method of study of art teaching, a strong commitment to the production of art as classroom behavior and a frequent loyalty to keeping up with the latest in gallery and museum art styles as modes of student art production.

If we designate this group by a particular name, which in some way symbolizes a general description of that cluster of ideas and do much the same for other significantly unique groups of attitudes, we find that our characteristic roles are five in number. Explained and identified by a cast of actors, our dramatic map of art education might be the following.

1. *The Magicians.* The name of this group of ideas is most appropriate since the word "magic" itself crops up in their writings. Irving Kaufman, for example, states this posture towards art education in unvarnished terms when he writes: "Any approach to art education has to be aware of the basic mystery of art, of its 'magic.' An individual teacher must himself or herself be artistic, in-herently sympathetic and sensitive to the play of the senses and the symbolic character of visual forms" (1966, p. 522).

An earlier and very similar exposition of this posture was articulated by Allan Kaprow at the Pennsylvania State Seminar in 1965. Although Kaprow is not, strictly speaking, an art educator—not being primarily concerned with the study of art teaching—he did present an important voice in the field, having been selected as one of sixteen major speakers at a federally funded art education conference. Kaprow writes (actually, as I recall, this was extemporaneously spoken, but recorded and later transcribed for the final report):

> The value of imagination cannot be taught to teachers-in-training, much less conveyed by them, if they aren't imaginative in the first place. Artists who have imaginations know this and it is the one thing they share with the very young, before it is stifled out of the latter. What school children need is a Pied Piper, lots of Pied Pipers, not social workers and lab technicians. The Pied Piper had magic and this is what is important about his story. Like magicians, artists deal in a sort of magic, and it is proposed here that some of them can double as Pied Pipers and lead school children along roads they are pressured to avoid and soon forget... In sum, what we are proposing is an approach to art education which has in mind only an awareness of the basic mystery of art and a belief (supported by ample evidence) that artistic people are best suited for revealing this to youngsters ... Eventually, all art teachers may be working artists. (1966, pp. 84-85).

If Kaprow's last sentence does not fill us with confidence about the future of art education as a separate field, nothing will! In fact, a cynic might observe that we are part of the way down that path already.

The Magicians are, at heart, metaphysicians, though they sometimes try to avoid it. (Kaufman, 1966). To the Magician the essence of art education is the act of creation and that act is essen-tially a mystery, an act of magic that cannot be and, in fact, should not be investigated or explained. The teacher should be, at best, an artist who exercises that ancient magical ritual—the creation of a work of art—himself or herself and can serve as mentor for the student as acolyte. For the Magician there are fundamentally two very different kinds of people: (a) the elite who create the magic of art and their devoted servants who worship the ritual and its products, and (b) the "others" who do not for whatever reason participate in the celebration. It is not that the Magician has contempt for those others; but, rather, when he or she thinks of them (as in relation to teaching all the children of a society), he has an often genuine regret that they are being cheated of that central experience of living. Thus, the Magician is an elitist, but not generally a vicious one. People of any social class or group are acceptable as long as they perform as artists or contribute the act of adoration with words or money. Then they, too, become Magicians. Harold Taylor is a striking example. A college administrator by profession, Taylor writes:

> Many of the students have come to an interest in the arts through growing up in the youth culture, and when they find that the works of art in the college humanities courses are treated as famous objects about which they are required to have information, they simply cannot gain aesthetic or intellectual nourishment from what they are asked to do ... What they need is to enter into the experience of the artist, to move from their existing state of aesthetic awareness, which is often minimal, to deeper levels of insight, intuition, and appreciation which can only come from learning to see, to hear, to feel, to experience in the way artists do.

> At a college or university which took the arts as a celebration of life on the campus there would be days and weeks of this kind all year, with noonhour happenings, dancing on the grass, parades with costumes, picnics with poetry readings, street theater, comedians, orchestras, experiments with jazz whistles, guitars, kazoos, washboards and suitcases, banners, posters, songs, choruses, chanting, children's fairs, all in the spirit of celebration of the arts of living. (1971, pp. 122, 127-128)

What is particularly appealing about the Magician's posture—one is led to suspect—is the delightful mindlessness which is all it requires as a scholarly position. After all, if the essential quality of art and art teaching is magic and mystery, why struggle to understand it? In fact, the sine qua non of Magicianism is anti-scientism and, more popularly, anti-technologism. The fault is not in our stars or in ourselves, but in that old devil, the machine. Pollution? Caused by cars and industrial machinery. Depletion of natural resources? Caused by over-mechanization. Military over-spending? The military buys machines, does it not? Of course, not even the most vehement Magician will give up shaving with an electric razor or traveling in jet aircraft or insisting on the latest technology in dental and medical facilities. Inconsistent? But, after all, consistency is a requirement of the scientist, not of the magician.

Those who know the field have already remembered the grandparent of art education's Magicians, Sir Herbert Read, who wrote.

> Independence, freedom, law and art—these are all implicit in esthetic education, and it is only in so far as we oppose esthetic education to scientific education, and to intellectual education in the tradition of the Renaissance, oppose it as a complete and adequate substitute for these bankrupt traditions, that any hope can be entertained for the future of our European culture ... The only habit that is enobling, penetrating to the frame and physique as well as the soul of man, is the creative activity in all its rituals, exercises, festivities and practical services. (1948, p. 14)

An uncompromising idealist in both the colloquial and philosophical senses of the word, Read saw "esthetic discipline" as the only influence to change individual moral consciousness and create a world of peace.

The whole burden of Plato's theory of education is to the effect that if only we bring up children in the contemplation of universal forms, in the practice of graceful and harmonious movements, in the active making of beautiful objects, then these children will instinctively recognize and choose goodness when they see it. Esthetic education develops ethical virtue. (Read, 1948, p. 7)

In another work Read (1943) clarifies his basic position as Magician and, incidentally, reveals what may be the main reason for his consistently wide popularity among many in the world of art and art education, "for art is nothing but the good making of sounds, images, etc. The aim of education is therefore the creation of artists—of people efficient in the various modes of expression" (p. 11).

However, seen in a larger perspective (and written at a later date) not even the inculcation of ethical virtue through esthetic education is enough. Instead, Read suggests:

Until we can halt these processes of destruction and standardization, of materialism and mass communication, art will always be subject to the threat of disintegration. The genuine arts of today are engaged in a heroic struggle against mediocrity and mass values, and if they lose, then art, in any meaningful sense, is dead. If art dies, then the spirit of man becomes impotent and the world relapses into barbarism. (1965, p. 187)

What a comforting thought to those of us who teach art to be, potentially, the saviors of humanity by creating artists in the classroom and supporting the "genuine arts of today."

Interestingly enough, the posture of the Magician is not merely a theoretical position. It is at this writing the official policy of the federal government of the United States, supported by a substantial amount of tax dollars. I refer, of course, to the Artist in the School Program, which, along with state and local funding in most instances, is the most ambitious single project in the history of art education. Despite its monumental scope, this program to date has had no thorough, careful evaluation (Eisner, 1974). In effect, the artist has "done his/her thing," performed the magic ritual, and almost three million public dollars later our children have had the benefits of the best art education can offer.

A small but inviting sub-group of Magicians is made up of those whose position is the extreme of Magicianism. These are the Mystics. Like the anarchist, the Mystic regards any ordering with suspicion—even that of the artist. All that can be depended upon is each individual's unique and private experience and even that is unexplainable. Where the Magician is anti-rational, the Mystic is proirrational. Consider the following.

In the kinesthetic flow of our body's spatiality we experience the living existence of our own consciousness. We experience in an immediate manner the embodiment of ourself through our sensuous, spatial movements. As we surrender ourself to the flow of sensuous spatious movement, we are not standing "outside" of it from a distance watching ourself doing the moving, for we are fused with the sensuous movement. We have become the movement itself. And in becoming the movement we allow ourself to be moved. We move with the attitude of being moved, for we are moved by the movement of our own moving. When we look at the world while we are being moved by the movements of our own moving, we do not experience our movements as contained in the spatiality of the world, but we "see" the rhythmical, spatially extended flows of bodily movement in and with the spatiality of the world. (Madenfort, 1973, p. 8)

The Mystic appears in what seems to be the most unlikely persons. Perhaps the most notable example in art education is Kenneth Beittel. A careful and diligent empirical researcher, Beittel (1973) confesses his basic mysticism in graceful prose. "The making of art, however, is intensely personal and experiential. Hence I have begun, and literally only begun, to journey up the qualitative prong (I think of it visually as the left prong) ... It is a long way to the region of the tip of the prong (the tip itself I take to be unreachable)" (p. 131).

Once we stipulate unreachability, once we assert the essential mystery of any problem, which is inherently unexplainable, life is much simpler and easier. After all, we can be forgiven any inadequacy in our efforts, since they really are—ultimately—pointless. This is a somewhat strange posture for an empirical researcher.

The popularity of the Mystic's stance among the young is, of course, no news to anyone. The celebration of the irrational on a mass scale is indeed one of the hallmarks of much of the quasiculture of the last two decades. Yet art educators as a group seem to have a smaller proportion representing this outlook than the general population. One reason might be that they are teachers and, thus, constrained by a sense of public obligation. However, another might be that magicianism is already available and attractive in the arts as a respectable position. Their craving for irrationality, their "rage for chaos" can be satisfied by the mystic mystique of the studio.

Despite their small numbers, however, Mystics carry considerable weight in art education. Not only do we courteously (art educators appear to be courteous to a fault, even in the presence of obvious sham and banality—as any convention goer can observe), avoid challenging their public insistence on private experience, but we seem even to envy their unfettered enjoyment of a disordered universe. It may be that there is a repressed mystic in everyone of us waiting to be released like the savage Tarzan casting aside the "thin veneer of the English lord" in those turgid works of Edgar Rice Burroughs. Perhaps we are fortunate to have the milder alternative of magicianism as an option.

Also hidden within the larger group of the Magicians like the Mystics is another posture deserving recognition as a second sub-group, the Manipulators. Although the Manipulator is es-sentially a true believer in the magic of the artist's ritual act of creation, the treasured emphasis in this case is on the actual handling of materials. Thus the Manipulator is often, in origin or currently, a craftsperson, a potter or weaver or jeweler. The following paragraphs explain the Manipulator's stance and kinship to the Magician.

In art all form emerges from art processes and art materials and, unlike the other arts, art depends on these elements for its vigor and its identity. It is these processes and materials which the child thinks of as "art" and which draw him to art as a means of communicating his ideas and expressing his emotions.

And it is in these processes and materials from which all art springs that we find the most effective means of motivation for art activity and the logical core around which to build an art program. (Lidstone, 1967, p. 7)

2. *The Mechanics.* As the name implies, this cluster of ideas represents the extreme polarity from our first position. Mechanics view the world (of art education, that is) as an orderly construction of quantifiable elements, built according to blueprint and understandable and even predictable by the patient accumulation of weights and measures. The Mechanic is the empiricist, the worshipper of scientific methodology, the researcher. The Mechanic sees the teaching of art through a screen of means and modes and standard deviations, the architecture, as it were, of educational psychology.

The Mechanic is easily recognized by never venturing an assertion without the support, by in-text or footnote citation, of an empirical study. A characteristic bit of Mechanic prose is the following:

In the art area one measure was found under each of these four personality factors and associated subgroups which contributed to the .800 Multiple R for the prediction of creativity by the spontaneous deliberate criterion (note Table A- 15). Since the art population was divided by the criterion judgments into four groups, this means that nine out of ten of the predictors based on the measurements of the student's personality structure agree with the actual or criterion placement in these four major categories. The rest of the error results from within-group deviations. Therefore, creativity in art and creativity in personality structure as they were measured in this study are very significantly related. (Burkhart, 1962, p. 215)

The as yet unassailable stronghold of the Mechanic is the doctoral program of the university. Here, substantially safe from those everyday problems for which no controlled testing has been devised, the Mechanic deftly juggles statistics, wields slide rule and equation, and meticulously reports every last Arabic numeral in endless masses of tables and charts. The paradigm of the Mechanic is, of course, the computer and for the full-fledged mechanic, the printout has an almost morbid fascination not at all unlike the Magician's obsession with the ritual of the creative act.

The voice of the Mechanic in professional circles is about evenly divided between *Studies in Art Education,* the research journal of NAEA, and research reports at national, regional, and local conferences. On these stages, the Mechanic can spread the gospel according to St. Stat., extinguishing—the Magician is quick to point out—all the joy and excitement of art with the stultifying crassness of an empirical outlook. A quick glance at most issues of *Studies* since the Fall of 1959 will reveal the scope of this numerical virus. For example, the third number of Volume 16 of *Studies in Art Education* (1975) has 16 numerical tables and figures, in 72 pages of text, a not uncommon proportion. What every conscientious Mechanic freely admits is that sample populations, limited contexts, and the manipulation of a minimum of variables clearly prohibits generalization from·a piece of research to the larger situation of art teaching. Nevertheless, studies reported with majestic rigor and dignified by methodological kinship to an engineered society, sustain a kind of impregnable authority even in the midst of the Magician's domain.

In art education the one figure which dominates all others as Mechanic par excellence is Viktor Lowenfeld. At heart a mystic (if the reader has doubts, I must insist, since he told me so himself), Lowenfeld almost alone brought empirical—in those days almost exclusively psychological—research into the purview of art education. However, the most visible current personal exemplar of this posture is Elliot Eisner. Fortunately for the field, since Eisner is an influential figure, he is a cautious Mechanic—a quality one might wish other Mechanics would emulate. Eisner explains his caution in these terms:

Practices are influenced in greater degree by the persuasiveness of leading ideas than they are by the conclusions developed by systematic research.

In many ways this is unfortunate.

It tends to lead people to hold ideas without the benefit of evidence. It tends to lead to an advocate-adversary conception of educational practice. Although many, perhaps even most, significant issues in art education cannot now be resolved by appeals to empirical evidence, I believe such evidence should be employed wherever possible. Commitment to an unexamined or untested doctrine is not, in my opinion, the most productive way to improve educational practices in art education. (1972, pp. 177-178)

3. *The Merchants.* More a technique for survival than a theoretical position, Merchantism illustrates our propensity for adopting the coloration of the contemporary mainstream. Perhaps the most characteristic quality of American life is its mercantilism and the apostle of mercantilism is advertising. What's good for General Motors is good for the country, and Madison Avenue will tell us just what that is. The most exquisite distillation of the Merchant's viewpoint in our field can be seen wherever one finds that fetching little yellow button (or T-shirt or bumper sticker) with its inspirational message: "You Gotta Have Art." If we can sell underarm deodorants, presidents, and compact cars, why not art education?

Of course the Merchant rarely appears to us in those vestments, but rather in the guise of that strong right arm of the businessman, the politician. Although some wit once claimed that politics is the art of the possible, it can be argued that he or she was, indeed, only half right and that politics is even more the art of the profitable. The political world of art education is for the most part limited to its professional associations of which NAEA is by far the most extensive. The Alliance for Arts Education and the Institute for the Study of Art in Education are smaller but distinctive bodies. Thus, the hierarchy of professional association politicians play the role of Merchant—at least during their tenure in professional office—selling art education to the world outside as well as to colleagues.

Carried away by evangelical ardor the Merchant sometimes rhapsodizes about the virtues of art so bombastically as to become absurd, probably convincing no one outside the field (more likely, offending them by an unconscious arrogance) but reassuring the faint-hearted within the field about the sanctity of their mission. The following is one clear example among many.

Technology without human understanding is like an answer without a question. True human understanding is only possible through the arts.

If education is learning to grow, learning to choose, to provide a medium for self-awareness and com-munication, then the integral role of the arts in the learning process is neither contrived nor tangential. (Rogers, 1975, p. 5)

We might also turn to the words of an art educator turned Merchant (Schwartz,[1]) temporarily:

The appropriate challenge for an organization seeking to make integrity—its cornerstone has more to do with making the goals of art teaching in the schools clearer than they have been before. There is a need to articulate and organize our arguments and then present these in the forums where educational decision making takes place. We must be able to point with insistence to those historical and social antecedents which designate the central place of the arts during the millenia of significant human development. (p. 5)

One might reasonably ask if the author is serious in assigning a principal (that is, more important than any other) role to the arts in human development and if he is, how he arrives at this monumental judgment. Isn't it just possible that politics, economics, religion, science, or philosophy might have had even as much to do with human development as the arts? But then exaggeration is the basic ingredient of the "hard sell," which is, in turn, a favorite tactic of the world of adver-tising and of Merchantism. It would seem that art education might profit from a truth in advertising regulation or at least a self-imposed obligation to give Brand X equal time.

However, if we wish to savor the ultimate in status for the arts, we must turn to a major professional politician, Nelson Rockefeller. Not only are the arts the *only* possible path to "true human understanding", in *the* "central place during the millenia of significant human development", but, as Mr. Rockefeller (1975) puts it:

Much of education involves a necessary shaping and training of the child's mind. Art education goes a significant step beyond these educational aims. Art education expands the mind ... teaches the child how to enjoy life, how to use the senses fully. And in so doing, the child not only adds to his or her pleasure, but begins to understand the greatest wonder of mankind, the quality which separates human life from all other forms of life, the capacity to be creative. It is this spark of creativity that lends a touch of the divine to the human race. And it is in art education classes that a child can first be made to perceive that wondrous spark. (p. 7)

What a terrifying responsibility for the art teacher, on top of all the others, to nego-tiate the child's perception of the divine—even if we are not dismayed by the potential Constitutional problems raised by the statement.

In contradiction to this kind of extreme claim is another tendency of Merchantism which is simultaneously strange and almost masochistic. Any consistent art education conventioneer will recognize this syndrome from its frequent appearances at our meetings. In descending order of frequency, artists, art historians, art critics and significant others are hired, paid, and applauded to appear before large groups of art educators and tell them that, in effect, all one needs to be a good art teacher is to be a good artist, a good art historian, a good art critic, etc. These not infrequent exercises seem to be a sort of *mea culpa,* a public confession by the profession—instigated by the Merchant who has the political clout—that they are indeed worthless and that any practitioner is by definition more valuable in the classroom.

One might offer in this context the immortal words of Nancy Hanks (who qualifies only partially as a Merchant, since the National Endowment is only partially concerned with art education, if at all) who said: "When you have a problem, it makes sense to turn to the person who knows most about the subject. None of us was satisfied with our progress in making the arts more central in education, and so we decided to look to the professional artist for help" (Cited in Morrison, 1975, p. 53). This idea seems very neatly to eliminate the need for a field of study such as art education, a consequence apparently unrecognized by those in the field who flock to embrace programs such as the Artist in the School. But then, that particular program is the only substantial source for profit in the field today and as an undernourished area of education, art can hardly be blamed for grasping the helping hand wherever it can. What is unfortunate is that our poverty is more than a dearth of vigorous ideas than of money and that this lack is only dimly recognized by the profession.

Needless to say, art education has had and still does have its own indigenous Merchants, behaving thus either by persuasion or by force of their professional responsibilities. Ralph Beelke, Charles Dorn, Harlan Hoffa and John Mahlmann have been or are Merchants by role definition—whatever other ideas they might have about the teaching of art. An even more impressive list of Merchants (since they did or do influence Federal purse strings) would include Katherine Bloom, Nancy Hanks, Forbes Rogers and Martin Engel. While they are not, strictly speaking, art educators (to the best of my knowledge), their positions confer considerable authority to what they have to say about the field. Having quoted two of them above, further elaboration of their approaches is probably unnecessary.

A dramatic current example of Merchantism rampant is the NAEA's building project. The particular Merchants responsible are, I suppose, the NAEA boards who decided and supported the policy. It has yet to be shown (or argued, for that matter) that an association monument of this sort will influence the art teacher's task in the classroom one way or the other, and, that is, many of us naively believed, the primary function of the association. What it might do, aside from making the NAEA staff more comfortable, is to advertise the stability and affluence of art education. It will, as the jargon has it, project an image and everyone knows that the advertised image need have nothing to do with reality.

An even more blatant example of Merchantism can be found between the covers of the October 1975 NAEA Journal, *Art Education.* Here the Vice-President of the United States and 27 U.S. senators mellifluously inform us of the vital role of art education in clichés so exhausted by usage as to prohibit careful reading. Would it be too harsh to suggest that no NAEA member could possibly learn anything new about the field from that issue except that these gentlemen had such opinions? However, a Merchant would probably respond that the October 1975 issue, whatever its intellectual level, was good PR, and that for a Merchant is reason enough for being.

4. *The Muckrakers*. The inheritor of an ancient and unpopular tradition in American culture, the Muckraker has a compulsion to turn over the flat stone and see what is on the other side and expects consistently to find a mess of maggots. The Muckraker comes out of Missouri and into this worst of all possible worlds, often breathing brimstone and fire and delights in the role of devil's advocate or gadfly. The highest priority in his or her pantheon of professional responsibilities is to question and particularly to question those beliefs all of us accept.

A pungent illustration of Muckrakerism appeared in 1963 with the publication of *Educationists and The Evisceration of the Visual Arts* (complete with Rembrandt's painting of a side of beef on the cover). The author, David Manzella, castigated art education with more than a little venom—appropriate or misplaced according to one's loyalties—going as far as to launch a now dated but then devastating attack on the personal qualities of the professionals.

> The educationist has, perhaps un-wittingly but nonetheless effectively, seen to it that the teacher of art generally knows as little about the history of art and is as indifferent to the practice of art as possible, They have accomplished this, most usually, by designing curricula for prospective teachers that assure no more than a superficial acquaintance with the history and practice of art while demanding a great portion of time in education courses. This philosophy has resulted in the usual art education major being a nice young woman of unexceptional abilities and little ambition to do anything with her art on a personal level; the young man in the program is usually interested in crafts and the decorative rather than in painting or sculpture and is often rather low in male hormones. (pp. 76-77)

Although this document stands as by far the most vitriolic attack on art education (at least within its own literature, if not anywhere) and represents an extreme of Muckrakerism verging, to some, on bad taste, there are numerous other examples. These range from Brent Wilson's (1974) gentle and scholarly questioning of child art practices in the classroom to Kenneth Marantz's virtually unparalleled and delightful public self-questioning as Merchant:

> For I find myself addressing a conference audience of a national institute with the thought that we may be conferencing ourselves to death. Surely part of this simplistic notion stems from a gross dissatisfaction with my performance as resident of ISAE. Without assuming the guise of the Aristotelean tragic hero I nevertheless share that feeling of selfdisillusionment. Nor can I identify a single flaw to account for my failure, although it would be so comforting to seek solace in a range of rationalizations ... Not that I shall gouge my eyes out nor run upon my sword nor even sip Socrates'

bitter brew in some splashy attempt to placate my personal gods and dissipate my frustrations. My masochism peaks in public self-denunciation; verbal suicide is the just vehicle for a word merchant. (Note 2, pp. 7-8)

Other examples can be found in Eisner's (1974) concern for the lack of evaluation of the Artist in the School Program and his (1973-74) critical analysis of myths in the field, and still another in Arthur Efland's speculation about the repressive influences of a "school art style" (1976). Perhaps the most persistent Muckraker in the field is this author (Lanier, 1976). (Having been free with the personalities of my colleagues, I may perhaps be forgiven for immodestly submitting my own.) In point of fact, this paper itself will qualify as a piece of Muckrakerism in its attempt to cast doubts on every position in the field.

The professional problem clearly posed by the often irritating efforts of the Muckraker is a consistent and discouraging negativism. Is nothing right with art education, is the unavoidable response to a thorough piece of Muckrakerism. It is not that the Muckraker has no point of view to cherish and present, but rather that the habit of doubt and questioning often makes even his or her ideals and ideas suspect. Both for this and other reasons, there are very few consistent Muckrakers in art education. Ultimately, the penalty for being "odd man out," as it were, is a kind of professional ostracism that only the thick-skinned can long endure. In any case, the Muckraker, like every other actor on this stage, should continually be challenged to produce a positive alternative to his or her negative assessment of an idea or practice.

5. *The Mosaicists,* Properly last in our cast of art education characters is the Mosaicist, the Renaissance person, the eclectic, who deftly or clumsily orchestrates all of the previously described postures into one grand pattern. The Mosaicist is at heart a chameleon, taking on whatever coloration is appropriate to the occasion, with costume and dialect to match. This process, however, is by no means insincere. Quite the contrary, the Mosaicist tries desperately to weave all the threads of ideas in the field into one tight fabric, seeing salvation in concep-tual togetherness.

Our most successful contemporary Mosaicist is without question Edmund Feldman, whose massive recent textbooks (1967, 1970) could each be subtitled, "All You Wanted to Know About Art (or Art Education) But Were Afraid to Ask." In fact, one symptom of Mosaicism appears to be sheer size. Once a volume hovers about the 500 page mark, one can be fairly certain that a Mosaic will at least be attempted. Other examples of Mosaicism (because of the scope and complexity of the role, a book rather than periodical article is usually its venue) can be found in the work of Reid Hastie and Christian Schmidt (n.d.), Kenneth Lansing (n.d.), James Schinneller (1968), and the earlier work of Italo de Francesco (1958). However, these efforts, one must suggest, are not as successful in their Mosaicism (whatever their other virtues) as the work of Feldman. They appear to possess a bias in posture that dilutes their catholicity.

Another powerful and master mosaicist was, of course, Manuel Barkan, and most of all in his last work (1970). *Guidelines* is a testimonial to the Mosaic spirit, having the size, the inclusion of every conceivable viewpoint and the ambition—if not the fulfillment—to combine diversity. It is, nonetheless, far less influential than its weight might suggest, and its weight, one might add, may well be the reason, In order to teach aesthetic education, as this volume would have us do, each teacher must be or become a Mosaicist juggling an overwhelming array of concepts and behaviors. To submit that few of us are equipped or disposed to play such a role is to state the obvious. The current destiny of *Guidelines* in the field is nicely illustrative of one of the problems of Mosaicism.

Another more pernicious problem is the Mosaicist's compulsion to ride several horses at the same time. Even in a field like art education where debate is rare, sizable differences in basic viewpoint do exist as we have seen above. To proclaim, "peace in our time" like Neville Chamberlain returning from Munich, is to ignore the ailments that plague our profession. The following passage from Feldman (1970 illustrates this difficulty:

> A great deal of the literature in art education endeavors to bring the mass of pupils up to the artistic level of that gifted minority. To be sure, this effort is carried out under the banner of enlarging the creative powers of *all* children. Alas, it often succeeds in convincing many of them that they are inadequate as *performers,* But their tremendous creative potentials as intelligent viewers, perceptive critics, and sen-sitive interpreters of the arts are left largely untapped. (p. vi)

One would think, based on this passage in the Preface, that Feldman was about to proclaim a commitment to an art curriculum which transcends the futility of our tempera paint drenched classrooms. But, alas, the Mosaic spirit requires that nothing be wasted, no idea be ignored. A later passage reveals this all-embracing quality nicely.

> From a humanistic standpoint, then, the artistic creativity of children and adolescents is seen in a new light. It ceases to be primarily a technical enterprise. Instead, the emphasis in teaching is on the humanistic purposes that art serves, the humanist would cause art to be created indirectly and incidentally, as it is created in the organic cultures of primitive men, for example, And in such cultures, we are fond of saying, there is no artificial separation between art and life ... There have to be "good reasons" as opposed to calculated and essentially artificial motivations, for the creation of art in schools. (pp. 174-175)

But, one might legitimately ask, what if most people's (children's) personal and social needs are satisfied by looking at art or by writing or dancing or singing instead of creating visual art? Surely a more authentic picture of any culture, living or dead, includes a variety of expressive options when there are "good reasons." In which organic primitive culture do we find all the people making visual art? To argue from an anthropological model one must remain true to the model.

Feldman's Mosaic argument for aesthetic education may be a good one if the creation of art is optional and assuming that artistic performance is only one of several modes of behavior embraced by an art curriculum.

One finds the same possible ambivalence in Eisner's (1972) picture of a multi-faceted aesthetic education curriculum—all in one paragraph.

A fourth characteristic of art programs at both the elementary and secondary level is their tendency to place almost exclusive curricular emphasis on the making of art. The vast majority of programs that are offered both children and teachers are aimed at helping them learn to create art forms, with making paintings, sculptures, and so forth, Now there is no good reason why the making of art forms should not be an exceedingly important part of every art program, Having children immerse themselves in the task of giving visible aesthetic form to their inner visions is clearly one of the goals that a large percentage of art educators would wholeheartedly endorse, But there is also no reason why the production of art forms must necessarily command exclusive attention in the art curriculum. Making art is important, to be sure, but there are other aspects of art education that are also important. (p. 126)

I suspect that the key sentence, "Now there is no good reason ... " might be called damning with faint praise. What a large percentage of art educators endorse (in the next sentence) could easily be all wrong for children and is certainly not a strong logical reason for prescription. Surely there are means other than visual for children to give "aesthetic form to their inner visions?" As with Feldman, we can ask why studio production remains obligatory for everyone in Eisner's Mosaic construct? One answer, of course, is that there is a price to be paid for Mosaicism.

It would seem that as long as art education has no single coherent and powerful sense of purpose and a rough agreement on how to achieve it, all the athletic horsemanship of the Mosaicist will only prolong the confusion. The problem of disparate directions in the field cannot be solved by the crazy quilt of the Mosaicist. It appears that the primary threads of thought in the field are truly contradictory and, therefore, incompatible. Again, the reader will have guessed that the most coherent and fruitful theoretical construct of art education's recent years, aesthetic education is a mosaicist concept, and, despite its many real merits, suffers from the disadvantages of that posture.

Moving, as aesthetic education does, from a single model of art behavior in the classroom (that of the artist) to a multiple model (a triumverate of roles, artist, historian, critic) the idea attempts to be, as it were, all things to all persons. Like being a jack-of-all-trades, it prohibits being master of any one. To seriously pursue a Brunerian "acting like an artist" is to take time, energy, even intensity. It is certainly not to dabble. The scope of potential for art activities in formal schooling being as limited as it is—and likely will be for some time, despite the sometimes frenetic claims of the Merchants—there is hardly the opportunity for exercising one model of behavior, much less three with any plausible degree of adequacy. Even worse, the three behaviors are sufficiently discrete as to inhibit transfer of any consequence. A curriculum which expects the student to maintain the agility necessary for leaping from one context to another with education profit, and digest the connections as well, is at least unrealistic. Thus, in spite of its laudable collective character Mosaicism seems to represent a band aid psychology—a small patch here, another one there, and perhaps the vehicle will move. It is probable, however, that our problems are more serious than a band-aid therapy will cure.

These, then, are the five faces of art education typified by those who play the roles most convincingly. But it will not do to simply describe the cast of characters and leave the play. The good critic feels obligated, by tradition if not by necessity, to offer judgment as well. Also, out of evaluation may grow the beginnings of a direction for the field which avoids the pitfalls of previous postures.

Perhaps the lowest common denominator of all five positions is an often unconscious but ever present elitism. Art education has been almost totally unable throughout its history to accept any but the Fine Arts of the gallery and museum into the body of content it negotiates with the young. While on the other hand, our citizens, both young and adult, enjoy a multitude of visual aesthetic transactions with nature, folk arts, popular arts, and mass media outside the preferred purview of the art and art education world.

Looked at in terms of socialization, our unfortunate myopia is far more serious in its educational consequences than simply to keep us from reaching the young with a broadening of their ability and desire to deal with all the visual arts. What our orthodoxy supports is a class structured social organization, with an art of the privileged--pungently illustrated by Mr. Rockefeller's $35,000 mink covered bed, and rather heartlessly unclothed by Tom Wolfe's (1975) essay and an art of the non-privileged, of the great majority. Like Henry Higgins' assessment of Liza's speech, we know our station in life from the art we profess to enjoy and no amount of dripping easels in our kindergartens or exhibits of child art in the Kennedy Center (which I have taken the liberty elsewhere (Lanier, 1971) to call the Potomac palace for the privileged) will alter this stratification. The elite thrill to David Smith, the rest of us to Kojak; and the twain do not meet, as they well might, in our classrooms.

Another damaging drawback of all five positions is an inability to conceive of art—in our case the visual arts, of course—as only one of a number of important instruments for satisfactory survival as an organism. As the celestial claims of our Merchants attest, we feel obligated to insist defensively—probably because of our heritage of second class citizen in education—that art is "the core" of education, that "you gotta have art," never daring to ask what might happen if we do not have art in the schools at all, either as core or cake-icing. Certainly the long history of the human race will not abruptly cease. Nor will people stop having legitimate aesthetic responses to visual phenomena of all sorts —except, perhaps, the preferred phenomena of gallery and museum. Nor, indeed, will people even stop being creative—whatever that means—in areas outside of art or even in art itself, as the history of art will indicate. In fact, one might argue that there would be no grave dis-advantage resulting from an elimination of art education from the school situation entirely, given the minimal chance we presently have of influencing the child and the poverty of our current means. But, that is another essay. It will suffice to say here that we should accept and admit that art in the schools is a luxury, albeit a valuable one and that a healthy society and one with reasonable financial means ought to be able to afford and provide the valuable luxuries of all the arts for all its youth.

A third difficulty or inadequacy of all five positions is a strangely unimaginative quality that pervades these varieties of thinking and renders them stagnant and barren in the face of the rapid changes of present history. For a group talking incessantly of creativity, art educators appear to be singularly uncreative people, at least as far as ideas about the study of teaching art is concerned. Except for those ideas which responded to the social pressures of the 1960s, all the major concepts of purpose and function for art education have had a long and usually unsuccessful history (Lanier, 1975). This is, of course, no reason to assume that a concept is inherently weak or inappropriate. It may, in fact, be the context of the school or the larger social situation which limits the success of an idea.

Neither antiquity nor custom makes an idea ineffectual by itself. What is catastrophically destructive about old ideas is their petrification as shibboleths. Once a concept is enshrined as sacrosanct, unexaminable, substantial and critical dialogue about its merits is stifled. No field of study can prosper under the burden of such millstones, and it can be shown that art education suffers from more than its share. It seems as if we need a regiment of Muckrakers to clean and sort our intellectual attic.

The reader who wishes an illustration of the shibboleth functioning in the field might study the fortunes of the idea of creativity. Questioned in its heyday in 1963 and again in 1974-75 (Lanier), it remains today, in all likelihood, the most popular single justification used for classroom art (and a splendidly ambiguous rationale for maintaining an exclusively studio curriculum, which is what most art teachers are interested in anyway). There simply is no critical dialogue in the literature about creativity even today and the Mosaicist, who is usually the most progressive in thought among us, invariably salutes it in passing, presumably out of a sense of loyalty or obligation, if not by conviction.

Perhaps the most significant assessment of these five positions one can note is the breadth of concepts they represent. As much as the unanimity of a party line is to be shunned, a little more coherence in the field might be healthier. As it is we seem to be straining mightily in a dozen different directions at the same time, with the altogether predictable result of running madly in place merely to stay where we are. David Templeton (1976) very neatly contrasted the earlier age of heroes in the field with the present era of celebrities. It is true that the loss of our heroes probably helps to insure that ideas will not conquer our thinking even in part because of the force of personality of their purveyors. We may now examine the ideas themselves more cautiously and more thoroughly. On the other hand, the same situation imposes a kind of leveling of the intellectual terrain. Where there are no heroes, there are no mountain peaks, only foothills, and art education seems to have a wide range of foothills today. One might almost wish for the old-fashioned hero (on a white horse, of course) to inspire us out of our insipid doldrums with an idea worth crusading for.

An even more jaundiced Muckraker than this author might ask who would listen to this contemporary hero? Not the Magician, for he or she already knows the answers to all the worthwhile questions. Not the Mechanic, who would need to reduce any idea to quantifiable terms and measure it. Not the Merchant, who has, after all, a heavy investment in the status quo. Not even the Muckraker would listen, but, rather, would look for ways to discredit the idea. Only the Mosaicist might listen, then hasten to include it in the mosaic, where even the strongest ideas are watered down to anaemic shadows.

These, then, are the five faces of contemporary art education, the actors in a drama which theatre people might call "off Broadway." We hope the play will not close, but the reviews have been something less than favorable.

References

Barkan, M., Chapman, L. H., & Kern, E. J. *Guidelines: Curriculum development for aesthetic education.* St. Ann, Missouri: Central Midwestern Regional Educational Laboratory, Inc. 1970.

Beittel, K. R. *Alternatives for art education research.* Dubuque: Wm. C. Brown Co. 1973.

Burkhart, R. C. *Spontaneous and deliberate ways of learning,* Scranton: International Textbook Co. 1962.

de Francesco, I. L. *Art education: Its means and ends.* New York: Harper & Bros. 1958.

Eisner, E. W. *Educating artistic vision,* New York: The Macmillan Co, 1972.

Eisner, E. W. Is the artist in the school program effective'? *Art Education,* 1974, 27(2), 19-23.

Eisner, E. W. Examining some myths in art education. *Studies in Art Education,* 1973-74, 15(3), 7-15.

Efland, A. The school art style: A functional analysis. *Studies in Art Education,* 1976. 17(2), 37-43.

Feldman, E. B. *Becoming human through art.* Englewood Cliffs: Prentice-Hall, 1970.

Hastie, R. & Schmidt, C. *Encounter with art,* New York: McGraw-Hill Book Co. n.d.

Kaprow, A. The creation of art and the creation of art education, In E, L. Mattil (Ed,), *A seminar in art education for research and curriculum development.* University Park: The Pennsylvania State University, 1966.

Kaufman, I. *Art and education in contemporary culture,* New York: The Macmillan Co. 1966.

Lanier, V. *Essays in art education: The development of one point of view,* New York: MSS Educational Publishing Co, 1976.

Lanier, V. Objectives of art education: The impact of time, *Peabody Journal of Education,* 1975, 52(3), 183-185.

Lanier, V. Schismogenesis in contemporary art education. *Studies in Art Education,* 1963, 5(1), 10-19.

Lanier, V. Conception and priority in art education research. *Studies in Art Education.* 1974-75, 16(1), 26-30.

Lanier, V. Letters to the editor, *Newsweek,* October 11, 1971, p. 9A.

Lansing, K. M. *Art, artists and art education,* New York: McGraw-Hill Book Co. n.d.

Lidstone, J. *Self expression in classroom art.* Worcester: Davis Publications, 1967.

Madenfort, D. Educating for the immediately sensuous as unified whole. *Art Education,* 1973, 26(7), 8.

Manzella, D. *Educationists and the evisceration of the visual arts,* Scranton: International Textbook Co. 1963.

Morison, B. Artist as teacher, *Saturday Review,* December 19, 1970, p. 53.

Read, H, *Education through art.* London: Faber and Faber, 1943.

Read, H. *Culture and education in world order.* New York: Museum of Modern Art, 1948.

Read, H. *The origins of form in art.* New York: Horizon Press, 1965.

Rockefeller, N. Untitled. *Art Education,* 1975 28(6), 7.

Rogers, F. In pursuit of significance. *Art Education,* 1975, 28(5), 5.

Schinneller, J. A. *Art/search and self-discovery,* Scranton: International Textbook Co. 1968.

Taylor, H, *How to change colleges: Notes on radical reform,* New York: Holt, Rinehart & Winston, 1971.

Templeton, D, Self gratification or shared goals? *British Columbia Art Teachers Association Journal.* 1976, 17(1), no pagination.

Wilson, B. The superheroes of J. C. Holtz. *Art Education,* 1974, 27(8), 2-9.

Wolfe, T. The painted word, *Harpers,* April 1975, pp. 57-92.

Endnotes

[1] Schwartz, F. R. President's message. *Vocational alternatives in art education,* Institute for Study of Art in Education/Abstracts, 1975, 1(1), 5.

[2] Marantz, K, A, Opening Remarks as Outgoing President. *Vocational alternatives in art education,* Institute for Study of Art in Education/ Abstracts. 1975. l(I), 7, 8.

ARTICLE SELECTION

Sandell, R. (1979). Feminist Art Education: An Analysis of the Women's Art Movement as an Educational Force. *Studies in Art Education*, 20 (2), 18-28.

Sandra Packard

Senior Editor, 1979-1981

The 1970s saw the start of two significant movements which are reflected in several articles published in *Studies in Art Education*. The first, the Women's Movement, resulted in the introduction of research on the status of women in art education and of feminist art education theory (Lovano-Kerr, Semler, & Zimmerman, 1977; Michael, 1977; Packard, 1977). A growing dissatisfaction with the exclusion of women artists and scholars in art education curricula, publications, and organizational leadership and the zeitgeist of the national women's movement led to numerous changes in art education These included the use of a blind review process for publication selection in *Studies in Art Education* which opened the journal to the research of significant numbers of women scholars.

The second, the Disciplined-Based Art Education (DBAE) movement, was brought about by a unique collaboration between art education theorists and the Getty Trust. The result of this unique partnership of mission, money and ideology resulted in the development and promulgation of new art education curricula and pedagogy. Simply put, DBAE supported the study of the knowledge base of four disciplines (art history, aesthetics, art production, and art criticism) that should be taught to children in order for them to truly understand, appreciate and participate in art (Clark, & Zimmerman, 1978; Kern, 1978).

In the 1970s, the two movements appeared separate and unrelated; the first having a predominately political agenda, and the second a predominately educational agenda. Rereading the 1970s *Studies in Art Education* articles, however, provides a different perspective, a common mission shared by both. Feminist scholars decried of the lack of gender-diverse curriculum content in art education and DBAE scholars encouraged the inclusion of the art of diverse groups in the education of children. Both agreed that an art education that was not inclusive was inadequate.

Sandra Packard is Chair of the Department of Educational Leadership, Past President, and Professor of Education at Oakland University. Prior to Oakland, she was Provost and Vice Chancellor at The University of Tennessee at Chattanooga, Dean at Bowling Green State University, and Associate Provost at Miami University. Currently a Trustee of the National Art Education Foundation, she was a founding member and the first President of the NAEA Women's Caucus. She has also been a Senior Fellow with the National Association of State Colleges and Universities and an Administrative Fellow with the American Council of Education.

With keen insight, Renee Sandell identified the overlapping mission in feminism and art education in her article, "Feminist art education: An analysis of the Women's Art Movement as an educational force" (1979). Feminist art education, which she defined as "a hybrid between feminism taken as an ideology, and the theory and practice of art education … can refer to the process either of educating an artist through feminism, or educating about feminism through art" (p. 18). Both, she believed, were necessary:

> Future teachers require some understanding of women's issues in the arts and education. With some formal feminist art education content, art teachers could transmit nonsexist values and concepts in the arts to their students, thus educate the younger members of our society and liberate them from unjust sexist influences. (p. 26)

Renee Sandell understood that education is both political and apolitical and that art educators must be prepared to wrestle with both: "Art education can contribute to a more truly humanized world in which both sexes have equal access to the visual skills and sensibilities necessary to play an active role in their self-actualization" (p.26).

References

Clark, G.A., & Zimmerman, E. (1978). A walk in the right direction: A model for visual arts education. *Studies in Art Education, 19*(2), 34-49.

Kern, E.J. (1978). The study of art. *Studies in Art Education, 19*(3), 50-53.

Lovano-Kerr, J., Semler, V., & Zimmerman, E. (1977). A profile of art educators in higher education: Male/female comparative data. *Studies in Art Education, 18*(2), 21-37.

Michael, J. (1977). Women/men in leadership roles in art education. *Studies in Art Education, 18*(2), 7-20.

Packard, S. (1977). An analysis of current statistics and trends as they influence the status and future for women in the art academe. *Studies in Art Education, 18*(2), 38-48.

Feminist Art Education: An Analysis of the Women's Art Movement as an Educational Force

Renee Sandell

In the '70s, for the first time, women's art began to be accessible in quantity. This has had two effects: One is that women artists could begin to work knowingly in relation to the work of other women: the other is that the traditional question-are men's and women's art different?—could be discussed again, but with adequate samples of women's art for the first time. (Alloway, 1976, p. 66)

Feminist art education is conceptually, as well as literally, a hybrid between feminism taken as an ideology, and the theory and practice of art education. Its current nature needs critical study. Art education refers both to the educating of artists and educating of people about art and its relationship to society. Feminism applied to art education can refer to the process either of educating an artist through feminism, or educating about feminism through art. A useful map of the terrain to be investigated is found at the intersections of feminism, the art world, and education; specifically, the women's art movement, women's studies, and art education (see Figure 1).

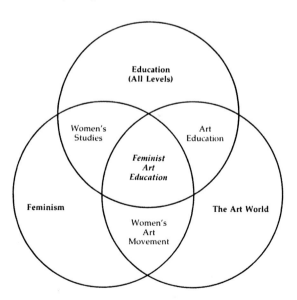

Figure 1. Feminist art education: Location within the universes of feminism, education, and the art world.

The purpose of this study is to suggest relationships between the women's art movement and feminist art education by noting historical and contemporary issues in the women's art movement with regard to art making and the marketing of art and by citing examples of educational efforts of the women's art movement. From these observations there follows a discussion of the role of the field of art education with regard to feminist, art, and educational issues.

The Women's Art Movement and Art

According to sociologist Jacqueline Skiles,[1] the women's art movement represented "the coming together of two streams of protest in the society: the feminist movement of the 60s and 70s and the artists' protest movement against both the existing art structures and the injustices and the support of the war by the society at large." Further, women artists, concerned with "achieving access to the career patterns and structures now open to male artists in the society" engaged in bringing about sexual-political reform in the established art world. Some feminist artists and art historians proposed a gender-based "revisionist" art history, which would reexamine art history and traditional aesthetics from a feminist perspective. This movement has had a positive effect on the making and marketing of women's art. The increased visibility and interest in women's art during the last decade implied in the introductory statement by Alloway, is the result of feminist ideology regarding sexual politics, revisionist art history, and female aesthetics, accompanied by actions of members of the women's art movement.

Women and the Making of Art

The movement's effect on the actual making of art objects has been subtle. The making of art is generally subject to three influential factors: an artist's training and practice, the prevailing historical and critical attitudes of the time, as well as the artist's social milieu and environment. Art making is, and always has been, a creative activity performed by individuals with the desire to visually express original and cultural ideas through their craft. However, traditional art which has been valued by its label "high art," in contrast to "crafts," has often been dependent on patronage and commission by institutions such as the church, royalty, or private patrons. Additionally, such art has been created by those individuals who have received and utilized formal art training.

Although the history of Western art is long and rich, the artistic heritage as we know it has been dominated by male contributors. Art historian Linda Nochlin (1971) has shown that, historically, art training for women has been limited. She blamed unfair institutional and educational practices for impeding women's access to art training and professional aspirations:

> to be deprived of this ultimate state of training [access to the nude model—available to men and a necessary experience in training to become a "history" painter] meant to be deprived of the possibility of creating major art. (p. 24)

Despite their lack of training and recognition, women have continued a tradition of art making, primarily in the form of crafts or decorative (minor) art in the convent, home, school, and studio (Collins, 1978, p. 14). Furthermore, most of women's aesthetic labors have prevailed over the traditional social constraints of motherhood and homemaking; these have been concomitant with deficient work facilities as well as a lack of monetary and social support. Given these factors, Nochlin (1974) hypothesized that a woman born with the potential of a Picasso would be more likely under the existing social conditions to become a wife and mother than a successful artist.

From the beginnings of art history through the first half of the twentieth century, the few women who managed to become successful artists (e.g., Rosa Bonheur, Georgia O'Keeffe and Louise Nevelson) have been regarded as exceptions. Regardless of such status, women artists and their art products have been subject to stereotypical attitudes. Art historians have furthered women artists' isolation as feminine talents that were somehow peculiar, either by underrepresenting their work or by overstating traditional feminine roles and attribute. For example Walter Shaw Sparrow wrote in the preface to his 1905 book *Women Painters of the World:*

> What is genius? Is it not both masculine and feminine? Are not some of its qualities instinct with manhood while others delight us with the most winning graces of a perfect womanhood? Does not genius make its appeal as a single creative agent with a two-fold sex? .... Style is the man in the genius of men, style is the women in the genius of the fair. No male artist, however gifted he may be, will ever be able to experience all the emotional life to which women are subject; and no woman of abilities, how much so ever she may try, will be able to borrow from men anything so invaluable to art as her own intuition and the prescient tenderness and grace of her nursery-nature. Thus, then: the bisexuality of genius has limits in art and those limits should be determined by a worker's sex. (p. 11)

In contrast to Sparrow's earlier study, Eleanor Tufts' (1974) book *Our Hidden Heritage: Five Centuries of Women Artists* has attempted to

> dispel some of the amusing and fallacious myths that have sprung up concerning women artists, such as that of the characteristic "female touch" and "female theme." In the same way that it is impossible to determine the sex of a writer by the individual's handwriting, there is, in general, no perceptible distinction between the touch of the male and female artist. (pp. xvi-xvii)

Tufts has endeavored to redress the imbalances in art history by rephrasing art historian Linda Nochlin's (1971) famous question "Why have there been no great women artists?" to "Why is so little known about great women artists of the past?" The answer, she felt, points to "a collective and rather recent cultural neglect."

This neglect, which is also linked to women's limited production of art, has, until recently, been sustained by attitudes regarding the notion of "feminine sensibility" or "female aesthetic." In her study of the feminine sensibility in art, Georgia Collins (1978) disclosed historical and contemporary attitudes which recognize the influence of an artist's gender on works of art. She concluded that while "the nature and potential of the feminine sensibility is in the process of being scrutinized and redefined by women artists . . . the concept of feminine sensibility should itself be open ended" (p. 17). Gloria Orenstein (1975), in exploring recent feminist debates over the notion of the "female aesthetic" expressed her feeling that

> the answer to the question of whether, indeed, there is something definable as a "female aesthetic" is ultimately less important than the fact that the issue has been raised, for it means that contemporary women are taking art history into their own hands and molding it to suit their own image. (p. 521)

Another significant debilitating factor to women's art production has been the social milieu of artists. Though artists have traditionally worked in a seemingly independent manner, they have often functioned in small groups in settings such as workshops, schools, or private circles. Until the mid-nineteenth century, many artists served an apprenticeship learning artistic skills, traditions, and history from masters. Modern artists, on the other hand, have tended to operate in intellectual circles, sharing their ideas, approaches, and values. Such circles have functioned as an ideological support system for the solitary visual artist who has been at the periphery of society. Women have been included in such circles but primarily in the roles of wives, mistresses, mothers, patrons, etc. Women have been second-class members of such supportive environments, since they have been supporters but not recipients of reinforcement or credit for creative work. Faced with obstacles to their artistic creativity in the school and studio as well as in professionally supportive groups, women have been particularly needy of a support system complete with female role models.

Women and the Marketing of Art

With an awareness that historians had "built women a bad art history" (Schwartz, 1973) and of the contemporary inequities in the acquisition of art skills and professional survival in the art world, some women artists in the late 60s and 70s united to form their own supportive groups. They aimed to change the current art system in which they had to survive as women who were artists. This move towards a unified support system for women in the arts was necessitated by the insular conditions in which women's art had traditionally been fabricated. Without this movement, women's art might have remained divested from dialogue with other historical and contemporary art forms (Lippard, 1976). However, the particular ways in which the women's art movement has fostered better conditions for women making art and secured a reevaluation of their contributions to the history of art can best be understood as part of the complex notion of the marketing of art, seen in an educational as well as economic context.

To understand what is meant by the marketing of art in an educational context, we need to examine the marketing process as well as the agencies and targets of the women's art movement. The term "marketing" has two meanings: "the act of buying or selling in a market," and "the total of activities by which transfer of title or possession of goods from seller to buyer is effected, including advertising, shipping, storing and selling" (*The Random House Dictionary,* 1966, p. 878). Though there most certainly exists an economic art market that fits the first definition, greater attention will be paid to the second definition, which deals with the marketing process, activities by which transfer of goods occur. The women's art movement has, first and foremost, attempted to help "sell" women's art, aesthetics, *and* ideology to consumers in a male-dominated aesthetic economy, the art market. The marketing process of the women's art movement has included: advertising—promotion of women's art and aesthetics; shipping-seeking viable means for transmitting women's art and aesthetics to members of society; storing-cataloging information about women's past and present art works; and selling-bringing women's art works, philosophies, and aesthetics to the art world and society in the economic, labor, and educational markets.

Gloria Orenstein (1975) has noted that feminist artists and critics have challenged the existing art market by asking

what cultural prejudices are at work when certain artifacts are judged to be "high art" while others are relegated to the supposedly inferior categories of "decorative arts and crafts"? [Furthermore,] ... radical feminist art historians are questioning the very bases of the economic structure of our society that force the artist to become dependent upon the approval of a wealthy elitist clientele of art collectors, patrons, and corporate enterprises for their financial survival. (p. 518)

Women artists have banded together to form cooperative galleries to regain control of exhibitions and sales of their works. In taking such actions, they have

been forced to become their own curators, dealers and critics; to do their own promotion; and to run their own businesses—which has, in turn, permitted them to gain expertise in all phases of the art market. (Orenstein, 1975, p. 518)

The Women's Art Movement: An Educational Model

The making and marketing activities by members of the women's art movement can be viewed as educational in purpose. The process of education occurs through the (a) personal, (b) informal and (c) formal educational "routes" diagrammed in Figure 2.

Personal Education

The first route taken by members of the women's art movement was that of obtaining information for their own personal education. This involved the sharing and developing of an ideology which would establish personal and professional support in the short run and build toward eventual non-sexist changes in the art world and society.

The first stirrings of the movement began with women artists, art historians, and art critics who were concerned about the discrimination they had experienced because of their gender. They recognized their weak position in the art-learning and teaching labor market (Harris, 1972, 1973; White & White, 1973) and in the art making and selling product market (Baker, 1971; Lippard, 1971; Tamarind, 1972). Women artists were first provoked by their realization of sexist conditions in museums and art galleries. They began to organize in 1969. Their actions, directed at establishing a fine arts community for women (Nemser, 1974; Alloway, 1976), would later effect changes in the older, male domi-nated systems within the art world. Temporarily, new support systems for professional women in the arts, based on shared philosophies and needs, were established. Some of

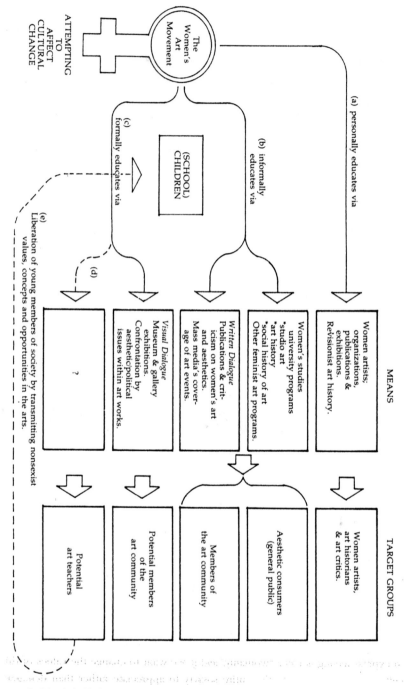

Figure 2. Model of the women's art movement as an educational force.

these began as consciousness-raising groups and developed into group art projects and cooperative agencies such as Womanhouse and the Feminist Studio Workshop (Chicago, 1975; Wilding, 1977).

Women's art groups first emerged on both the East and West coasts, and later spread nationally and internationally. The process of self-identification and education for women in the arts occurred in and through the following neoteric agencies:

1. Organizations and cooperatives for women artists such as Women Artists in Revolution (W.A.R.), Los Angeles Council of Women Artists (L.A.C.W.A.), Red Stockings, Women Art Students and Artists for Black Artists' Liberation (W.A.S.A.B.A.L.), Women's Ad Hoc Committee (which protested the Whitney annual), West-East Bag (W.E.B.), Artists in Residence (A.I.R.), Where We At, Women in the Arts (W.I.A.), Women's Interart Center, Washington Women's Art Center (W.W.A.C.)

2. Women's caucuses in existing established professional organizations such as the Women's Caucus for Art (which emerged from the College Art Association) and the National Art Education Association Women's Caucus, with special programs and publications.

3. Exhibitions of women's art such as: "X to the 12th Power"; "Unmanly Art"; "13 Women Artists"; "Women Artists Here and Now"; "26 Contemporary Women Artists"; "Ten Artists (Who Also Happen to be Women)"; "Women Choose Women"; "Womanhouse"; "Old Mistresses: Women Artists of the Past"; "The Dinner Party"; "Women Artists: 1550- 1950."

4. Publications of various sorts to disseminate information to and about women in the arts such as *Women and Art; The Feminist Art Journal; Womanspace; Women Artists Newsletter; Heresies; Chrysalis; Women's Caucus for Art Newsletter; The Report* of the National Art Education Association Women's Caucus; *Visual Dialogue; Womanart.*

5. Programs for women to participate in: slide registries and directories of women's art such as the West-East Bag (W.E.B.) and The Women's History Research Center (Berkeley, California); women's art workshops in settings such as Feminist Studio Workshop in The Women's Building (Los Angeles), Women's Interart Center (New York City) and the N.Y. Feminist Art Institute as well as special sessions at the College Art Association Meetings and the National Art Education Association conventions.

These agencies of the movement not only helped educate women artists but also provided women with access to the process of exhibiting—the consummation experience for the professional artist. The exhibitions, as well as the caucuses and workshops, provided women with a haven in which to work out their particular concerns. Both women artists and viewers were encouraged to "get in touch with their feelings" in these participatory environments as well as with the feminist content in the art works. For example, as Judy Chicago (1975) wrote after the success of the Womanhouse exhibit,

to express feeling is to be "womanly," and if we want to change the values of this culture, we must educate the entire society to appreciate rather than denigrate "womanliness" in art and in life. (p. 131)

Not only were a variety of conceptions of "woman" presented by and to many women in a contemporary context, but the history of women in art had become important. Women artists, historians, and educators sought information on historical female artists in an attempt to establish models and recover a lost correspondence of feminine sensibilities *and* liabilities within a patriarchal society. As part of the seven day Women's Art Festival at the California Institute of the Arts in 1974, women who had actively participated in the Feminist Art Program published their ideas with pictorial results in *Anonymous was a Woman* in which they also included a collection of solicited letters to young women artists from established contempo-rary female artist or art historian models. In introducing their book, they raised these points:

> What does it mean to make art as a woman? Some themes seem to repeat themselves: covering and uncovering, central imagery, intimacy, sensuality, personal symbology. What about the art made by women working in the mainstream? The more we learn about our sensibilities, the more complex and beautiful they become. We have come to redefine ourselves as pioneers in this strange territory. A long process of removing layers of social conditioning has kept our vision unformed, confused and repressed. Our marks are now a poetic outcry against the void of history. We have the audacity to be faithful to this dream. (Schapiro, 1974, p. 1)

In sum, the personal education "route," was a self-constructed path by which women artists, art historians, critics, educators, and students, with strengthened individual and collective professional identities, could enter, transcend, and transform the art market. From such initial educational efforts would later emerge feminist art education.

Informal Education

Beyond their attempts at personal education, members of the women's art movement educated other women and men through informal means—that is, outside of the traditional formal classroom. Their target was the members of the established art world and the general public. The educational process included visual and verbal dialogues, which threatened existing aesthetic and social attitudes.

A *visual dialogue* which confronted the public and the art world, was conducted through the special exhibitions of women's art in museums and art galleries as well as by the aesthetic and political issues contained within the art works themselves. Women artists were "bringing the 'private' sphere (usually maintained by women) into the light, making the private public, and in doing so taking a large step towards bridging the culture chasm between men and women" (Chicago, 1975, p. 131), which subtly lies in our societal divisions of a male public universe vs. a private female cosmos. Artist Judy Chicago (1975) felt that,

> not only do women have to move into public life, but men have to share the burdens of private life before any real change can take place. This means that men have to be educated emotionally, and the first step in that education is to be made to 'see' women, to feel with us, experience our point of view. (pp. 130-131)

The works which purported to share these female aesthetic views, or sensibilities, paralleled other current directions in contemporary art, but established its own categorical importance by the segregated mode of presentation, which excluded art made by males. Feminist art, as opposed to feminine art, could be "taken seriously" because of its political intent (Nemser, 1976). In surveying current art by women, Nemser noted these trends: political art, autobiographical art, a conscious search for archetypal imagery, exploration of female sexuality, and a return to crafts and decorative arts which are historically associated with women. Some women artists such as Helen Aim Roth[2] and Kate Millett[3], have advocated greater use of popular media such as video-tape arid graphics, in order to reach a wider audience. In sum, the new visual dialogue of the women artists with art audiences was expressed in different dialects and tones, while communicating through the contemporary visual vocabulary.

A *written dialogue* which included "painted words" (Wolfe, 1975) and feminist rhetoric accompanied the visual dialogue. It was carried on by and between art critics and art historians sympathetic to and often strongly identified with the women's art movement, such as Linda Nochlin, Patricia Mainardi, Carol Duncan, Lucy Lippard, Cindy Nemser, Elizabeth Baker, Gloria Orenstein, and Lawrence Alloway. Verbally articulate artists such as Judy Chicago, Miriam Schapiro, June Wayne, and Pat Sloane also participated by writing their ideas and experiences. Sociologists such as Jacqueline Skiles added other perspectives to the written dialogue.

The written dialogue has resounded in a distinctive but varied body of literature found in subject-specific journals and articles, books and monographs that survey the work of women artists, exhibition catalogues, bibliographies, and newsletters. All of these publications deal with the subject of women and art, past and present. They present and debate a variety of aesthetic and political issues. In addition to the specialized art publications, regular agents of the mass media have included coverage of the events and ideas surrounding the women artists' efforts to enlighten the general public (Hughes, 1972, 1977; Davis, 1973; Glueck, 1977; Hess, 1977).

Formal Education

Beyond personal and informal enlightenment of the art world and society, the women's art movement has had an impact on formal education, primarily in higher education. It has affected the contents of university art galleries as well as art and art history curricula. College art departments have expanded their slide collections to include women's art works and offered special seminars on women's art. The creation of separate feminist art institutions such as the Feminist Studio Workshop in the Women's Building in Los Angeles was another formal, albeit alternative, educational effort within the women's art movement. These attempts have fostered greater awareness of historical perspectives as well as current personal and professional needs of women (White, 1976).

Since the 1970s, courses in fine arts and art history have been offered by university women's studies programs around the country. These attempts at formal education constitute "feminist art education." Feminist art education, as an outgrowth of the women's art movement, refers to instruction on issues and topics relevant to feminism in the visual arts, taking place in formal classroom and alternative learning environments (Sandell, 1978). A representative sample of some courses of study was compiled for the Women's Caucus for Art of the College Art Association (Spear & Gellman, 1975; Fine, Gellman & Loeb, 1978). These courses deal with various issues raised by the women's art movement, but attempt to explore them in academic and non-academic settings. They vary

in quality and level, [and] are divided into three main categories: studio courses for women art students; art historical courses on women artists *and/or* on the image of woman in art; socially-oriented courses on the role and fate of women in the art world. (Spear and Gellman, 1975, foreword)

Some courses have been offered only once, indicating perhaps a lack of interest, funding, or adequate instructional materials. Other courses have been perennially revised and renewed. These courses and their derivative exhibitions and research projects are on-going, influencing the *potential* art community as well as supportive aesthetic consumers.

The Women's Art Movement and Art Education

Thus far I have identified issues related to women's art making and marketing and outlined a model of the women's art movement as an educational force. The educational actions of the movement have been characterized as (a) personal, (b) informal and (c) formal, the latter constituting feminist art education. Although the women's art movement has functioned educationally, the relationship and role of the field of art education with regard to women's issues and feminist art education remains to be examined.

Art educators examining current sexual-political concerns in art and society may note that the educational efforts of artists, art historians, and art critics who comprise the women's art movement have for the most part by-passed school-age children (see Figure 2). Despite advances made by these feminists, only minute portions of their efforts have been directed toward formal non-artist-oriented art education which takes place in agencies such as the schools. Further, members of the movement have paid little attention to the specific role that the field of art education might play in helping to eradicate sexist influences in art and education. This is ironic since many feminists and educators from other disciplines, believing that "a woman's place is the curriculum" (Trecker, 1971; Howe, 1973), have been campaigning actively for the implementation of nonsexist amendments in school subjects such as math, social studies, language arts, physical education, etc., to form a more androgynous education for both sexes. This has taken place in early and middle school curricula as well as in high school and college women's studies courses.

This is not to say that feminist concerns and activities have not surfaced in the field of art education. Since 1974, a number of art educators have responded to women's issues and have worked toward the goal of nonsexism in art education. This has been done in personal and informal ways: through the programs, publications and task forces of the National Art Education Association's Women's Caucus as well as by personal statements (McFee, 1975; Packard, 1974) and individual research efforts. Three major areas of research include: awareness of women's roles and sexism in art and art education (Acuff & Packard, 1974; Bastian, 1975; Collins, 1977, 1978; Dobbs, 1975; Loeb, 1975; Snyder-Ott, 1974; Whitesel, 1975, 1977); sex-differences in art preferences (Chalmers, 1977) and in children's art production (Feinberg, 1977; Majewski,[4]; and sex-related issues bearing on professionalism and leadership in art education (Michael, 1977; Lovano-Kerr, Simmler & Zimmerman, 1977; Packard, 1977). Additional qualitative and quantitative research on sex-related issues in art, education, psychology, and art education will be a requisite for appropriate non-sexist revisions in art education theory and practice.

More practical and direct educational efforts such as curricular modifications in art teacher education will be needed if we are to fully recognize the increased potential of woman's place in art and art education. As shown in Figure 2, most art teachers-in-training are not currently part of the educational process of the women's art movement. These future teachers require some understanding of women's issues in the arts and education. With some formal feminist art education content, art teachers could transmit nonsexist values and concepts in the arts to their students, thus educate the younger members of our society and liberate them from unjust sexist influences. Inclusion of feminist art educational content would be both compensatory and important in the training and cultivating of art teachers (the majority of whom are women), since they influence and train the general public to make and appreciate art, a small percentage of whom actually become artists. Additionally, this process of training art teachers would be a more efficient way of educating society against sexism than the current combination of educational processes of the women's art movement.

The field of art education needs to sensitize itself to issues such as these and become a more active educational force against the condition of sexism in art and society. By this adjustment in values, art education can contribute to a more truly humanized world in which both sexes have equal access to the visual skills and sensibilities necessary to play an active role in their self-actualization. A first step in that direction is the nonsexist training, or re-training, of art teachers.

References

Acuff, B. & Packard, S. Women's views. *Art Education,* 1974, 27(9), 24-25.

Alloway, L. Women's art of the 70s. *Art in America,* May/June 1976, pp. 64-72.

Baker, E. Sexual art-politics. *Art News,* 1971, 69(9), 47-48; 60-62.

Bastian, L. Women as artists and teachers. *Art Education,* 1975, 28(7), 12-15.

Chalmers, C. Women as art viewers: sex differences and aesthetic preferences. *Studies in Art Education,* 1977, 18(2), 49-53.

Chicago, J. *Through the flower.* New York: Doubleday, 1975.

Collins, C.. Considering an androgynous model for art education. *Studies in Art Education,* 1977, 18(2), 54-62.

Collins, C. Reflections on the head of medusa. *Studies in Art Education,* 1978, 19(2), 10-18.

Davis, D. Women, women, women. *Newsweek,* January 29, 1973, p. 77.

Dobbs, S. Women in the arts: an optimistic forecast. *Art Education,* 28(7), 24-26.

Feinberg, S.G. Conceptual content and spatial characteristics in boys' and girls' drawings of fighting and helping. *Studies in Art Education,* 1977, 18(2), 63-71.

Fine, E.H., Gellman, L., & Loeb, J. (Eds.), *Women's studies and the arts.* New York: The Women's Caucus for Art, 1978.

Glueck, G. The woman as artist. *New York Times Magazine,* September 25, 1977, pp. 48-68.

Harris, A.S. The second sex in academe. *Art in America,* 1972, 60(3), 18-19.

Harris, A.S. Women in college art departments and museums. *Art Journal,* 1973, 32(4), 417-19.

Hess, T.B. Women's work. *New York,* October 17, 1977, pp. 90-93.

Howe, F. Sexism, racism and the education of women. *Today's Education,* 1973, 62, 47-48.

Hughes, R. Myths of 'sensibility.' *Time,* March 20, 1972, pp. 72-77.

Hughes, R. Rediscovered-women painters. *Time,* January 10, 1977, pp. 60-63.

Lippard, L. Sexual politics, art style. *Art in America,* September/October 1971, pp. 19-20.

Lippard, L. *From the center-feminist essays on women's art.* New York: Dutton, 1976.

Loeb, J. Our women artist/teachers need our help: on changing language, finding cultural heritage, and building self-image. *Art Education,* 1975, 28(7), 9-11.

Lovano-Kerr, J., Semler, V., & Zimmerman, E. A profile of art educators in higher education: male/female comparative data. *Studies in Art Education,* 1977, 18(2), 21-37.

McFee, J.K. Society and identity-A personal perspective. *Art Education,* 1975, 28(7), 5~8.

Michael, J.A. Women/men in leadership roles in art education. *Studies in Art Education,* 1977, 18(2), 7-20.

Nemser, C. The women's art movement. *Feminist Art Journal,* 1974, 2(4), 8-10.

Nemser, C. Towards a feminist sensibility: contemporary trends in women's art. *Feminist Art Journal,* Summer 1976, 5(2), 19-23.

Nochlin, L. Why have there been no great women artists? *Art News,* 1971, 69(9), 22-39, 67-70.

Nochlin, L. How feminism in the arts can implement cultural change. *Arts in Society,* 1974, 11(1), 80-89.

Orenstein, G.F. Art history. *Signs,* 1975, 1(1), 505-525.

Packard, S. A personal statement on discrimination. *Art Education,* 1974, 27(9), 25.

Packard, S. An analysis of current statistics and trends as they influence the status and future for women in the art academe. *Studies in Art Education,* 1977, 18(2), 38-48.

The Random House Dictionary of the English Language. New York: Random House, Inc., 1966.

Sandell, R. Feminist art education: Definition, assessment and application to contemporary art education. Unpublished doctoral dissertation, The Ohio State University, 1978.

Schapiro, M., Ed. *Anonymous was a woman-a documentation of the women's art festival and collection of letters to young women artists.* Los Angeles, California: Feminist Art Program, 1974.

Schwartz, T. They built women a bad art history. *Feminist Art Journal,* 1973, 2(3), 10-11, 22.

Snyder-Ott, J. The female experience and artistic creativity. *Art Education,* 1974, 27(6), 15-18.

Sparrow, W.S. *Women painters of the world-from the time of Caterina Vigri 1413-1363 to Rosa Bonheur and the present day.* New York: Hacker Art Books, 1976. (First published in London: Hodder & Stoughton, 1905.)

Spear, A.T., & Gellman, L. *Women's studies in art and art history* (2nd ed.). New York: The Women's Caucus for Art, 1975.

Tamarind Lithography Workshop, Inc. *Sex differentials in art exhibition reviews: A statistical study.* Los Angeles: Author, 1972.

Trecker, J.L. Woman's place is in the curriculum. *Saturday Review,* October 16, 1971, pp. 83-86.

Tufts, E. *Our hidden heritage: five centuries of women artists.* New York: Paddington Press, Ltd., 1974.

White, B.E. A 1974 perspective: Why women's studies in art and art history? *Art Journal,* 1976, 35(4), 340-344.

White, B.E., & White, L.S. Survey on the status of women in college art departments. *Art Journal,* 1973, 32(4), 420-422.

Whitesel, L. Women as art students, teachers and artists. *Art Education,* 1975, 28(3), 21-26. Whitesel, L. Attitudes of women art students. *Art Education,* 1977, 30(1), 25-27.

Wilding, F. *By our own hands: the women artists' movement, Southern California 1970-76.* Santa Monica, Ca.: Double X, 1977.

Wolfe, T. The painted word. *Harpers,* April 1975, pp. 57-92.

Endnotes

[1] Skiles, J. *The women artists' movement.* Paper presented at the annual meeting of the American Sociological Association, New Orleans, LA, August 28, 1972.

[2] Roth, H.A. Interview at The Women's Graphic Center, The Feminist Studio Workshop, Los Angeles, Ca., June 19, 1977.

[3] Millett, K. *Women and power: The position of women in the arts.* Author's notes from a lecture given at The Ohio State University, Columbus, Ohio, May 25, 1977.

[4] Majewski, Margaret Mary. *The relationship between the drawing characteristics of children and their gender.* Paper presented at the National Art Education Association Convention, Houston, Texas, March 17, 1978.

Selections
from the 1980s

1960s
1970s
1990s
2000s

STUDIES
in Art Education

ARTICLE SELECTION

Degge, R. M. (1982). The Classroom Teacher as Inquirer. *Studies in Art Education,* 24(1), 25-32.

Ron MacGregor

Senior Editor, 1981-1983

Whether Paul Pohland, Elliot Eisner, or one of their contemporaries first introduced the notion of participant-observation to art education may be a matter for debate. Certainly, Robert Bersson (1978) summarized in his *Studies in Art Education* article procedures characteristic of field observers, as well as arguing the "insider-outsider" role for the investigator, and discussing questions of validity and reliability. Equally indisputably, the first issue of *Studies* to be entirely devoted to the application of ethnographic method (with particular emphasis on participant-observation) appeared in 1982.

From the articles in that issue, I have chosen Rogena Degge's as a pioneer example of giving individual identity and freedom of response to persons who, in an earlier generation of statistical studies, would have been labeled with a generic S (for subject), and been the target of questions predetermined by the researcher. Degge's questions, by contrast, are open-ended, designed to help the respondents reflect on who they are, what they do, and why they do what they do, all within the setting of the art classroom.

A large part of the National Art Education Association's membership consists of teaching practitioners and members in higher education who have ongoing involvement with teachers, as advisors, or consultants, or collaborators in the preparation and support of the teaching force. This constituency is therefore both extensive and diverse, and it is this audience for whom articles like Degge's are particularly relevant.

Ron MacGregor taught art education at the University of Alberta in Edmonton, Canada from 1967 to 1982, then was Head of Visual and Performing Arts in Education, and a member of the Faculty of Education at the University of British Columbia in Vancouver, Canada. The author of three books, and an editor of *Art Education,* he has contributed internationally to most art education journals on topics ranging from aspects of visual perception to the investigation of art teacher practices. He retired in 1997 and currently lives on Vancouver Island.

Rogena Degge asks essential questions such as: What patterns of inquiry do teachers follow? What questions do they ask? What resources do they have? What methods do they use? From the responses her informants provide, she assembles a configuration that is multi-layered, rich in detail, and containing its share of the loose ends, contradictions, and lapses in thinking that accumulate over time in a familiar working environment, and that beg for remediation.

Of course, remedies are only possible with a supportive infrastructure, and in that respect, the ultimate prospect of benefits for Degge's informants was (and probably still is) poor. While journals like *Human Organization* were at that time filled with ethnographically-influenced case studies conducted in hospitals, industrial plants, and other settings where the clear intent was to learn from the findings and implement changes where necessary, little of the kind happened in education. Largely, I suspect, this was because educational ethnographies were conducted mostly by graduate students, who were neither remunerated for their work, nor consulted about their findings by the school district in which they were working.

At least, those who conducted field observation studies benefited from the experience, and often went on to assume positions of influence in the field, making use of what they had learned. Rogena Degge's article stands at the far end of a vein of art education research since mined by many educators working in the spirit of participant-observation (or in latter-day manifestations such as action research) to ensure its continuance as an effective research tool.

Reference

Bersson, R.D. (1978). The use of participant-observation in the evaluation of art programs. *Studies in Art Education,* 19(2), 61-67.

The Classroom Art Teacher as Inquirer

Rogena M. Degge

Inquiry may be a quest for information, a search to extend knowledge, or a systematic investigation of a matter of interest. When undertaken by classroom art teachers, that quest is logically directed at developing, adding to, changing, and improving the teaching of art.

With that in mind, at least four clusters of questions seem worth pursuing. First, what are the patterns of inquiry practiced by art teachers? What are their questions? What resources do they use? What are their methods of inquiry? Why are certain patterns predominant? Second, what do teachers say and do in the art classroom that may reveal their instructional modes of inquiry and their range of concerns? Third, what are the realistic expectations of a classroom teacher as inquirer? How can our teacher preparation programs and inservice offerings affect the development of inquiry modes and skills? What content for inquiry can be carried into and applied to teaching? Fourth, how do the resources art teachers now utilize compare in content and form to those that educators of teachers provide? What do teachers want, and can it be provided without compromise? While this paper does not attempt to provide complete answers to these several issues, each cluster of questions is considered in turn to suggest implications for art education research and practice in these contexts.

Patterns of Inquiry Practiced

While little about the patterns of inquiry practiced by classroom art teachers is revelationary, they do assume configurations that are useful for decision making. Resources used to summarize the predominant patterns of inquiry practiced include personal interviews with eleven art teachers, written responses from twenty-seven practicing secondary art teachers, data collected by undergraduates observing in classrooms over a six year period, review and recall of classroom case studies, and personal experience and "grounded speculation."[1]

Teachers' Questions and Kinds of Inquiries

Three kinds of inquiry seem prevalent. The first centers on the desire for new or additional information related to media, and especially process. Questions center on what to do and how to apply it in the classroom, what needs to be known, and what students need to know to apply the process and produce art products. The second kind of inquiry focuses on new ideas for presenting a concept. "I know what I want to teach, but how to teach is what I'm after," said one experienced art teacher. The pattern of inquiry includes securing new, more interesting ways to present a familiar concept through an art project, and deciding whether the concept could be taught through dialogue in an historical or societal approach, or whether the concept can best be learned through production alone. Concern for keeping teaching and learning exciting for students and the teacher is a prime motivator. Tied to these inquiries is a continual search for visual imagery that will stimulate students' ideas for production or that will elaborate or clarify a concept. The third kind of inquiry seeks effective ways to transmit to parents, students, and administrators the potential value of art knowledge for students, and the impact that this knowledge ultimately may have on the community and larger society.

Inquiry Methods and Resources

Literature search and studio practice seem currently to constitute the major vehicles for art teacher inquiry. Among many teachers, "doing it before teaching it" seems paramount. Taking studio classes at universities, two-year colleges, and local art centers is often coupled with literature resources centered on design, drawing, sculpture, crafts, or the art of a person or culture. In a sample of eleven secondary art teachers interviewed, art education textbooks and journals were not mentioned unless asked about, even when the teachers were subjected to what I thought was careful prodding. Frank responses indicated that, though respected, these are least used by the experienced art teacher. Practical journals designed specifically for the classroom art teacher are seen as very useful by the new teacher, but are seldom consulted after one or two years' experience. Many new teachers compiled extensive files of materials from these practical journals, but later used them infrequently.

A range of resources was considered important in providing general, ongoing personal stimulation for the art teacher. Philosophy, criticism, reviews, picture books, and exhibits were highly valued in heightening personal enthusiasm for teaching. Of this material, picture books are most likely to be carried into the classroom. Seldom, it seems, are these or other personal resources directly incorporated into course content. Literature that is taken into the classroom is frequently and primarily in the form of how-to books and art (as distinct from art education), nature, geography and science journals. These and the picture books are used to stimulate students' imaginations, to provide ideas for art production, or to explain concepts.

Artists and other art teachers, workshops, students, parents, television, films, art educators, and professional meetings are among additional, common resources mentioned. My experience leads me to believe that the larger percentage of classroom art teachers does not belong to state and national art education associations. Those who are members receive the journals and newsletters and occasionally attend conferences, but the utilization of these resources, by comparison, is very low (Scholfield-Sweet et al., Note 1).

Art teacher patterns of inquiry seem related primarily to the still prevailing studio artist model. In this regard, Erikson has warned that "the artist role model for the practitioner works against his or her valuing and making use of art education research" (1979, p. 12). In all likelihood this pattern will persist if current educational practices continue to give no serious attention to the classroom art teacher as inquirer.

Clues to Instructional Modes of Inquiry

Recently, observations of a high school art program provided exemplary evidence of how one teacher made use of a literature resource he had found in the fine arts section of a local bookstore—the well-known *Drawing on the Right Side of the Brain*

(Edwards, 1979). A student observer provided a brief recounting of its classroom utilization (Dunkum, Note 2).

At the front of the room an ancient overhead projector sits with a white screen pulled down in front of it. Beside the projector, on one of the long cluttered tables, is Betty Edwards' book. The first page projected on the screen is a series of before and after drawings. They are of people's faces. Evidently the assignment for yesterday was the drawing of faces. The teacher points out the tremendous differences and attends to the amount of time it took each individual to achieve that difference. The next page projected onto the screen is another before-and-after drawing. "The individual whose work we're looking at is Vincent Van Gogh," the teacher says. "How many of you know who Vincent Van Gogh was? Van Gogh didn't actually start drawing until he was 27 years old. Even artists must study and learn how to draw." The teacher briefly reiterates what he talked about yesterday [split brain theory]. "We're going to try to enable you to switch modes. Think of your stereo switch. When you switch it to one or the other you hear the same thing, but you hear it a little differently, in a different way."

Students are given five sheets of paper. The first two were used to loosen up, working in continuous and diagonal lines, creating patterns. The third paper was used to draw their names or signatures with a focus on style. The teacher states, "When thinking of style, think back to your signature. No two signatures look alike." For the fourth drawing he says, "I want you to think in your mind's eye about what a profile is-your stereotyped idea about profile. Start at the top of your paper and think about forehead, nose, lips, and chin. As you draw, think about that feature you're drawing. If you are right-handed, draw your first profile on the left-hand side of your paper. Now, when drawing the second profile, I want you to think about the *why* in relation to the forehead, nose, lips, and chin; not their names, but where the curve starts, where a point is relative to another. Think about the top of the page in comparison to the bottom."

"O.K., I'm going to stop you now. I'd like for you to try to verbalize what you've drawn." One student says, "A vase." Another says, "Two profiles facing one another." Students agree that drawing the second profile was tougher. The teacher says, "The confusion should have lessened once you started to realize the relation between the lines-the right brain taking over." Time has flown. Class is just about over. "You should all be very proud of yourselves. Whether or not you know it, you've made some progress today," says the teacher. "Just walking around the room I can see it."

The student-observer, from whose notes the above passage is excerpted, later commented, "I can only assume that a total review of the book might have benefited the teacher." Admitting that it had been a long time since he had read it, and adding" I really ought to sit down and read it again," the observer went on to say, "I think that the teacher would have felt genuinely more comfortable if he had more facts, more insight, more instances and examples when dealing with the concept of split brain theory. I guess I find it hard to believe that so little thought was spent on a subject that would lead these students through numerous exer-cises in the coming weeks. Surely they are not just new exercises to take up time?"

A number of similar examples could be added to this one. In the literature there is more than one article pointing out cautions and considerations regarding split-brain research, particularly as it may be applied to teaching art. Youngblood (1979) provides such a critique under the title "The Hemispherality Wagon Leaves Laterality Station at 12:45 for Art Superiority Land." As unforgettable as the title is, one only has to note that it is published in *Studies in Art Education* to realize that very few classroom art teachers will seek it out unless guided there in a graduate art education class. Clearly this guidance is part of our task as art educators responsible for preparing teachers. But how, and in what form, do we get this kind of information to more teachers effectively? Youngblood followed up his "Hemispherality Wagon ..." article with a similar one in *Art Education* (1981), a journal received by more art teachers and no doubt more widely read. His message was clear, direct, and cautionary. Surely it, and critical articles like it, deserve to reach our art teachers as pervasively as Edwards and many others have. This one example, arbitrary as it is, would seem to suggest we look more carefully at how resources and manners of inquiry are implemented in classrooms.

Developing Skills, Modes, and Resources for Inquiry

An experienced junior high art teacher whom I interviewed as representative of that group of teachers noted that her greatest recurring frustration was keeping students interested, involved, and behaved. One of many recently trained in assertive discipline, she noted that applying assertive measures seemed to quell some student behavior but did little or nothing to increase student interest. How to resolve this persistent problem was her greatest concern and one for which she has found too few useful answers in her continual search. Equally importantly, she said she did not know what she should be inquiring about. She had no means of access to the problem.

In general, teachers are aware of the relationship between what they teach and student interest. They seem much less aware of what the interests, needs, and levels of their students actually are, so that these can be assessed, and so that what they might teach could offer substantive quality and knowledge, rather than primarily skill and therapy, in their students' current as well as future lives.

A range of commentary on these very issues may be found in art education research and literature. But can we reach teachers with these and other concerns in more impactful ways? The thrust of research, theory, and such curricular material is not irrelevant to the classroom teacher; it is merely, in most cases, unattractive or useless in its initial form, not easily accessible, indecipherable, or unknown to them. Modes of inquiry used by classroom teachers take them more often than not to resources outside art education, as well as outside their own classrooms. Also, most research methodologies utilized by researchers in art education often are not reasonably or easily applied by the inquiring classroom art teacher. More important, perhaps, is that they have not been trained to use and value inquiry methods that may be useful and desirable.

Considering this and all that has preceded, it would seem that those engaged in art teacher training have at least a three-fold responsibility to the classroom art teacher as inquirer. Undergraduate programs should be constructed in such a way that aspiring art teachers will enter the classroom with some practical, useful, and feasible inquiry skills that they can easily and reasonably employ, and know why. Appealing and responsible resources should be provided for beginning art teachers that will meet their needs, not only as educators of teachers see their needs, but as teachers see them. Practical, useful materials should be provided and inquiry skills taught to experienced, inquiring art teachers that will not only help them assess their programs and students, but will direct them to other resources that both teachers and teacher educators feel are appropriate. Responsibly addressing these areas of need is clearly a task larger than the scope of this paper. Even so, some suggestions for consideration are attempted.

The Aspiring Art Teacher as Inquirer

A method of research effectively used by students placed in the field to learn in ongoing classroom settings, as well as by teachers in the classroom, is derived from the ethnographic (or educational criticism) model (Eisner, Note 3). To some degree teachers employ this mode of inquiry daily as they interact with, observe, and listen to their students. Providing teachers-in-training with skills and issues to extend and enhance their ability to inquire, analyze, and evaluate within the context in which they will function and for which they will plan instruction is clearly important. Mills (1980, p. 5) suggests that "to become adept at learning to teach, teaching, and improving their teaching, student teachers must be trained to investigate teaching-learning events critically." She suggests that, to facilitate their adjustment, initial and ongoing clinical observations be made so that they become "aware of certain critical school and classroom variables ... including norms, rituals, formal organizational patterns, management systems, and academic programs." Though these are reasonable suggestions, inquiries of this sort and others need to begin in earnest prior to the first week of student teaching.

Ongoing changes in state certification requirements have frequently necessitated an increase in the number of field experience hours to be completed prior to student teaching. What those experiences might include regarding inquiry and the acquisition of knowledge, therefore, becomes increasingly a national concern for art educators. Systematic observation and critical analysis throughout students' field-based experiences are more likely to be rigorous, enlightening, and effective when the aspiring teacher spends several hours a week in an art classroom for perhaps ten to twenty weeks prior to student teaching.

Observation and Analysis Guidelines for the Novice Inquirer

Deciding what to inquire about is an important first step that the novice is not always able to determine without guidance. What follows is offered from a range of issues as examples for the aspiring (or experienced) art teacher seeking to understand some of the complexities of teaching and learning.

The Environment. Classrooms, schools, and community environments, when carefully described, compared, and analyzed, provide a foundation for art education students to make important if somewhat speculative assumptions about the beliefs, attitudes, and interaction patterns that shape the process of education at the practical level. What the physical classroom environment reveals about the teacher and students, what the designed and controlled environment of the school reflects regarding beliefs and attitudes about schooling and the learning environment, what the community environment can suggest about the people who live there are issues for study. When these are observed, written about, and discussed, student understanding of these relationships between environment and those who help to make them is improved.

Considering how these aspects are integrally related to a teacher's roles and responsibilities should be central to the goals of this kind of inquiry. Excerpts from one undergraduate student journal regarding the environment provide insight to the potential of such inquiry:

The neighborhood has a general population of lower to middle class income, university affiliated families. There are a few remaining elderly people still living there, but for the most part the homes and buildings are university-owned and maintained. The university's rights for eminent domain have marked the neighborhood for potential development and university expansion. The homes are older and have individual character. No two are exactly alike. Toys are left out on the sidewalks and in front yards suggesting there are quite a few kids and that it is a safe and trustworthy environment for them to play outside unattended. Trees line the sidewalk, and a network of alleyways divides the blocks into two. From these alleyways clotheslines and gardens are visible, showing that a certain amount of self-sufficiency is maintained by the residents.

The teacher's personality dominates the room. The furnishings and their particular arrangement are all reflections of the teacher's personal taste ... what is placed on the many white bulletin boards has a haphazard and random feeling to the arrangement. One entire white expanse has only a small art postcard of a Calder reproduction. Yet, overall, the arrangement of the room shows thought and ingenuity as well as a sense of purpose and intention. The partitioned off areas allow the children a moderate amount of privacy and are designed to foster a sense of independence in their play. However, the inflexibility of the arrangement prevents the children from getting actively and personally involved. In spite of the clutter and the busy look to the room, the general feeling is one of sterility and control. When I am in the room, I feel as though I am a guest in someone else's home. Finally, I wonder how the children and teacher alike are affected by the subterranean feeling the room maintains with the only available natural light coming down from the ceiling. I am curious as to how this element may affect the children's sense of perspective and personal stature within the environment (Lupton, Note 4).

On-Going Phenomena and the Nature of Dialogue. Approaches to successful and unsuccessful teaching vary in several ways that often go unnoticed by the unskilled or undirected observer. Systematic looking and subsequent analysis allows the breaking of ongoing phenomena into manageable parts that enhance understanding: recording entire class periods at timed intervals, mapping patterns of action, recording or analyzing the complexities of dialogue, movement, and behavior of a teacher or students, as well as recording the observed responsibilities of a teacher.

From these data teacher dialogue, for instance, can be separated into at least two general categories for the purpose of analysis. The first is dialogue that is instructional and motivational regarding the subject being taught. In sorting out art teacher talk, the undergraduate can categorically discern the quality of talk and percentage of talk time spent on art production or media, art criticism, history, socio-cultural considerations, artists and their works, or on traditional and popular arts. Clues to teacher preferences, biases, concerns, and training emerge from such inquiries.

The second is dialogue that is not directly related to the teaching of art. What teachers say often reflects expectations that are social or value-laden in nature. How students are expected to behave, conform, interact, and even believe can be discovered through teacher dialogue and manner. What this implies regarding a teacher's social values and the role of the school as a socialization force is revealing to the undergraduate student observer. This kind of inquiry would help aspiring teachers become more aware of how dialogue and other patterns and behaviors can serve to reveal their own choices and actions within the art classroom, and how these may in turn have potential effects on student learning and actions.

What is Taught and How It is Evaluated. What is actually being taught and why, what is being learned, and what is being evaluated can be pursued through observations and interviews with teachers and students to determine some of the range, quality, and cohesiveness of teaching as well as expected and actual learning. The degree to which there are or are not logical connections between content taught and learning evaluated is often particularly revealing, as is the fact that student evaluation is often based as much on behavioral matters unrelated to learning as it is on learning. Such data are frequently perplexing for the student teacher who has been taught that evaluations or grading should logically be connected to what is being taught as content. Particularly intriguing are those intuitive evaluations purportedly based on categories of craftsmanship, originality, and creativity, carried out in classrooms where none of these is addressed or discussed by the teacher doing the evaluations. Bases for choices of instructional content and evaluation, as well as how these choices are carried out, are obviously aspects worthy of inquiry and analysis for the art education student who will soon have to face these decisions responsibly and alone.

Students in the Art Classroom. Perhaps the most important of these suggestions for inquiry is the need to consider the students enrolled in school art classes. Their many school and non-school interests, their characteristics, levels of knowledge and ability in art, their daily encounters with art and what that range of art is, and their attitudes about art are worthwhile subjects for investigation. Observation, eavesdropping, informal interviews, questionnaires, assessments of classwork, and performance are methods and tools useful in constructing group and individual profiles that can help in assessing student interests, needs, and levels. Not only are these kinds of data valuable in determining what the relevant content of instruction might be, it is intriguing and revealing to compare these findings with what students are actually being taught. How one devises art instruction that is of student interest, is level-appropriate, and is responsible in content are issues better addressed when real students in real contexts can be studied and speculated about.

These and other tools and modes of inquiry must necessarily be connected to philosophical, theoretical, and curricular foundations in our field in palatable and reasonable ways. Guiding the preparing teacher to make sound choices regarding instructional strategies and content, and to select and utilize curricular materials in art education responsibly and efficiently might be enhanced with rigorous inquiry experiences and training prior to entering the art classroom.

Not all undergraduate art education students are able to spend extensive hours in classrooms prior to student teaching. In these cases, written as well as videotaped or filmed case studies can be invaluable for group inquiry and analysis regarding classroom practice. When these kinds of documents are coupled with on-site observations, both are enhanced. Mrs. Allen, a studio-based junior high teacher (Degge, 1975); Mr. Allen, a college art teacher (Sevigny, 1977); Mr. Jewel, who teaches high school art history (Alexander, 1980); and Bruce, the new art teacher (Hawke, 1980) are useful additions to our body of research. Studies of this nature extend art teaching inquiry into new dimensions and offer undergraduates not only interesting and entertaining reading, but valued information upon which to base their inquiries and teaching considerations.

Beginning and Experienced Art Teachers as Inquirers

Hawke's study, "The Life-World of a Beginning Teacher of Art," includes a review of research findings that reveals new teachers "felt unprepared to cope with the wide range of student abilities and interests," were "surprised by the lack of enthusiasm in their students toward learning," were "by the end of the first year of teaching" no longer utilizing the methods of teaching which they began with because pre-service education was too idealistic "in terms of their present school situation," and, very importantly, "were now using methods similar to those of their colleagues" (Hawke, pp. 28-29).

Inferences may be drawn from this about the content of undergraduate programs, but even more directly about the needs of teachers already in the field where the responsibilities of teacher educators are less clear cut and manageable. The art education community has gone some way toward meeting the needs of new teachers by sponsoring and publishing practical journals. Unfortunately, the National Art Education Association reduced likely contact with the beginning art teacher by eliminating the publication *Art Teacher.* Perhaps it is because we know too little about the needs and inquiry practices of art teachers that these kinds of journals seem only marginally useful to the experienced teacher. That may explain why practically oriented art teacher journals are so inconsistent and often unfocused in purpose, lacking a substantive, operational framework that gives credibility to the field and offers quality to the teacher.

Fortunately experienced teachers are often required to take additional coursework after initial certification. In my own state, practicing teachers must now take a graduate research course along with other art education courses for their required second endorsement, which provides a chance to explore inquiry modes that teachers do and might employ.[2] The effects of my recent in-depth work with 27 art teachers enrolled in such a course are only partial at the time of writing. However, the research methods explored and students' enthusiasm for developing plans of investigation to match their specific teaching situations were more than I had anticipated. They designed research proposals around major problems or frustrations that hampered their effectiveness as teachers, and outlined plans to initiate their research plans in the upcoming school year.

One of these students was the teacher reported on previously who had conducted the lesson on left brain-right brain drawing. He arrived at a proposal to determine why a higher number of his students made more gains in their drawing using split-brain techniques. His literature review suggested that there was no conclusive evidence that the right or left hemisphere of the brain functioned exclusively verbally, visually, or holistically. He hypothesized that achievement was related to concentration rather than to the hemispherality issue, and he proposed to investigate a possible correlation between levels of attention or involvement and achievement in drawing. Techniques suggested by Edwards and Nicolaides were selected to be used with experimental and control groups. The problems and flaws associated with this proposal are usual and characteristic of an inquirer doing research for the first time. The outcome of the inquiry may prove inconclusive even for its author. But the genuine enthusiasm and commitment to an issue at the heart of this teacher's concern that he know more about why his students learn and don't learn is important.

The range of proposed inquiries by the remaining 26 students was diverse both in methodologies selected and problems addressed. Their reviews of literature, limited as these were, did not provide satisfying answers to many of their particular problems. The solution was to investigate these themselves. The task of doing that, of course, is large and takes time and commitment. Some will carry them through, others will not. Perhaps for some, discovering that they can seek answers methodically and in varied modes will mean more in the long run than whether their first research proposal is carried out or is successful.

Summary

The classroom art teacher as inquirer plays a crucial part in art education. This paper has presented a threefold message discussing how that role might be nurtured. Regarding the most extensively discussed point, that we prepare our teachers to be more efficient inquirers, Packard reminds us that "each new art teacher confronting his or her first class must ask and answer the question, 'What are my goals and how do I accomplish them?' This question is asked from the start of one's teaching career to the end" (1980, p. 5).

The second and third points are reflected in a reminder from Erikson, which states that "the ultimate value of knowledge generated in art education research is in the service it can provide to the practitioner" and that "too few art education researchers make enough effort to ensure that the knowledge they generate is made available and usable to the clientele which they serve" (1979, p. 12). While all research in art education need not be directed at the art teacher, I suggest that we can more efficiently and effectively get research findings to those whom they purport to serve. I believe we have not been responsible enough in providing guides to and models of art instruction and inquiry that are, in form, really usable or appealing. I suggest that we educators of art teachers cannot stay inside our hardcover textbooks, general references, curriculum guides, and journals talking to each other, and still hope to have our convictions put into practice. Additional research related to or centered on the inquiring art teacher is needed as well as that which is useful for the inquirer.

What we investigate regarding teacher performance, learning, and inquiry; how we better insure that research is made available and usable; and the methods of inquiry that we prepare teachers to use hold exciting promise for classroom art teachers, who persistently and with commitment do inquire in order to improve their teaching and enhance their students' learning.

Reference Notes

1. An unpublished study, *The NAEA: A Sampling of Our Society*, by K. Scholfield-Sweet, B. Jones, G. Kensler and J. McFee, 1976, revealed that out of 196 teachers who responded to a national survey, 10070 read School Arts, and 66% read Art Teacher as resources for teaching art.

2. Used by permission from the observational notes of Robyn Dunkum, an undergraduate art education major at the University of Oregon, and by gracious permission of the anonymous art teacher.

3. Eisner devotes a chapter to educational criticism in his book *The Educational Imagination* (1979).

4. The excerpts were taken from the observational notes of Courtney Lupton, used with her permission.

References

Alexander, R. R. Mr. Jewel as a model: An educational criticism of a high school art history class. *Studies in Art Education,* 1980, 21(3), 20-30.

Degge, R. M. A case study and theoretical analysis of the teaching practices in one junior high art class (Unpublished doctoral dissertation, University of Oregon, 1975). *Dissertation Abstracts International,* 1976, 36, 5750. (University Microfilms No. DAH 76-05157)

Edwards, B. *Drawing on the right side of the brain.* Los Angeles: J. P. Tarcher, Inc., 1979.

Eisner, E. W. *The educational imagination.* New York: Macmillan Publishing Co., 1979.

Erikson, M. An historical explanation of the schism between research and practice in art education. *Studies in Art Education,* 1979, 20(2), 5-13.

Hawke, D. The life-world of a beginning teacher of art (Doctoral dissertation, The University of Alberta, Edmonton, 1980).

Mills, J. R. A guide for teaching systematic observation to student teachers. *Journal of Teacher Education,* 1980, 31(6), 5-9.

Packard, S. Editorial. *Studies in Art Education,* 1980, 21(2), 5.

Sevigny, M. J. A descriptive study of instructional interaction and performance appraisal in a university studio art setting: A multiple perspective (Doctoral dissertation, The Ohio State University, 1977). *Dissertation Abstracts International,* 1978, 6477. (University Microfilms No. DDK 78-06199)

Youngblood, M. Hemispheric amphigory. *Art Education,* 1981, 34(4), 9-11.

Youngblood, M. The hemispherality wagon leaves laterality station at 12:45 for art superiority land. *Studies in Art Education,* 1979, 21(1), 44-49.

Endnotes

[1] To my knowledge, there is no published, definitive study centered on the inquiry practices of art teachers. The sources used here from which to draw conclusions about inquiry patterns are informal and may suggest a need for an in-depth study of the topic.

[2] To remain certified, secondary teachers in Oregon must complete a Standard Endorsement program of forty-five credit hours within six years following Basic Endorsement. To receive Standard Certification teachers are required, by the Oregon Teacher Standards and Practices Commission, to have preparation in diagnostic, prescriptive, and evaluative techniques, and in research.

1980s

ARTICLE SELECTION

Lanier, V. (1984). Eight Guidelines
for Selecting Art Curriculum
Content. *Studies in Art Education*,
25(4), 232-237.

Terry Barrett

Senior Editor, 1993-1995

Having accepted the request to choose an article for this volume, I first narrowed my choices to authors, and then selected Vincent Lanier, based on personal bias as well as considered opinion. When I was young, teaching art in a black school in the heart of the St. Louis ghetto, I heard of an article titled "The Teaching of Art as Social Revolution" (Lanier, 1969, *Phi Delta Kappan*, 50(6), 314-319) by an author unknown to me. I knew very little of the literature of art education, or that art education was even a field of study, having graduated with a Bachelor's degree in art and philosophy and no art education classes. Upon graduating, I quickly and spontaneously accepted a high school teaching job to avoid the Vietnam War. At that time of the build-up of the war, teachers were exempted from the draft. I was opposed to the war and I was for civil rights. I began teaching with no prior experience. Lanier's article title alone gave me courage.

Years later, having been converted to accepting "art educator" as an identity while an instructor teaching courses centered around photographic media at The Ohio State University, I had the honor and privilege of being a visiting professor at the University of Oregon to fill in for Vincent Lanier while he was on leave but still in town. I taught courses related to "newer media" that Lanier had brought to the attention of the field. These newer media were primarily the lens-based media of film, photography, and television, which Lanier had positioned within the domain of popular art.

June King McFee was my chairperson, Rogena Degge my friend and colleague, and Vincent became a friend and a newly chosen "mentor," although the term was not in use in education at the time. That brief stint in Eugene, Oregon, was a formative period of my young academic life.

"Eight Guidelines for Selecting Art Curriculum Content" reinforces many of the themes for which Vincent Lanier is best known: a serious consideration of "all visual phenomena,

Terry Barrett is Professor of Art Education with a joint appointment in the Department of Art at The Ohio State University, where he is the recipient of a Distinguished Teaching Award for courses in art criticism and aesthetics within education. He has authored five books: *Why Is That Art? Aesthetics and Criticism of Contemporary Art; Interpreting Art: Reflecting, Wondering, and Responding; Criticizing Art: Understanding the Contemporary* (2nd ed.); *Criticizing Photographs: An Introduction to Understanding Images* (4th ed.); and *Talking about Student Art.* He is editor of the anthology *Lessons for Teaching Art Criticism.*

including natural objects, popular arts, commercial and industrial forms, as well as the fine arts" (p. 233). The article also reinforces Manuel Barkan's call 3 years prior for art educators to include the study of aesthetics in the curriculum of art education. Lanier asks in his article that we incorporate "the content from the literature of aesthetics" (p. 233) to engage the young in wondering "about the existence of the universe and the meaning of life, problems philosophers engage" (236). He also calls for us "to deal with the contemporary arts whenever possible" (p. 234). He continues his advocacy of including in the curriculum "popular art" (a contentious issue at the time) and "fine art." He also encourages the study of what were derogatorily considered the "minor" arts, such as jewelry and fibers. His call for philosophically investigating the meaning of life through the contemporary arts remains pertinent today, about 25 years after he wrote the article.

Eight Guidelines for Selecting Art Curriculum Content

Vincent Lanier

[Editor's note: At the time this article was published] Vincent Lanier is [was] Professor of Art in the Art Education Program, Department of Art. The author was a participant in the Penn State Seminar, for which he wrote a research proposal entitled "Aesthetic Decision— Making in Adult Life Situations." He also was a faculty member of the 1983 Getty Institute for Educators on the Visual Arts, and a member of its advisory committee.

Problems of curriculum content selection in art education may derive in part from the abundance of available and appropriate material rather than any poverty of content. A colossal mass of crafted artifacts reflecting the aesthetic proclivities of a broad variety of cultures clogs our museums, galleries, and media. Despite sometimes obvious, sometimes obscure inequities in quality, the range of objects promoting aesthetic response is disturbingly large. If we are conscientious about recognizing this span of material and, particularly, if we pay more than nodding attention to the so-called vernacular arts, we need to devise criteria for selection of curriculum content. This paper attempts to provide such guidance.

Since any curriculum is dependent upon the instructional purposes it supports, an initial criterion for content selection must stipulate the ends-in-view for which learner activity is mobilized. The traditional distinction between intrinsic and developmental purposes appears to be a valid starting point for deciding this first guideline (Lanier, 1964). It is not premature to emphasize intrinsic purposes; our long and barren preoccupation with developmental purposes such as creativity, therapy, visual literacy, humaneness, academic motivation, right-brain development, and a host of other not necessarily art-related purposes seems finally to have withered. The most powerful influences in the field hold that there is much to learn in and about art; indeed art is a serious discipline not unlike other "hard" school subjects. Further, learning about art should take precedence over those benefits (mainly psychological developmental) that are alleged to occur through art. This position is a consequence of believing that art is of value for itself, intrinsically, more than for what it might do for the individual's behavior outside of art.

If we consider the extremely limited time allotted to art in the school calendar (a situation that is not likely to expand drastically in the coming years), we must arrange priorities of learning with commensurate strictness. In such an exercise, the importance of learning about art as opposed to developing non-art behaviors through art is slowly growing. Thus, the first principle for content selection can be said to be *to identify art content that will best present the knowledges and skills calculated to enhance our negotiation of objects we see aesthetically.* In some contexts, this principle now travels under the new and appealing title of discipline-based art education. It appears likely to be the direction of the future and can boast a sturdy history in the literature of the field.

As simple and forthright a statement as this first guideline might appear to be, it conceals a problem of some magnitude and points to the second guideline recommended here. Most major writers in the field, even when they concede that all seen objects can be aesthetically provocative, do not take arts other than fine arts seriously. What the literature suggests, either overtly or by implication, is that museum and gallery art is the sine qua non of aesthetic experience and that all other objects or visual phenomena can be regarded as inferior as a class. Sometimes the justification for this assessment is that the fine arts are more abstruse and require more learning about than other less honorific art forms; sometimes it is that the fine arts deal with nobler thoughts and feelings than the others *(Report of the NAEA Commission on Art Education,* 1977, p. 36-39). In consequence, this second guideline may be applauded in rhetoric and ignored in application, at least insofar as the breadth of classroom art content is concerned.

It is not enough to include in the art curriculum a covey of Eisenstein or Bergmann films or to deal with *Civilization* or *Masterpiece Theatre* and thus conclude that the popular arts and the media have been in-cluded. This is to implicitly deny the genuineness of aesthetic response to Dallas or the repeated sagas of Dirty Harry. The response exists, whatever its particular qualities, and we might be more effective as teachers of art if we use it as a possible starting point to our efforts instead of ignoring it. Therefore, our second guideline is to *examine aesthetic response to all visual phenomena,* including natural objects, popular arts, commercial and industrial forms, as well as the fine arts.

A third guideline for the selection of curriculum materials is the idea that *content be centered on artifacts well within the cultural milieu of the learners.* Looked at seriously (and no one would suggest that we look at art any other way), works of art carry meanings enmeshed in the society in which the works are produced. In order to fully absorb these meanings, without which response to art can be superficial and unsatisfying, complex structures of knowledge are called into play by the viewer, usually without conscious effort or even recognition of the process during or after its occurrence. We look, we see, and we understand, having made large numbers of complicated associations for which previous learnings about the cultural context in which we live have prepared us. These associations are made at a speed rivaling the most awesome computer and their scope can involve accumulated data of a seemingly irrelevant nature.

Clearly this guideline questions a fashionable practice among art curriculum makers, that of using esoteric artifacts from exotic cultures to develop what is called cross-cultural learning. New Zealand art educator Bracey (1979) questions this practice on logical grounds: "If the means we use to give form to our ideas about the universe determines the nature of those ideas, then it would seem to follow that cross-cultural studies are logically vain attempts to understand what cannot be understood!" (n.p.) Allison (1978) raises the same question within the context of research.

One might view the issue on psychological grounds as well; dealing with the art of another culture, the universe of associational cues we depend on for proper insight is missing. Using the gold weights of the Ashanti or the prints of Hokusai as curriculum content in an American high school art classroom without considerable preparation has little currency. Better, at least at first, to concentrate on the learner's own present environment, which at times is itself difficult to fully understand.

A fourth guideline, derivative in some part from the first, involves *the use of content from the literature of aesthetics*. To ask and answer questions about the nature of art and of our response to art should be an early order of business in art curriculum. This is not to say, of course, that the answers we provide are in any sense definitive. The content of aesthetics is largely theoretical rather than empirical, and interpretation is a matter of belief or reason. Furthermore, alternatives of theory are fairly widespread. Nevertheless, the issues confronted in this content constitute the bedrock material of the study of art as a discipline, material which over 100 years of art education in the United States has carefully avoided and which some might still believe too complex for the young learner.

Barkan, who was perhaps the most influential pioneer in the development of aesthetic education and those who followed closely his specific orientation, consider the content of aesthetics just as relevant to the study of art as the more commonly recognized disciplines of artist, art historian, and art critic (Efland, 1979; Lanier, 1982). In fact, aesthetic education, the precursor of discipline-based art education, has suffered from an unfortunate misnaming; it never did concern itself with aesthetics, but rather limited its curricular purview to the three art behaviors noted above. This restricted interpretation occurred despite Barkan's (1966) clear injunction for the addition of a fourth behavior, that of the aesthetician.

> To the detriment of art education ... we have anchored curriculum almost entirely in relation to the artist, only slightly in relation to the art historian; we have ignored the aesthetician and the critic. Art curriculum is faltering, not because of efforts to attend to art history, but rather, because we have not learned to use the art historian. (p. 253)

The issue of using aesthetic theory as content for art teaching, emphasized by Barkan almost twenty years ago, will be touched upon later in this paper.

A fifth guideline to be recommended here raises more problems than it answers. This injunction is to *structure the content of art curriculum so that it moves from the familiar to the unfamiliar.* As with so many other ideas that are initially persuasive, this concept appears to be simple and obvious. Nonetheless, it is neither. While art educators have written and talked about the scope and sequence of curriculum for some years, it is not always clear what principle of sequence is being suggested. There are several time-honored sequences frequently and correctly used in present-day art curricula. One of these is the idea of moving from simple to complex material, so that the learner progresses from naive to sophisticated insight. Another is the guideline noted above, that of leading the student from the familiar to the less well known. As third, basically a reflection of our long preoccupation with studio curricula, arranges sequence on some basic pattern of art production.

Still another form of sequencing the art curriculum can be found in art critical dialogue prepared for art teaching. A notable example of such a structure appears in Broudy's aesthetic scanning, in which the chronology of the process moves from sensory properties to formal, then expressive, and finally technical properties. It is not clear if this pattern is seen as inherent in dealing with works of art new to the viewer, but it is recommended as a specific method of approach that will allow the viewer to analyze the piece more efficiently. A slightly similar sequence structures Feldman's art critical dialogue, from description to formal analysis, interpretation, and evaluation, although Feldman does not appear to insist on that particular chronology. In both cases, it is not unreasonable to suggest that the work of art itself, or the object evoking the aesthetic response, might present some characteristic that will demand initial attention, superceding the imposed structure; indeed this is the most likely nature of our experience of art or anything else. A piece of intricate carving seen for the first time might well impose immediate attention to this technical property, no matter how faithfully we attempt to respond in that order ordained by theory.

Finally, there is the chronological sequence favored by art historians. A legitimate sequence since it does report what occurred with accuracy, the chronology of art history is an inherent sequence native to the body of knowledge of art, which can be and is used in art teaching on any level. Unfortunately, it is not always the most provocative, particularly for the young, and other formats for approaching historical material are often used to replace historical chronology. A frequently appropriate sequence grows out of the social functions of art, the curriculum following those divisions that represent how art is used in the community or by both artist and viewer. An example can be found in one projected outline for an elementary art curriculum that moves upward through the grades by focusing on ever-widening social centers of art: home, school, community, nation, other cultures, historical cultures, and the future (Lanier, 1983). Other examples can be located in the more recent curricula in which such studies parallel studio activities (Greer, 1981).

The principle of sequence, as much as we endorse its theoretical applicability to art curricula, requires much careful study. There are those who have for some time taken the position that there are no "cumulative hierarchical structures" (Efland, 1968, p. 5) in the arts, and that the content of the arts within the learning context can start at "any one of a number of entry points" (Templeton, 1971, p. 23). One significant issue that might be examined with profit is the differentiation that might be made between those sequences of content in some way inherent in some aspect of art, and others of an artificial or imposed nature, which are superimposed upon the body of art for pedagogical purposes. This is not to suggest any judgment; a sequence inherent to art is not in any way necessarily superior to one that is artificial. What the distinction implies is simply that our understanding of the origins of our ideas about classroom art content should be as clear as we can make it.

A sixth guideline is the injunction *to deal with the contemporary arts whenever possible.* If there are viable options in selecting illustrative material, priority should be given to the most recent appropriate examples. The issue raised in this point has to do with the desirability of having learners of any age become conversant with the visual arts that surround them. This is not to say that the art of the past, distant or recent, is of little importance; it is indeed of significance. What is implied and should be understood is that the contemporary arts are those that will loom largest on the horizon of any level of student, and that knowledge about those objects is essential and practical for the enhancement of aesthetic experience to a level appropriate to those who share the good things of the society in which they live. Understanding the work of Giotto or Corot, while of great worth, can come second to the understanding of Christo or Duane Hanson. Future art will probably develop out of the contemporary arts-though, in fact, it may grow out of the past as well—and knowing how and why today's art is formed may support subsequent insight. Further, there is a consideration that the artist of today is the one who needs desperately to have the kind of approval and financial endorsement that such knowledge might provide.

The seventh guideline suggests that the art curriculum *should employ as models for study an adequate number of forms of art other than drawings, paintings, and sculpture.* Of particular significance are what used to be called the "minor arts." Areas such as jewelry, fibers, furniture design, glass, clay, metal, and others have only recently attained a proper equity with the older expressive arts and their use as objects to be studied with care and affection will nurture that equity. It is also useful for the learner to realize that with specific variances deriving from function or technique, much the same formal elements and relationships, potential for expressiveness, and art skills of all sorts, structure all of these forms of art. It is reassuring to the stranger to art to recognize these commonalities that can serve to make a dense and difficult topic less abstruse. Most of all, this fundamental democracy of materials dilutes the elitism and hierarchy with which the arts have been traditionally burdened. For artist and viewer alike, this equality greatly enlarges what is available for appreciation in the arts without lessening the artistic rigor with which the arts are created. Such expansion of opportunity would seem to most of us both logical and humane and is certainly defensible in the context of education.

The eighth and final guideline involves *the selection of material for curriculum content relevant to the largest portion of the learner group.* Despite many years of concern for what has been called individual differences, it is not unreasonable to suggest that considerable areas of commonality exist within groups and particularly within groups of similar maturational level or curricular interest. No doubt there are differences of instructional significance involved in some art behaviors among individuals in any sort of grouping; for example, the spread between divergent and convergent thinking hypothesized by the research on creativity may not only have merit but relevance to artmaking. Thus, one would expect the teacher of art or elementary classroom teacher to attend to this or other differences in directing art production. If on the other hand, the primary consideration in view is learning about art, as has been suggested here, these differences among individuals are greatly minimized and curriculum can be selected and constructed for the largest portion of any group.

Having returned, as it were, to the beginning of the paper, by reference to the critical nature of the purpose of the teaching situation, it is appropriate to examine that particular issue with more care. Once having admitted that art teaching has to do with learning about art, it is still necessary to specify the roads to be taken to achieve that goal. History provides us with some alternatives and it would be well to examine these. The quotation noted above from the writings of Manuel Barkan attends to four ways in which art can be studied: production, art history, art criticism, and aesthetics. As most readers are aware, the combination of the first three has been called aesthetic education and has been well described and represented in the literature of the field during the last 15 years or more.

The fourth area, however, had been ignored by most of those who write in the journals and publish the books that influence our sense of our discipline until the last very few years. Now we have begun to insert the idea of examining the nature of aesthetic response into the avenues relevant to learning about art. This expansion of methodology and curricular content provides the first indication of a high level of concern for the response of the viewer to the aesthetic object. Although the other three activities include such consideration, the emphasis in all three is unequivocally on the object of art, a focus which is certainly fitting in the study of art, but which is also limiting to the learner. This more recent addition, to some extent a part of what is now being called discipline-based art education, intends to make the learner aware of how and why aesthetic experience takes place. The assumption that this knowledge can then serve to enlighten subsequent aesthetic encounters does not seem unreasonable.

Further, as was pointed out in the discussion of the fourth guideline, this type of knowledge is conceivably applicable to the learner's experience with other forms of art, specifically music, drama, and dance. The commonalities that appear to exist among the various arts are sufficiently general at this point so that the modalities through which the various arts are experienced assume less significance. It may be that through the study of aesthetics in the art curriculum (or in the curriculum of music, dance, or drama) a genuine art education might be possible, a bonus for including aesthetic study within the avenues of art learning. For those of us who in earlier years enjoyed the type of classes then called "arts and humanities," the impulse toward teaching the combined arts might be satisfied. However, unlike these earlier courses, the backbone of such study should be aesthetic theory, rather than literacy or cultural materials.

Another issue relevant to content selection (though more properly critical to curriculum construction) is the matter of viewing the desired outcomes of art teaching as modeled on the behaviors of adult artists, art critics, or art historians. This behavior model idea, originating in the work of Bruner (1961), became the structural frame of reference of aesthetic education and deserves careful review. The idea manifests some serious prob-lems, including the question of which artist, art critic, or art historian to select as the model; the differences among members of each group being considerable (Simpson, 1972). Without repeating previously published arguments at some length (Lanier, 1983), an even more troublesome problem arising from teaching towards an adult behavioral model is the validity of the concept itself. Bruner's hypothesis that the pupil learning physics is a physicist may have currency in the sciences; that a child learning art is an artist or art critic or art historian may well be another matter and open to serious question.

For example, perhaps the most definitive attribute of the artist is the recognition and command of formal, visual relationships in the formation of artistic objects. Surely it can be argued that children (and other naive shapers of objects) do not manifest that recog-nition or command consistently and, therefore, are not behaving as artists. This is not to demean the aesthetic worth of children's production with art materials, nor to deny the desirable learnings produced by critical or historical activities. It is to suggest that if Bruner's dictum is in error, those who deal with art curriculum should view the sources of content somewhat differently. The problem with teaching toward an adult behavioral model is the assumption that youngsters in the classroom perform or can be taught to perform in any way meaningfully similar to the adult role model. Like small children performing "surgery" on candy animals, the motions may be highly reminiscent of the adult activity, but the understanding of the complexities involved is largely missing. Fortunately, there is no easily observed reason to keep us from using the terrain of the role models (artist, critic, historian) as content material for art curricula; what we might avoid is the inclusion of content that reflects procedure rather than substance in each behavioral domain.

Finally, including the study of aesthetics in the art curriculum permits a theoretical level of motivation unavailable in dealing with art history or art criticism and quite different in its nature and impact from the production of art in the school situation. Surely all of us, including the young, are more than a little puzzled about the character of experiences that seem to take up so much of our lives. Whatever our attitude about the contemporary popular culture, it cannot be denied that these media engross enormous numbers of young people in ways analogous if not similar to the aesthetic experiences of museum, gallery, theater, and concert hall. The observation that ideas about aesthetics, even as they are examined by philosophy, are too complex or too esoteric for the majority is a specious one. Even the simplest of mortals (whatever the parameters of that simplicity) has wondered about the existence of the universe and the meaning of life, problems philosophers engage under the rubric of metaphysics. The many hypotheses that answer these questions can be simplified enough so that the young might confront the range of ideas available in the history of thought. In fact, such basic philosophical specula-tion, made understandable to all learners, is long overdue in the general curricula of our schools.

So it is with aesthetics, which in rudimentary form might enlist the sense of wonder native to youngsters in the study of a question of more than a little importance in their lives. Although it is difficult to simplify the often abstruse concepts of aesthetic spec-ulation without undue injustice to their complexity, it is a necessary step and can be done. Some initial material of this sort is available in textbooks in the field. Feldman (1970) examines the social and personal purpose of art—a part of the turf identified as aesthetics, as does Chapman (1978), and a more recent pair of texts explore in simplified terms both the purposes and the nature of art (Lanier, 1982, 1984).

Perhaps the most significant statement one might make about curriculum and its content is to assert that the materials used in art learning are best for the task when they have been selected and put together by the individual teacher for a specific group. If the guidelines noted above have merit, they do so on the basis of what they have been called: guides for the teacher to bear in mind while selecting content for a particular situation. The so-called teacher-proof curricula described in textbooks, published by agencies of the governmental education establishment, and even sold commercially, are themselves only guides for the art teacher who knows the subject of art, and understands the group of learners. The point at which these curricula become vital to wholesome art teaching is in the elementary school, where the classroom teacher is almost without exception inadequately prepared. The one course in art education during a teacher education program, without the support of additional coursework in art during college, which appears to be the best we can expect or assume for the elementary teacher, is hardly enough to provide a confident independence in the selection of content and construction of curricula for the elementary grades. Fortunately, a variety of curriculum guides and suggestions exist in published sources to assist the teacher who feels inept in this area. The guidelines of this paper can be used to assess or develop such curricular materials as well.

It may well be that no curriculum or statement about content can compete with the inspired teacher who knows the subject of art. Perhaps the enthusiasm that comes from the love of a body of knowledge and the desire to transmit that affection to others, which is the peculiar attribute of the good teacher, is far more important to the learning process than any descriptions or prescriptions. Such engagement is undoubtedly infectious to the learner and the best guarantee of successful learning. However, most of us in teaching are something less than inspired zealots; like the majorities in any other profession, we are at best competent workmen. We can use the help of the theorizing and study of others to guide our efforts.

References

Allison, B. (1978). The relationship between child arts and their cultural foundations. Paper presented at the *INSEA Arts Education Research Conference,* Adelaide, Australia.

Barkan, M. (1966). Curriculum problems in art education. In E. L. Mattil (Ed.), *A seminar in art education for research and curriculum development* (USOE Cooperative Research Project No. V-002) (pp. 240-255). University Park: The Pennsylvania State University.

Bracey, E. N. (1979). *Cross cultural studies: Problems and prospects.* Unpublished manuscript.

Bruner, J. S. (1961). *The process of education.* Cambridge: Harvard University.

Chapman, L. H. (1978). *Approaches to art in education.* New York: Harcourt Brace Jovanovitch.

Efland, A. D. (1968). Some problems of structure in art and their curriculum consequences. *Studies in Art Education,* 9(3), 2-11.

Efland, A. D. (1979). Conceptions of teaching in art education. *Art Education,* 32(4), 21-33.

Feldman, E. B. (1970). Becoming human through art. Englewood Cliffs, NJ: Prentice-Hall.

Greer, W. D. (1981). *SWRL elementary art program.* Bloomington, IN: Phi Delta Kappa.

Lanier, V. (1964). *Teaching secondary art.* Scranton, PA: International Textbook.

Lanier, V. (1982). *The arts we see.* New York: Teachers College, Columbia University.

Lanier, V. (1983). Beyond aesthetic education. *Art Education,* 36(6), 31-37.

Lanier, V. (1984). *The visual arts and the elementary child.* New York: Teachers College, Columbia University.

Report of the NAEA Commission on Art Education. (1977). Reston, VA: National Art Education Association.

Simpson, 1. E. (1972). *Aesthetic education as art education theory.* Unpublished doctoral dissertation, University of Oregon.

Templeton, D. E. (1971). The learner's search: Beginnings of structure in art. *Studies in Art Education,* 12(3), 23-30.

1960s

1970s

1980s

Selections from the 1990s

2000s

STUDIES
in Art Education

ARTICLE SELECTION

Garber E. (1990). Implications of Feminist Art Criticism for Art Education. *Studies in Art Education*, 32 (1), 17-26.

Candace Jesse Stout

Senior Editor, 2005-2007

Looking backward at modernism with its soft segue to Discipline-Based Art Education and looking forward toward the liberating perspectives of feminist poststructuralism, Elizabeth Garber's article sits Janus-like in the literature of art education. *Implications of Feminist Art Criticism for Art Education* (1990) is a writerly piece, as Barthes would say, one that should be read and interacted with again and again. Once inside this article the reader finds it productively challenging, broaching leading-edge conversations for readers of *Studies* in 1990 and, still, acutely relevant for art educators today. In a time when the discipline of art education was suspended in ambivalence between DBAE (a pedagogy that worked in some pragmatic ways, a pedagogy sweetened with Getty funding), and the postmodern turn, Elizabeth opened wide the door to disciplinary self-consciousness, providing authorial acknowledgment and instigating reader admission that it was time to re-structure the practice of art criticism in art education. Most essentially, what she called for was a re-conceptualization of what art might be and what it means to interact with the richness in the visual realm of human creativity. Drawing interdisciplinarily and pluralistically on the formative work of feminist scholars like Nochlin, Lippard, Frueh, Lacy, as well as from a variety of art educators, postmodern critics and philosophers, Elizabeth points out the stasis embedded in modernist art criticism pedagogy, that well-ingrained tradition of remaining "inside" the work, attending to formal and expressive properties and keeping with the "reality" of the artist's readerly biography. As we see it today, it is a tradition that insists on a monocular equilibrium, one that denies subjectivity, that is, all the richness, complexity, and diversity inherent in multi-perspectival collaboration with art. In her own words:

> I advocate feminist criticism because it is based in consequential and contextual theories of art, recognizing art as a meaningful element of and response to culture and society. Feminist criticism poses not a single method, but draws on a variety of critical approaches whose foci are understanding art in relationship to social values

Candace Stout is Professor of Art Education at The Ohio State University. Her research and instructional interests focus on alternative forms of writing in arts-based qualitative inquiry. She has single-authored books and published articles both within arts education and in a variety of interdisciplinary journals and has served as keynote speaker in state, national, and international forums. Having devoted the first half of her life to teaching language, literature, and humanities to high school students, she has an abiding interest in the dynamics of classroom learning.

and ideologies, to power struggles, and to economic, class, gender, ethnic, and racial considerations. (p. 19)

As I read this article so long ago and as I read it again with 21st-century eyes, I see a well-crafted and theoretically explicit text. It is a piece that calls for an opening, an insistent opening of a conversation about the ways we as art educators might involve our students in critical considerations about our visual world. I think she was and is, in her words, "on to something." From this early article and its tandem interaction with art educators of like mind, we began a transformation from the conception of classroom art criticism as the holding of court with the students on trial for enculturated competence, to engaging young minds in a process of learning that is "understood as fluid and ongoing, beginning with an individual's conscious realization of himself or herself in relationship to the world about...." In the author's most timely assertion: "Criticism as such can become a student's active response and intervention to the world" (p. 24).

Implications of Feminist Art Criticism for Art Education

Elizabeth Garber

In this paper, I will argue feminist art criticism as a basis around which to restructure the practice of art criticism in art education. This focus is stimulated by calls from feminists, educators, and art critics-theorists that art be understood in relation to its ideological context and its social relevance. It is further activated by the current recognition in education that experiences and multiple world views of people of different genders, classes, ethnicities, races, and nationalities be respected. Moreover, diversity should permeate our approaches to knowing and understanding. The reflection of these changes in dictums of governance is important. Education, however, is realized as the underlying instrument for change. The need is as great in art education as in any other field.

Feminism, Art, and Art Education

Feminism in the arts and humanities during the last decade has undergone two important changes. The idea of a universal "woman" has been supplanted by the concept of differences between women, where gender, race, ethnicity, class, sexual preference, age, and disadvantagedness are understood to contribute to differences among women. Approaches for implementing change in social attitudes have altered from demands for equal opportunity and for a straightforward "gestalt switch" (Alcoff, 1988, p. 414) in how we as a society value women's accomplishments and traditional deeds, to detailed analyses of the implications underlying social, institutional, ideological, and psychological structurations of gender, race, class, and other factors. Drawing on critical methods such as poststructuralism, Marxism, and psychoanalysis, feminist critics in the arts and humanities are at the forefront of practices that work to strategically undermine the status quo.

Feminists reject the thrusts of modernism in art that have emphasized genius, originality, and self-referentiality—qualities associated with male development (Lipton, 1988; Parker & Pollock, 1981; Pollock, 1987). Over the course of the past century and a half, *artist* has been thought of as an antisocial, antidomestic free-thinker, while women's roles have been associated with social reproduction and cultural refinement. Such associations are understood by feminists to be socially, not ontologically, determined.

Art is not a free, autonomous activity of a superendowed individual ... [but] occurs in a social situation, is an integral element of the social structure, and is mediated and determined by specific social situations. (Nochlin, 1971, pp. 488-489)

These social situations include education. Modernism has determined what is taught as art in the schools. Hence, a hierarchy of values in education relative to gender as well as class and race is perpetuated (Collins & Sandell, 1984; Nochlin, 1971; Pollock, 1986; Sandell, 1978).

Art education has also been undergoing changes, in integrating art criticism, art history, and aesthetics with the studio curriculum (a host of discipline-based art education literature could be referenced here; among the most well known are Clark, Day, & Greer, 1987; Getty Center for Education in the Arts, 1985; Greer, 1984; Greer & Rush, 1985). With less publicity yet ample poignancy have come renewed calls for a socially based, socially informed art education that includes art criticism components (Congdon, 1989; Hamblen, 1986; Nadaner, 1984). Art is understood as a carrier of ideas, values, and beliefs, and must be taught and discussed with the larger world in mind. Critical talk about art is a primary means through which these ideas, values, and beliefs are conveyed. Most attention to art criticism in art education, however, results in an examination of the formal or expressive properties of works of art. Some art educators recognize this as problematic. In the words of Dan Nadaner (1984), an emphasis on formalism and self-expression is compatible with a social ideology that isolates meaning within the individual, and looks to an individualistic psychology to explain meaning ... it is not cognizant of wider, equally relevant horizons .... Sociology, morality, and ethics must enter the debate if the debate is to be adequate to its subject. (p. 25)

He specified faults with the ever-popular critical method put forth by Edmund Feldman, arguing:

Feldman outlines three criteria for evaluation: formalist, expressivist, and instrumental. While the instrumental category is meant to include social dimensions of experience, it does so by placing them outside of the ontol-ogy of the work itself. (p. 21)

Nadaner noted lack of social awareness in students from a study he did in film education, and argued they needed encouragement to consider different world views. He suggested that within the purview of art education, ideologies be examined and critiqued. He cited feminist art criticism as a means through which social values concerning art are considered.

Karen Hamblen (1986) perceived similar deficiencies, identifying art educators' reliance for meaning on traditional aesthetics (with issues of value and truth in relationship to beauty) as insufficient. She concluded that sociological relationships in criticism, the social significance of art objects studied, and cross-cultural aesthetics need to be studied as foundations to art criticism in art education.

Kristin Congdon (1989) argued for a language of criticism that permits recognition of the world views of a variety of people. The familiar formats of criticism used in art education, she argued, were created by Western, academically oriented Caucasians. These formats "may hamper our enjoyment of art," she continued, as well as "unnecessarily limit our intellectual growth" (p. 182). Although Congdon did not focus on gender in this article, her arguments extend to differences between the sexes. Academia being overwhelmingly dominated until recently by males, the formats are also masculine biased, hence intellectually and experientially limited to the Western Caucasian male's ideas and values about art. Given parallel concerns of feminists and these educators, and the opportunity for change that education presents, what is the model of feminist art criticism?

Feminism, Art Criticism, and Art Education Varieties of Feminist Art Criticism

I propose feminist approaches to criticism to displace the methods currently used by art educators for structuring art critical talk—methods that reproduce the modernist emphasis on originality, genius, and formal and expressive elements. I advocate feminist criticism because it is based in consequential and contextual theories of art, recognizing art as a meaningful element of and response to culture and society.[1] Feminist criticism poses not a single method, but draws on a variety of critical approaches whose foci are understanding art in relationship to social values and ideologies, to power struggles, and to economic, class, gender, ethnic, and racial considerations. As advocated here, feminist art criticism does not isolate and overrepresent gender in critical discourse: class, race, age, sexual preference, ethnicity, nationality, and additional influences hold parallel positions. Finally, feminist art criticism, being grounded in a social and political movement outside art, has as its conceptual bases the relationships between art's meaning and social understanding.

Utilization of diverse critical strategies by feminist art critics reifies as different practices.[2] I have organized these practices into three groups that will be examined first as *bases,* then as *strands.* This is to emphasize that underlying the different practices or strands are common bases. Bases are shared purposes and goals of mainstream American feminist critics. They are *social analysis, political activism,* and *self-knowledge.* The focus of the social analysis basis is social systems and their effect on valuation and discrimination in the art world. Structures underlying our social institutions are analyzed for their underlying roles in constructing how we view and value women, and other marginalized groups in relationship to art. Analyses adapt and synthesize extra-feminist critical methods such as Marxism, psychoanalysis, and poststructuralism. The focus shifts in the second and third bases from social systems to women. The focus of the second basis, political activism, is the political nature of feminism itself and social changes that are to result from the feminist movement. The third basis, self-knowledge, holds subjective experience as valid and important for the individual's own self-worth, as well as in creating awareness of women as social and political classes. In the original consciousness-raising efforts that were begun by the New York Radical Women in the late 1960s,[3] subjectivity and self-knowledge were connected to political consciousness-raising. Although consciousness-raising as a technique became focused on the individual, and is remembered outside its larger political and social foci, self-knowledge in feminist art criticism recalls these original social and political foundations.

All three bases are apparent in the contemporary feminist art criticism of mainstream American feminists. Each basis is emphasized in distinctive form in one of the three strands mentioned earlier. *Analytic feminist critics* focus on exposing and undermining social and cultural forces that oppress *women. Activist feminist critics* emphasize particularly the political projects of feminists by reporting the political content of feminist art and championing its political causes. For *woman-centered critics,* the validation of subjectivity that is part of self-knowledge becomes a celebration of what one critic has termed "personal engagement" with works of art and a celebration of women (Frueh, 1985b). The emphasis of each strand varies, its motivating impulses vary, and the approaches practitioners take and methods they prescribe to effect change differ.

A brief example of each type of criticism should help to clarify their differences. Analyses of how structures underlying our social institutions construct what women are and their places in society characterize the writing of analytic feminist critics. They locate gender as a dynamic element in all human experiences. Gendered experience and the structure of gender, as projected by analytic feminist critics, are changing elements, shaped by their historical con-text. In an analysis of Sherrie Levine's photographic appropriations,[4] Abigail Solomon-Godeau (1985) also focused on cultural codes:

> The rephotographed Walker Evans photographs, whose graininess and obvious screen clearly attest to their already reproduced status, underline the cultural and representational codes that structure our reading of (respectively) The Great Depression, the rural poor, female social victims, and the *style* of Walker Evans. (p. 7)

Solomon-Godeau claimed that by copying images of other artists, Levine rejected originality, authorship, subjectivity, and the authority of an artwork. Solomon-Godeau discussed Levine's rejection of these criteria that are basic to Modernist practice in art (Kelly, 1984), calling the work a challenge to art in a capitalist system and to art governed by a partriarchal system. Solomon-Godeau's (1985) interpretation arrives at the juncture of feminism, Marxism, and semiotics. A Marxist critique of capitalism bears upon what the author equally associates with patriarchy. The valuing of originality, authorship and individual self, and authority are understood to be emphasized in males and patriarchal culture, and are often argued by feminists to be in opposition to what women are taught to cultivate and value in themselves (Parker & Pollock, 1981). Thus, the roles women most often play in art are those of observed subjects and carriers of meaning rather than makers, spectators, or interpreters. Solomon-Godeau (1985) utilized the strategies of semiology-the study of connotations implied by the images which are understood by so many viewers that they become signifying codes—to explain what these images (both Evans' and Levine's copies) signify to audiences.

Lucy Lippard's criticism exemplifies activist feminist art criticism. In fact, she has termed her writing "advocacy criticism." She reports on and defends activist art. Suzanne Lacy is an example of the kind of artist Lippard discusses. Lacy's performance pieces have included rap sessions on oppression, a demonstration for women murdered by the hillside strangler, and a performance on aging. Although Lacy's work culminates in what Lippard (1984) has described as "recognizable 'art pieces' ... in fact the real work includes the yearlong organizing and workshops that led up to it, as well as film and documentation that may follow" (p. 343). Lacy's process involves community participation and an effort to raise the awareness of audiences about needed social changes and political actions that will implement change. Lippard champions the art of many kinds of art activists, such as Tim Rollins, a high school teacher in the South Bronx who with his students works on community consciousness-raising projects.

Finally, woman-centered criticism emphasizes self-knowledge in a celebra-tion of women that is individually and politically instrumental. In an article on allegory for *Art Journal*, feminist critic Joanna Frueh (1985a) interpreted Margaret Bailey Doogan's *Basic Black with Pearls*. She begins, "You probably wouldn't want her. She screams at other women and men. She grimaces and smirks, as if she knows some disgusting truth and sees through your lies;" and ends, "Because she makes the ugly faces of a real woman, she is uncommonly beautiful" (p. 326). Frueh projected strong women independent of men and male culture. She communicated a woman in touch with herself who rejects socially established standards for what women should be. This gestalt switch (Alcoff, 1988, p. 414) of a traditional woman stereotype (the "bitch") should be understood as a political strategy that undermines the concept of woman as either madonna (good) or whore (bad). Through Frueh's interpretation, we must reconceptualize beauty and goodness in this woman to include strength and self-knowledge.

I emphasize that these different practices in feminist art criticism are not mutually exclusive, because the importance of self-knowledge, the political nature of feminism, and the active intervention of feminists into the status quo of our defining social institu-tions are projects motivating all three strands of feminist art criticism. The translation of bases into strands identifies primary emphases within different practices.

Feminist Education: Pluralistic Voices

Recent scholarship in feminist education is based on the premise that be-cause diverse peoples experience the world differently, "comparative ap-proaches in which each of several perspectives augments and challenges the others" are to be emphasized (Maher & Rathbone, 1986, p. 216). Subjectivity and perspective are not only recognized, but under-stood as inevitably contributing to "the form and content of the evolving knowledge" (pp. 216-217). Frances Maher and Charles Rathbone, writing on implications of feminist theory for teacher education, arrived at general pedagogical implications. They called for a comparative strategy in presenting information, using different perspectives. Their strategy utilized an interactive, collaborative, cooperative style of teaching.

Another strategy can utilize comparison of differences within a particular area, such as feminist criticism, as a model towards understanding the existence of variety and its legitimacy. Allowing for a breadth of perspectives in interpreting art and making students aware (in part through criticism) of different perspectives on art allow for greater breadth of meaning in understanding art. Patrocinio Schweickart (1985) proposes a "conversa-tion" between pluralisms.[5] The aim of the conversation is comprehension, not agreement. Schweickart seeks coherence, though this need not be bound by consistency and unifor-mity. Within the art education classroom, the goal of art criticism becomes coherence in diversity and respect, rather than a unity of logical consistency.

If respect for diversity is one projected outcome of criticism in art education, another is an extended understanding of "Otherness," the concept that originated with Simone de Beauvoir and examined by feminists for the last score of years. The "Other" defines each individual of every cultural group: Otherness is a potential within each of us as we relate to different cultures. "The master ... discovers ... that he is just an other among others" (Minh-ha, 1986/1987, p. 3). In other words, "everyone is someone else's 'Other.'" (Ellsworth, 1988, p. 15). The educational outcome of conversations of plurality, and of our own self-definitions as sometimes contradictory and sometimes other, support an understanding of self as a process of becoming. The process, not the outcome, is emphasized.

The result of comparison, as argued by feminist educator Elizabeth Ellsworth (1989), is that we come to see that all knowledge is partial and biased. We come to see that the true enemy is not the unknowable but systems of belief that efface the partial nature of any understanding.

What would it mean to recognize not only that a multiplicity of knowledges are present in the classroom as a result of the way difference has been used to structure social relations inside and outside the classroom, but that these knowledges are contradictory, partial, and irreducible? They cannot be made to "make sense"—they cannot be known, in terms of the single master discourse of an educational project's curriculum or theoretical framework. (p. 32)

Ellsworth has recognized the need for the existence of pluralism as an educative model as opposed to a norm of a single universal truth. Within feminist art criticism, woman-centered criticism, centered on a celebration of women's traits and bonds between women as a route for change, may not be reconcilable with analytic criticism, where .the concept "woman" is perceived as a social construct. The plural isms and their differences can be taught as acceptable. Recognizing and respecting differences should be the focus of learning, not judging one as superior by all standards.

We might also come to see that we are, within ourselves, different things at once. Judith Mayne (1987) has asked, for instance, why women enjoy commercial Hollywood films that were created from a male viewpoint, with women portrayed as objects of the male gaze. Spectators of these films, female or male, can identify with the woman in them through two routes: as voyeurs or as objects of the looking. The female spectator is caught between the two, in continuous conflict and tension. We are caught, as Teresa de Lauretis (1984) proposed, between *"woman*—the configuration of patriarchal ideology—and *women,* historical subjects who live in a tangential relation to that configuration" (p. 16). Mayne (1987) understood this state as one of positive tension that she called "both/and." She quoted historian Linda Gordon in concluding, "'This in-between would not imply resolution ... [it] is rather a condition of being constantly pulled, usually off balance, sometimes teetering wildly, almost always tense'"(p. 18). The focus in teaching is realization of these internal and external differences, and that individuality is produced through self-reflection on our internal processing of our external worlds.

In proposing three approaches for integrating feminist scholarship into education, it is the pluralistic approach that Georgia Collins (1981) has advocated. Pluralists work towards "a reconstructed inclusive art community with institutions embracing a variety of values and practices, drawn from both the male art establishment and the female countermovement .... The individual would be free to seek congenial situations and audiences without prejudice or penalty." (p. 87). Activist and analytic feminist criticisms work toward such reconstruction, although most practitioners go beyond pluralism in envisioning a reconstruction of such extreme dimensions that it might be understood as revolutionary.

Feminist Education: Political Ramifications

In thinking through these implications, judgments against pluralism in art call into question its use in effecting an education of social relevancy. The endpoint of pluralism is often to "better enjoy life" noted David Lodge (1985) through his novel's character, the old-school academic Philip Swallow (p. 317). Critics of pluralism include Gablik (1984) who has argued that it presents us ultimately with no true value or meaning. Amorality underlies pluralism. Anything goes. Pollock (1983) indicated it allows many styles without challenge to the status quo or its underlying ideology. It rests uncomfortably close to the exaltation of self-expression as an endpoint. Pluralism as used in recent modernist art allows for the singular and exclusive aesthetics of modernism. Enjoyment of life does not result in a better—more socially caring—populace, as Walter Benjamin (1979) observed when he linked cultural documents (such as literature and art) to barbarism (p. 359). Transformation cannot occur in isolation from a social context (Eagleton, 1983). Accepting a variety of positions in feminist art criticism should not be understood to be pluralistic in the sense of art in the 1970s—that anything goes. Feminist critics assume conscious positions relative to feminist goals and perceptions of the current social context. The strategies for change differ, reflecting different perceptions and needs. Feminist criticism is consequentially, contextually, and politically based.

At a recent talk by art critic and aesthetician David Carrier (1989), I was struck by his model for teaching art history. He proposed teaching a plurality of interpretations of artworks to students as expressions of various cultural-historical eras. Sixty-eight interpretations of a northern Baroque painting by Caravaggio exemplify the ideologies about art that were popular in the era each was written. I think he is on to something, building from an ideological exploration. But once we arrive at some understanding of ideological expression, are we any closer to social relevance? What I am arguing for is an extension of Carrier's model. The critical endpoints at which students arrive need to be dissected in terms of their sociopolitical ramifications. Students learn to identify and construct critical interpretations, cognizant of their ideological implications. They will learn also that art and criticism are not simply illustrations of culture; they are signifying practices which produce meanings and construct images of the world that effect particular ideological representations of the world (Pollock, 1987). Lest this sound like brazen support of nonobjective thinking, let me call to mind Carrier's (1987) conclusion about Clement Greenberg's theory of modern art—a theory that was centered in the medium and not the illusion of painting, with abstract expressionism as the sine qua non of modernism. The theory, asserted Carrier, reflects a matter of taste. Greenberg probably admired "Pollock but not Dali, [so] he was naturally led to produce an explanation of his experience" (p. 35). An ideology, in addition to taste, informs why we like and ultimately support a work of art, a style, or medium. The connection of Greenberg and the abstract expressionists to Marxism in the 1940s, and their turn to nonobjective painting in response to blacklists of the McCarthy era, indicate not only taste but ideological issues. Greenberg and the abstract expressionists acted in full awareness of political and ideological implications (Herbert, 1985). Each of the strands of feminist criticism outlined above is backed by such awareness and with intent to effect change towards a society which respects without prejudice differences in gender, sexual preferences, race, ethnicity, and ableness. As Greenberg's criticism constructed a particular world view, each strand of feminist criticism consciously and openly acts as a signifying practice to effect feminist world views.

Feminist art criticism, in its bases and strands, is undergirded by a political initiative. It should be understood not as another "approach" or singular "perspective," but as part of a broader political struggle (Pollock, 1983). It should be understood as fluid and ongoing, beginning with an individual's conscious realization of himself or herself in relationship to the world about, and developing as consideration of socially relevant meaning is undertaken. Criticism as such can become a student's active response to and intervention into the world.

References

Alcoff, L. (1988). Cultural feminism versus post-structuralism: The identity crisis in feminist theory. *Signs: Journal of Women in Culture and Society,* 13(3), 405-436.

Benjamin, W. (1979). Eduard Fuchs, collector and historian. In *One-way street and other writings.* Quoted from T. Eagleton (1983). *Literary theory: An introduction* (p. 208). Minneapolis: University of Minnesota Press.

Carrier, D. (1987). *Artwriting.* Amherst: University of Massachusetts Press.

Carrier, D. (1989, October). *Teaching the new art history.* Keynote talk presented at The Second Penn State Conference on the History of Art Education, The Pennsylvania State University, University Park, PA, October 12, 1989.

Clark, G. A, Day, M. D., & Greer, W. D. (1987). Discipline-based art education: Becoming students of art. *Journal of Aesthetic Education,* 21(2), 129-193.

Collins, G. (1981). Feminist approaches to education. *Journal of Aesthetic Education,* 15(2), 83-94.

Collins, G. & Sandell, R. (1984). *Women, art, and education.* Reston, VA: National Art Education Association.

Congdon, K. G. (1989). Multi-cultural approaches to art criticism. *Studies in Art Education,* 30(3), 176-184.

Deckard, B. S. (1983). *The women's movement: Political, socioeconomic, and psychological issues.* New York: Harper and Row.

de Lauretis, T. (1984). *Alice doesn't: Feminism, cinema, and semiotics.* Bloomington, IN: University of Indiana Press.

Donovan, J. (1985). *Feminist theory: The intellectual traditions of American feminism.* New York: Frederick Ungar Publishing.

Eagleton, T. (1983). *Literary theory: An introduction.* Minneapolis: University of Minnesota Press.

Eaton, M. M. (1988). *Basic issues in aesthetics.* Belmont, CA: Wadsworth.

Ellsworth, E. (1989). Why doesn't this feel empowering? Working through the repressive myths of critical pedagogy. *Harvard Educational Review,* 59(3), 297-324.

Frueh, J. (1985a). Allegory: An-other world. *Art Journal,* 45(4), 323-329.

Frueh, J. (1985b). Towards a feminist theory of art criticism [part 1]. *New Art Examiner,* 12(4), 41-44.

Gablik, S. (1984). *Has modernism failed?* New York: Thames & Hudson.

Getty Center for Education in the Arts. (1985). *Beyond creating: The place for art in America's schools.* Los Angeles: The J. Paul Getty Trust.

Giroux, H. A (1983). *Theory and resistance in education.* South Hadley, MA: Bergin & Garvey.

Giroux, H. A (1989). Schooling as a form of cultural politics: Toward a pedagogy of and for difference. In H. A Giroux & P. McLaren (Eds.), *Critical pedagogy, the state, and cultural struggle* (pp. 125-151). Albany: State University of New York Press.

Greer, W. D. (1984). A discipline-based art education: Approaching art as a subject of study. *Studies in Art Education,* 25(4), 212-218.

Greer, W. D., & Rush, J.e. (1985). A grand experiment: The Getty Institute for Educators on the Visual Arts. *Art Education,* 37(1), 24-35.

Hamblen, K. (1986). Three areas of concern for art criticism instruction: Theoretical and research foundations, sociological relationships, and teaching methodologies. *Studies in Art Education,* 27(4), 163-173.

Herbert, J. D. (1985). *The political origins of abstract-expressionist art criticism: The early theoretical and critical writings of Clement Greenberg and Harold Rosenberg.* Stanford Honors Essay in Humanities, no. 27. Stanford, CA: Humanities Honors Program, Stanford University.

Kelly, M. (1984). Re-viewing modernist criticism. In B. Wallis (Ed.), *Art after modernism: Rethinking representation* (pp. 87-103). New York: New Museum of Contemporary Art.

Lippard, L. (1984). Trojan horses: Activist art and advocacy. In Brian Wallis (Ed.), *Art after modernism: Rethinking representation* (pp. 341-358). New York: New Museum of Contemporary Art.

Lipton, E. (1988). *Looking into Degas: Uneasy images of women and modern life.* Berkeley: University of California Press.

Lodge, D. (1985). *Small world.* Harmondsworth: Penguin.

Maher, F., & Rathbone, e. (1986). Teacher education and feminist theory: Some implications for practice. *American Journal of Education, 94*(2), 214-235.

Mayne, J. (1987). Feminist film theory and women at the movies. *Profession,* pp. 14-19.

Minh-ha, T. T. (1986/1987, Fall-Winter). Introduction. *Discourse,* (8), pp. 3-9.

Nadaner, D. (1984). Critique and intervention: Implications of social theory for art education. *Studies in Art Education, 26*(1), 20-26.

Nochlin, L. (1971). Why are there no great women artists? In V. Gornick & B. K. Moran (Eds.), *Woman in sexist society: Studies in power and powerlessness* (pp. 480-510). New York: Basic Books.

Parker, R., & Pollock, G. (1981). *Old mistresses: Women, art, and ideology.* London: Routledge & Kegan Paul.

Pepper, S. C. (1963). *The basis of criticism in the arts.* Cambridge, MA: Harvard University Press.

Pollock, G. (1983). Women, art, and ideology: Questions for feminist art historians. *Woman's Art Journal, 4*(1), 39-47.

Pollock, G. (1986). Art, art school, and culture: The individual after the death of the artist. *exposure, 24*(3), 20-33.

Pollock, G. (1987). Feminism and modernism. In R. Parker & G. Pollock (Eds.), *Framing feminism: Art and the women's movement 1970-1985* (pp. 79-124). London: Routledge & Kegan Paul.

Sandell, R. (1978). *Feminist art education: Definition, assessment and application to contemporary art education.* Unpublished doctoral dissertation, The Ohio State University.

Sarachild, K. (1975). Consciousness raising: A radical weapon. In Redstockings (Ed.), *Feminist revolution* (pp. 131-137). New Paltz, NY: Redstockings.

Schweickart, P. (1985). What are we doing, really? - Feminist criticism and the problem of theory. *Canadian Journal of Political and Social Theory, 9*(1-2), 148-164.

Solomon-Godeau, A. (1985). Winning the game when the rules have been changed: Art photography and postmodernism. *exposure, 23*(1), 5-15.

Endnotes

[1] Contextual theories of art bring the history of an artwork to its interpretation. Such historical context includes relevant cultural attitudes, beliefs, and politics during the period the artwork was created; influences on the artist; art contemporary to the artwork under consideration; critical interpretations of this and other artworks; art theory; artist's intent, and relevant details of the artist's life. Consequential theories place aesthetic value on objects that produce or are associated with something else that is culturally valued. For an overview of contextual and consequential theories of art, the reader is referred to Eaton (1988), chapters 5 and 7, and Pepper (1963), chapter 3.

[2] The organization of feminist art criticism that I explain now is based on that written by white American and British feminists. This delimitation should be understood as a preliminary one that should be expanded by further research into feminist racial, ethnic, class, and sex-preference minorities.

[3] The group known as New York Radical Women are credited with adopting consciousness-raising into the feminist movement from the writings of Karl Marx. Their first use of the technique was true to Marx's intent that it be connected to a revolution led by the oppressed. In the case of the New York Radical Women, women were "the oppressed." To accomplish a revolution led by the oppressed, Marx argued as a preliminary step the necessity of forming class consciousness in dialectic opposition to the ideology of the ruling class. In the New York Radical Women's con-sciousness-raising, women's thoughts, perceptions, and experiences were to be collected as a basis for revising extant ("patriarchal") ways of thinking about women. Women would become aware of themselves as a social and political class, and their culturally prescribed roles would be unlearned. For more information, see Deckard, 1983; Donovan's (1985) chapter on feminism and Marxism; and Sarachild, 1975.

[4] Levine has copied the photographs of such well-known photographers as Walker Evans, Edward Weston, and Eliot Porter, and signed her name to the copies.

[5] Although Schweickart is focused on the pluralisms within feminist literary criticism, I am extending her conceptual model of the conversation to the art classroom.

Graeme Sullivan

Senior Editor, 2001-2003

ARTICLE SELECTION

Wilson, B. (1994). Reflections on the Relationship Among Art, Life, and Research. *Studies in Art Education*, 35(4), 197-208.

Brent Wilson's article is based on his *Studies* Invited Lecture given at the 1993 NAEA national convention. Two small items in Enid Zimmerman's introduction caught my eye. Enid mentioned that she first became aware of Brent listening closely to a conference presentation, while intently "filling his sketchbook with an abundance of words and images." The second reference was when Enid became more aware of his scholarship when she was on the committee that awarded Brent and Marjorie Wilson the 1980 Manuel Barkan Award. The acknowledgment was for their 1980 article that compared the drawings of children from different cultural backgrounds. For me, these two anecdotes acknowledge the inextricable relationship between visual and scholarly inquiry. These themes are key concepts explored in Wilson's 1994 reflection on art, life and research, and the issues he raises echo with even greater resonance amid discussions today about art, culture, and educational inquiry.

Wilson begins his argument with a visual reference that captures what research is supposed to do—and that is to explain things. The research genealogy he presents is a braided tapestry of seminal art sources, art educational issues, exploratory projects, reviews, and publications, which reflect the interweaving of his research life. His visual account seeks to explain in a causal fashion what glues this matrix of issues, ideas and actions together. The inference is that 'art' holds the key. I think he is right.

When I was a graduate student in the early 1980s I was intrigued by Brent and Marjorie Wilson's quest for a socio-cultural explanation of children's drawing that was grounded in cultural production. My understanding was fashioned by reading the artifacts of research—the journal articles, research reports, and books. But it was only recently that the links between art, life, and research, that Wilson alludes to came into full view. The moment was when I had the opportunity to closely examine the sketchbooks that Enid Zimmerman mentioned. There were over 70 of them, and they recorded Wilson's visual history of art education, from the early 1980s to the present time.

Graeme Sullivan is Professor of Art Education, Teachers College Columbia University. He received his Ph.D. from The Ohio State University, Columbus, Ohio in 1984, and taught at the University of New South Wales, Australia from 1988, before taking up the position at Teachers College in January 1999. He has published extensively. In 1990, he was awarded the Manuel Barkan Memorial Award for his scholarly writing by the National Art Education Association (NAEA), and in 2007 the Lowenfeld Award for significant contribution to the art education profession.

Here I found visual snippets, jottings about everyday events, historical footnotes, and images that revealed private thumbprints of ideas that may have been pressed into action later. It was in a sketchbook from the early 1980s where I found the visual idea that seemed to account for the research insight I read about as a graduate student regarding the cultural necessity of children's drawing. Brent had copied drawings (made by Egyptian children) he had stumbled upon in the back streets of Cairo. It was a moment of discovery, captured in a sketch--it was a visual research question. Here was a glimpse of the artist-researcher in action. Wilson's more public writing as an art educator calls us to look into the world of children as they see it and how we might frame it. His art captures how he sees it and anticipates why we might need to think about it. This is where art, life, and research still converge today.

Brent Wilson. Children's wall drawing, Cairo. Page from sketchbook, 1980.

Reflections on the Relationships Among Art, Life, and Research

Brent Wilson

There is one major idea that underlies this paper: I want to try to illustrate the relationship between one's research and one's life. I wish to echo Foucault who said, in an interview about his book, *Archeology of Knowledge,* "I believe someone…who is a writer is not simply doing his work in his books, but that his major work is, in the end, himself in the process of writing his books." He went on to say "the work includes the whole life as well as the text" (Ryan, 1993, p. 14). Although an active research life is composed of many parts, in the end, a researcher would like to see his or her own interests, values, and assumptions about life and human purpose interwoven with the themes and topics of one's inquiry so that their tapestry has a vivid pattern of meaning-for the researcher and the readers of research.

Although we research what we are, what we think, value, and feel, others may not see the patterns and connections to our lives that we, the researchers, do. Then again, it is possible we have only imaged the patterns. I wish to take a retrospective look at my research as it relates to a larger life in art and to point to patterns that I think are there. To make my points, I'll present a diagram and tell some brief stories about some of the people, ideas, times, and places that have given form my research. I wish, at the end of the paper, to point to the educational research I would like to see as we approach the 21st century.

Art Educational Campaigns

I have a long-standing aversion to military metaphors, and yet I wish to refer to a disastrous campaign that resulted in what is perhaps the most elegant visual display of information ever drawn. In 1861 Charles Joseph Minard drew a diagram that in one four inch by seven inch rectangle captures with "brutal eloquence" (Tufte, 1983, p. 40) Napoleon's Russian campaign of 1812. Tufte (1983) suggests the diagram may well be the best statistical graphic ever drawn and describes it in this way:

> Minard's graphic tells a rich, coherent story with its multivariate data, far more enlightening than just a single number bouncing along over time. Six variables are plotted: the size of the army, its location on a two-dimensional surface, direction of the army's movement, and temperature on various dates during the retreat from Moscow. (p. 40)

On receiving the invitation to present the *Studies* Lecture I began to envision a graphic that would capture the multivariate relationships among the components of my research and inquiry in art and art education. However, I wanted my diagram to be the reverse of what Minard showed in his. He visualized a thick band that represented Napoleon's army of 422,000 men as it invaded Russia in June of 1812. By September, when it reached

---

the sacked and deserted Moscow, the army had declined to 100,000 men. An increasingly narrower black band shows the tragic loss of human life as the army retreated to its starting point—arriving at the Polish/Russian border with a mere 10,000 men. One's professional life should not diminish like a misguided campaign. Rather, it should grow in magnitude, purpose, and clarity.

The human mind is vastly more complex than a military campaign.

Nevertheless, if I could manage to produce a diagram of my mind's battles in and around art and art education, I would wish it to show how a few small threads eventually spun into a thousand colorful strands that over a lifetime were woven into one brilliant tapestry. I would wish to illustrate that as the tapestry widened, its design became increasingly parsimonious, elegant, and integrated as it illustrated the profoundly important consequences a good art education could have for an enlightened citizenry. (See Figure 1.)

The Bands and Strands of Art Educational Inquiry

In Figure 1, I show two pages from one of my sketchbook/journals in which I make a sketch for a diagram of my various campaigns in art education.[1] Times, places, and institutional settings provide opportunities to interact with individuals and ideas. In my sketch I first established a timeline and place-line—one that started in 1950 in Idaho and extended through Utah State University from 1952 to 1956; Cranbrook Academy of Art from 1956 to 1958; serving as the Art Supervisor in Salt Lake City, Utah from 1959 to 1966 (with two years' leave to work on a Ph.D. at Ohio State); the years 1966 to 1974 at the University of Iowa (with one year's leave to teach at the Birmingham, England Polytechnic); to 1974 and my present position at Penn State (with two very important sabbatical semesters, one in Egypt and the other in Japan). I didn't quite know how to graph the fact that from 1987 onward I have spent nearly as much time away from than at Penn State—first to do the research for the National Endowment for the Arts' *Toward Civilization* and then, beginning in 1988, to work as the cross-site evaluator for the six Getty Center for Education in the Arts Regional Staff Development Institutes in Florida, Minnesota, Nebraska, Ohio, Tennessee, and Texas. In art, my timeline runs from surrealism and abstract expressionist high-modernism, through pop, to postmodernism, and in art education from creative expression to Discipline-Based Art Education.

The left hand column of my diagram presented problems. I wanted to show a logical and hierarchical relationship between my research and its sources. I knew that I wanted to begin with the philosophical and theoretical sources on which I have drawn, but what should come next? Finally, I settled for the following: first, "Theories, Philosophy, and Intellectual Climate": and second, a classification, "Art World and Its Social Climate, Artists, Works of Art, Styles, Purposes and Practices." In this art world classification I wanted to show my own works of art and their relationship to conducting art educational research. Thus the third classification was "Education and Art Education-Theories, History, and Practice." It is only when I arrive at the fourth, "Child's Art World," that I begin to point, in the rectangular shapes, to my own research. The fifth classification points to research

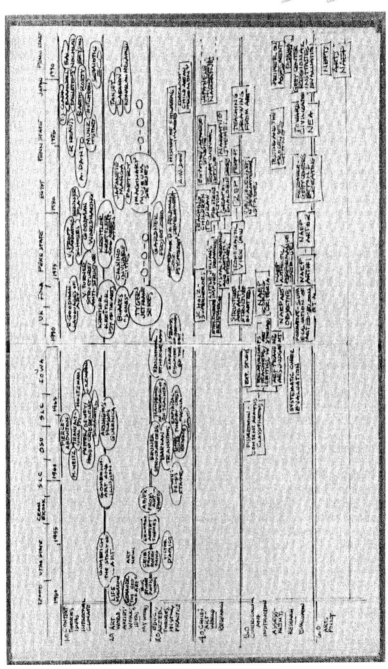

Figure 1. Failed Graphic: Some of the Parts, Few of the Connections

relating to "Curriculum, Instruction, Assessment, and Evaluation." Finally, I end the left hand column with a sixth classification:"Arts Education Policy."

My crude sketch has none of the elegance of Minard's graph. Nevertheless, by organizing in a matrix, times and places; art, philosophical, and art educational sources; and my own research, I have begun to see patterns and relationships that inform the things I wish to say about inquiry in art education. Perhaps sometime I will be able to graph to my satisfaction the connections among these variables. For now, however, I will have to be satisfied with merely using words to point to factors and relationships.

The World of Art and the Realms of Art Education Research

Our field is composed of art and education. For some art educational researchers, I have the feeling that education comes first. For me, however, art has always held the preeminent position. I have always tired to go directly to the art world for my ideas about art, not to the world of art education where notions of art are frequently narrow, shallow, and outmoded. Usually our field provides only a delayed reflection of the art world and we art educational researchers are like generals who continue to fight the battles of previous wars, rather than the ones in which we currently find ourselves. While art continually redefines itself, we tend to direct our research toward artistic content and values from previous eras.

Learning about the Art World

Let me explore this relationship between the art world and art educational research in a personal way. Does any teenager have aspirations to be an art educa-tional researcher or even an art teacher? My early ambitions were directed toward being an artist. When I made my first firm career decision at age 16 my unconscious thought must have been: "Well, if you are going to be an artist, you had better find out what art is." Living on a farm in Idaho, my primary window to the art world, at least the one outside Idaho, was *LIFE* magazine in whose pages, from the early 1940s onward, I saw and read about contemporary art and the history of art. I didn't have the foresight to tear out the art pages and my parents didn't save back issues, but my aunt and uncle did. In the summer of 1950 I spent weeks in their basement going through eleven years of *LIFE* tearing out every article on art and mounting them in thick wallpaper catalogues. That same summer I traveled east for the first time and in New York bought Emily Genauer's book, *The Best of Art* (1948), which contained reproductions and critical reviews of 50 paintings from New York exhibitions from the 1946-1947 season. For the next two years, in the private studio that I organized in the storeroom adjoining my high school art room, I painted dozens of oil paintings in the styles of my *LIFE* and *Best of Art* sources. Stuart Davis's abstractions were the basis for my predominant style. I also played with the themes and subjects of others' art. Although I didn't know it at the time, I had violated one of the sacred tenets of modern art education. I had copied, and borrowed, from everything in sight.

My pattern of borrowing continued. At Utah State, during a painting critique, I remember a fellow student saying,"Wilson's work doesn't look like the rest of ours." I also remember thinking at the time, "Yes, because the rest of you don't know what I know about art."

I may have known a little of that far-away art world that now came to me through the pages of *Art News,* but I didn't have clear ideas about what I wanted to do in my art. Through my undergraduate years and while I worked on my MFA at Cranbrook Academy of Art, my work was highly eclectic and had no central theme. As I served as the art supervisor in Salt Lake City and as I taught at the University of Iowa, I had been nagged by a conversation with Harrison Groutage, one of my art instructors at Utah State. In my studio one afternoon, the usual teacher/student barriers dissolved as he told me about his desire to create a personal art that reflected the uniqueness of what has been called the "Great Basin Kingdom." As he sketched for me the works he wished to paint, I resolved to find my own artistic theme that truly reflected my interests, values, and purposes. My twelve-year quest yielded no profound thematic result as I worked through years of abstract expressionist figurative paintings and welded steel and polished cast bronze sculptures that were a cross between Brancusi and Boccioni.

It wasn't until I was teaching in England in 1971 that I finally arrived at my theme. I had resolved during my stay in England to read lots of William Blake's poetry; it seemed the appropriate thing to do. One morning as I was reading the "Guardian" I saw a sinister looking silhouette of the British Harrier jet plane. Immediately, I thought "That's Blake's Tyger." For several years and literally hundreds of little paintings of "tyger-jet planes" and collages, I explored Blake's lines from "The Tyger" in *Songs of Innocence and Experience:*

When the stars threw down their spears And water'd heaven with their tears:
Did he smile his work to see?
Did he who made the Lamb make thee?

In these lines Blake asks something like "If God created the world and its goodness represented by the Lamb, then did he also create evil personified by the tyger?" Finally, I had my powerful universal theme, and in the Vietnam era a tyger-jet plane was a particularly sinister symbol. The adventures of the tyger-jet plane became a cosmic narrative of the oppositional forces of good and evil. The tyger-jet still appears occasionally in a series of paintings, "museums of the imagination," where I am the curator of exhibitions I have concocted and mounted in actual museum settings—especially the Kroller-Muller in the Netherlands and in my own fabricated museums.

Through the tyger-jet paintings, I had learned that universal themes, drawn from the art of another era can be reinterpreted in light of contemporary interests. I also learned that this theme-borrowing, if it is to be done sensitively, must be based on a thorough interpretation of the source-works. I did some of my own interpreting, but mostly I relied on a shelf of critical works on William Blake's poetry. It was my first in-depth encounter with literary criticism. Through my quarter century of experience with art and literary criticism I have become increasingly concerned that we art educators are not good interpreters of art. Yet, if we are to be good art teachers and art educational researchers we must first become insightful critics. My most serious criticism of contemporary art education is that art teachers do not understand how to help students make meaningful thematic connections between the works of art they study and the works they create—the very thing that artists have always done.

From Art to Art Educational Research

What does painting have to do with research in art education? At the very time I was making my tyger-jet paintings I realized that in his superhero stories the young J. C. Holtz (Wilson, 1974a) was depicting the same struggles between good and evil that I was. When I wrote about "Little Julian's Impure Drawings," (Wilson, 1976) I recognized that the young Julian Green was investigating human sexuality-one of the sub-themes of my tyger-jet series. In J. C. Holtz's and Julian Green's work I recognized that the schemata of young peoples' graphic images stemmed more from society than from self—just as in my own works. This line of inquiry, informed by my own image- and idea-borrowing, was reflected in Marjorie Wilson's and my "Iconoclastic View of the Imagery Sources in the Drawings of Young People" (Wilson & Wilson, 1977). In a very real sense we were reporting on my method of artistic creation that is, in fact, almost everybody's method.

There is an even more important point I wish to make. Through my experiences as an artist I approached my art educational research with the assumption that worthwhile art—art that functions well in the educational context—must be about ideas that touch on profound human purposes. I strove for these ideas in my own work and I saw them in the art of gifted young people. Without my grounding in art and without my insights into the world of art, I could not be the kind of art educational researcher that I wish to be. To pursue art educational research with little understanding of the ideational power of art makes research trivial. Artistic ideas are, of course, conveyed through form and style. This is the subject of my next short story.

Child Art, the Riddle of Style, and Some Ideological Riddles Yet to Be Addressed

The uproar from the "Iconoclastic View" article had a series of consequences; it led to studies like the "Case of the Disappearing Two-eyed Profile," (Wilson & Wilson, 1981); a series of studies of cultural influences on children's drawings (Wilson, 1992a; Wilson & Litgvoet, 1992; Wilson & Wilson, 1979a, 1980, 1984, and 1987); and the books, *Teaching Children to Draw* (Wilson & Wilson, 1982) and *Teaching Drawing From Art* (Wilson, Hurwitz, & Wilson, 1987). Let me try to connect a thread between my artistic interests and the study of children's images in the manner of art historians.

Through much of this century our modernist blinders have forced us art educators to look only to the universal features of child art. As I began to study children's art, however, it was obvious to me that their works were as stylistically distinct as the art of adults. Why was this so, and why hadn't we art educators noticed it? Curiously, for me the answer, at least one answer, was in the second art book I purchased when I was 16 or 17 years old—E. H. Gombrich's *The Story of Art* (1950). It was an auspicious purchase, although I didn't know it at the time. The first page of the book's introduction contains enough "aesthetic puzzles" to last a lifetime, and they must have, unconsciously, fed my curiosity about why any art looks as it does.

When Gombrich's *Art and Illusion* was published in 1960, I bought the book immediately and it provided another confirmation of my belief that art comes from art. In our research, Marjorie Wilson and I have shown that Gombrich's theory of "schemata and correction" is far more broadly applicable than Gombrich himself believed. We discovered that the schemata children use in their drawings are nearly as predictable as the words and grammar of their native languages. Moreover, we have shown that the styles and features of children's drawings change over time just as the works of adult artists do (Wilson and Wilson, 1981). In short, the theories that explain the history of adult art provide the basis for explaining children's art.

In our postmodern era, however, Gombrich's theories are beginning to seem a bit conventional. The new feminist, semiotic, political, critical, and sociologically based art histories (Bal, 1991; Bryson, 1988; Clark, 1984; Nochlin, 1989) have perhaps even more important implications than Gombrich's work does for a theoretical grounding of the study of children's art and art education (Wilson, 1992b). We art educators have virtually no understanding of the history of school art styles, of the hegemonies to which we subject our students in the art classroom, or of the ideological underpinnings of *all* art instruction. If we fail to see school art and art teaching from historical, social, and ideological perspectives we will never understand it, nor will we understand art education. This largely unexplored area of inquiry, akin to cultural criticism and the sociology of art as well as to art history, could inform our teaching immensely.

A Short Story on Cross-cultural Graphic Narration

By now I hope I have made the point that my art educational research is grounded in what I know about the world of art, but it is also affected by other interests. How does one account for these interests that compel us to pursue one research topic rather than another? As a young child of four, I remember going in my imagination to England to see what the people who lived there looked like and how they dressed. During World War II, when German prisoners of war were brought to my valley to harvest sugar beets, I followed them for days to hear them talk about their country, its schools, and to listen to their views on Hitler. When Mexican laborers were hired to dig by hand a mile-long trench for an extension of a water line, I volunteered to carry water for them day in and day out so I could hear about their country. I devoured books that told me about New York City, Switzerland, India, and Scotland, and I eagerly listened to missionaries and soldiers tell about the countries from which they had just returned. My interest in Japan was kindled by my favorite uncle's vivid letters telling about the American occupation.

When Marge and I observed that many of the gifted children we studied drew to tell stories, that it was narration that led them to greater and greater graphic means so that they could tell better and more stimulating stories, and that their stories pre-sented encapsulated views of themselves and their society, I decided it was time to collect story drawings from different countries (Wilson & Wilson, 1979b, 1979c, 1982a, 1982b, 1983, 1984a, and 1984b). It is not unlike collecting stories from German prisoners and Mexican laborers. The sets of graphic narratives I have collected from over a dozen countries show me how little the children's conceptions of the world are affected by their art education, and how powerfully the popular media and the art of their peers affect the way children draw stories that provide astonishing views into their societies.

Currently I'm investigating how young Japanese children use Doraemon, an atomic-cat from *manga-Japanese* comic books, to explore the realities of their lives and their society. This little character materialized from the top drawer of his friend Nobita's desk one day and the drawer became the gateway to the fourth dimension. Doraemon has a kangaroo-like pouch from which an amazing variety of gadgets are produced and used to solve problems and resolve difficulties (Schodt, 1983, p. 14). Doraemon also provides a way of symbolically fulfilling wishes by taking his friends on odysseys. When asked to draw stories, many young Japanese children draw Doraemon stories.

Why are children attracted to the Doraemon character? I have concluded that it is because he is little, like a child, and he's also "cute." More importantly, he is clever and he has the power—one that a young child might like to have—to go to whatever exciting place he wishes to go. Those places represent the unknown—Doraemon's journeys represent the future, a whole series of possible futures. When Doraemon gets into difficulty, he possesses the "inner resources" needed to solve the problem—in his pouch. When children draw Doraemon stories they symbolically rehearse ways to overcome difficulties.

My speculation about Doraemon has led me to speculate about the entire Japanese *manga* industry, with its savvy creators of mass media who know that kids will be attracted to a cute little character with marvelous powers. Doraemon's creators also know that the exploration of the fourth-dimension with its relentless stories of what happens and what happens next, of tension and release, of equilibrium lost and regained will attract an eager audience for each new publication.

In their own graphic narratives, through the employment of Doraemon and countless other *manga* characters—either co-opted or invented—Japanese children experiment with life's themes. They can invent situations that enable them to observe such things as cause and effect, growth and development, threat and overcoming, good versus evil, the process of creating and destroying, and on and on. They reconstruct their own little graphic words along manga-lines and then experiment endlessly with how these worlds are, how they might be, and with the many ways in which individuals encounter life's joys and cope with its challenges.

I have concluded that creating new fourth-dimension worlds (futures), overcoming difficulty after difficulty, and symbolically solving endless problems is very good practice for kids in a small nation with few natural resources such as coal, timber, steel, and oil—a nation whose very survival depends on the development if the one natural resource it has in abundance, the minds of its young people. The nation must assure, when its young people enter the work force, that they will contribute to the prosperity of the country by creating a never-ending series of technological miracles. (I should add that I doubt whether either the adult creators of *Doraemon* or their young imitators have a conscious understanding of the role played by the character in furthering their national well-being.)

When I view children's graphic narratives, as signs of things not present for which the signs stand, I gain insights into children, their minds, and their art; but, more importantly, I gain insights into their societies, values, and conceptions of reality. In my application of semiotics to the study of graphic narratives, I continue to satisfy my long-standing curiosity about other times and other places. Now, however, semiotics provides an interpretive means for understanding—a means that at one time, I could not even imagine.

Philosophy, Theories, and the Grounding of Art Educational Research

When I look back on my undergraduate education, I find it disappointing to see how little exposure I had to philosophies and theories of art that would have provided metaphors for organizing a comprehensive view of the art world. Even at Cranbrook Academy of Art, where I listened to my first lectures on aesthetics, I resisted Nathaniel Champlain's neo-Deweyan philosophy of art, primarily because I was required to leave the studio to listen to him.

I spent the 1950s avoiding theory and philosophy and the 1960s drinking in as much as I could. At Ohio State, while I worked on my doctorate, I decided that I wanted to verify art educators' claims regarding the outcomes of art education. The claims I investigated centered on the way art education was supposed to change individuals' "perception" to make them more sensitive to the aesthetic features of the world. Rather than testing whether or not art education changed individuals' perception of everything, as some art educators claim—an outcome that assumes an enormous transfer of learning—I decided to study the conditions under which art education changed students' experience of paintings. Even testing how students experience works of art posed difficult problems. In the end, I made the most simple choice imaginable; I merely asked individuals to tell me what they saw in works of art and analyzed what they told me.

I was taught that good science involves explanation and that explanations have greater power if they are grounded in theory. I am still astonished at the number of theoretical sources I encountered at Ohio State. The last work of Dewey written with Bently (*The Knowing and the Known,* 1960), Randall's *Nature and Historical Experience,* (1962), Pepper's *Basis of Criticism in the Arts,* (1965) and the work of the transactional psychologists (Kilpatrick, 1961). Through these transactional theories I came to understand that the meaning of the work of art is not to be found in the art object. Rather, through experience and interpretation each individual constructs their own conception of the work of art. My interest was in examining how individuals' verbal reports provided evidence of the works of art they constructed from their experiences with art objects.

A Set of Categories

I reasoned that almost anything that students learned in art classes would be reflected in their talk about art. I made no assumptions that there would be an isomorphic fit between language and experience with art; nevertheless, I thought I would get a general idea about the works of art individuals "constructed" through their experiences with art objects. Consequently, I constructed a set of categories designed to classify virtually any kind of verbal response individuals should make about art objects. My categories, like my art, were borrowed from a variety of sources—from my reading in aesthetics, art history, and even the categories designed to analyze inkblots (Holzman, 1961). The categories were as comprehensive as I could make them: ranging from media and technique; through sensory and formal features; to the symbolic, allegorical, and historical; and ending with evaluative criteria. Although I borrowed categories wherever I could, I also used my own practical experiences as an artist to confirm their validity.

I found the content analysis procedures I used tremendously useful in studying the various outcomes of art education. I found there was little difference between elementary and high school students' responses to art objects when they had only the usual general art education courses (Wilson, 1966). In experimental and com-parative studies I showed the positive effects of various kinds of art education (Wilson, 1972). I used expanded versions of the categories in analyzing the results of the first two National Assessments of Educational Progress in art (Wilson, 1981)—using procedures that now go by the name of "authentic assessment." The categories were used as the basis for a chapter in the Bloom, Hasting, and Madaus book on formative and summative assessment (Wilson, 1971). More recently, another version of the categories found its way into the work of the National Board for Professional Teaching Standards/Early Adolescence through Young Adulthood Art committee.

The categories reflect little of the depth of the theories that informed them; nevertheless, they may be the most useful thing I have done in the field. Perhaps more than anything else, they reflect my view that in art education we should always take a holistic view of art and art experiences. We should avoid getting stuck studying only one dimension of our field. This brings me to the last point I wish to make—how we might broaden the scope of art educational research beyond anything that we seem to have imagined.

If I Could Do Only One Piece of Art Educational Research, What Would It Be?

I have taken to asking art educators, "If you could list only one goal for art education, what would that one big goal be?" Most certainly it would not be to nurture a students' ability to discriminate between organic and inorganic shapes in design. My own "shorter" answer to the question is that I want students to create works of art in which they investigate and express ideas or feelings about themselves, the worlds in which they live (and the worlds from which our current worlds arose), speculate about future worlds, and examine the normative reality of good and evil. I also want students to interpret the meaning of their own works in light of the themes, subjects, ideas and styles of works created by others. I am especially fond of Rorty's notion that works of art are "honorary persons" that we have no right to treat narrowly, wrongly, or badly. A good art education would be to approach the creation and interpretation of a work of art (or a person or thing or text) "hoping that person, thing, or text will help you to want something different—that he, she, or it will help you to change your purposes, and thus change your life" (1992, p. 106). That is what an education through works of art should be about.

If we were to ask a similar question relating to research, "If you could do only one research study, what would it be?" My answer is that it would not be any one that I have done, because none of my studies have examined sufficiently the relationship between art education and life. We just don't know much about how their education in art affects students' lives after they leave our classrooms. I did once begin to examine this question, and some day I hope to pick it up again.

In England in 1971 I learned of an unusual art classroom in a working-class neighborhood in a large city in the Midlands (Wilson, 1974b). The highly unusual classroom had the expected institutional look at the studio end and on the other it was a cross between a living room and the Victoria and Albert Museum. The refectory table and chairs could have been in the Victoria and Albert and the display cabinets held objects and artifacts that revealed the history of Britain from Roman to contemporary times. Because the classroom presented such a complete model of the art world, and because the teacher was a carrier of an enormous amount of information about different dimensions of the art world, I set about to find out what happened to the students who passed through the classroom 10 and 15 years earlier. For the better part of two years, I sought out and interviewed former students and visitors to the classroom. I listened to students tell about how their lives had been changed because of their experiences in the classroom—how they had become artists, designers, or how their tastes in interior design and collecting had changed, how some had even claimed that they moved from the working-class to the middle-class because of their experiences in the classroom. I also found that only a few students were invited to enjoy the special features of the classroom, the rest looked on from the institutional side.

As I puzzled about how to explain my findings, I encountered the work of Victor Turner (1969) and his explanation of change in tribal societies—how most change occurred during rituals and rites of passage. I began to see that the tension between structure and anti-structure in the school explained most of the changes that took place in the classroom. The changes didn't occur during the normal school day; students spent as much as 20 hours a week in the classroom, living with and creating art objects. They made collecting trips together, received visits from former students and artists, ate together, and in myriad ways subverted the usual look, feel, and function of the normal structure of the school. Most of the changes in the students' lives occurred because of things that happened outside the normal school schedule.

I discovered that an unusual art teacher in an unusual classroom could have an unusual effect on a few students' lives; but what effect does a usual art classroom have on a large number of students? A piece of research that might have provided a bit of insight into the possible influence of art education on individuals' lives, David Halle's *Inside Culture; Art and Class in the American Home* (1993)—a study of how the works of art people collect and display in their homes provide a means for self-definition—has no mention of art education. Do we make a difference in peoples' lives? Through their contact with us and through the works of art we have them create and interpret, do we change individuals' purposes—do we change their lives? This is the one big study we need in art education.

References

Bal, M. (1991). *Reading "Rembrandt": Beyond the word-image opposition.* Cambridge: Cambridge University Press.

Bryson, N. (1988). *Calligram: Essays in new art history from France.* Cambridge: Cambridge University Press.

Clark, T. J. (1984). *The painting of modern life: Paris in the art of Manet and his followers.* Princeton: Princeton University Press.

Dewey, J. & Bentley, A. (1960). *Knowing and the known.* Boston: Beacon Press.

Genauer, E. (1948). *Best of art.* Garden City, NY: Doubleday.

Gombrich, E. H. (1950). *The story of art.* London: Phaidon.

Gombrich, E. H. (1960). *Art and illusion.* Washington, DC: Pantheon.

Halle, D. (1993). *Inside culture.* Chicago: University of Chicago Press.

Holzman, W. (1961). *Inkblot perception and personality.* Austin: University of Texas Press.

Kilpatrick, F. P. (1961). *Explorations in transactional psychology.* New York: New York University Press.

Nochlin, L. (1989). *The politics of vision: Essays on nineteenth-century art and society.* New York: Harper and Row.

Pepper, S. C. (1965). *The basis of criticism in the arts.* Cambridge, Massachusetts: Harvard University Press.

Randall, J. H. (1962). *Nature and historical experience.* New York: Columbia University Press.

Rorty, R. (1992). The pragmatist's progress. In U. Eco (S. Collini, Ed.) *Interpretation and overinterpretation.* Cambridge: Cambridge University Press.

Ryan, A. (1993). Foucault's life and hard times. *New York Review of Books,* XL(7), 12-17.

Schodt, F. L. (1983). *Manga, manga!: The world of Japanese comics.* Tokyo, New York, and San Francisco: Kodansha International.

Tufte, E. R. (1983). The *visual display of quantitative information.* Cheshire, Connecticut: Graphics Press. Turner, V. (1969). The ritual process: Structure and anti-structure. Chicago: Aldine Publishing Company.

Wilson, B. (1966a). An experimental study designed to alter fifth and sixth grade students' art-trained individuals' statements about Picasso's *Guernica. Studies in Art Education,* 12(1), 31-39.

Wilson, B. (1966b). The Development and Testing of an Instrument to Measure Aspective Perceptions of Paintings, Doctoral dissertation, The Ohio State University, Columbus, Ohio.

Wilson, B. (1971). Evaluation of learning in art education. In B. S. Bloom, J. T. Hastings, & G. F. Madaus, (Eds.), *Handbook on formative and summative evaluation of student learning,* (pp. 499-558). New York: McGraw Hill.

Wilson, B. (1972). The relationship between years of art training and the use of aesthetic judgmental criteria among high school students. *Studies in Art Education,* 13(2), 34-43.

Wilson, B. (1974a). The superheroes of J. C. Holtz plus an outline of a theory of child art. *Art Education,* 16(1), 2-9.

Wilson, B. (1974b). The other side of evaluation of art education. In G. Hardiman & T. Zernich, (Eds.), *Curricular considerations for visual arts education: Rationale, development and evaluation.* (pp. 247-276). Champaign, Illinois: Stipes Publishing.

Wilson, B. (1976). Little Julian's impure drawings. *Studies in Art Education,* 17(2),45-62.

Wilson, B. (1981). The triumph of American culture over the art educational establishment: Findings from the U.S. National Assessment of Educational Progress in Art. In *The product of a process: A selection of papers delivered at the 24th INSEA world congress* Rotterdam, The Netherlands, Amsterdam: DeTrommel.

Wilson, B. (1992a). Primitivism, the avant garde, and the art of little children. In D. Thistlewood, (Ed.), *Drawing: Research and development,* (pp. 14-25) Harlow, Essex, England: Longman.

Wilson, B. (1992b). Children's schooled and unschooled images from the nineteenth and early twentieth centuries: Art education, cultural hegemony, and the "intentions" surrounding three sets of visual artifacts. In P. Amburgy, et al. (Eds.), *The history of art education: Proceedings from the Penn State conference,* 1989. (pp. 226-233). University Park, Pennsylvania. Reston, VA: The National Art Education Association.

Wilson, B., Hurwitz, A., & Wilson, M. (1987). *Teaching drawing from art.* Worcester, MA: Davis Publications.

Wilson, B. & Litgvoet, J. (1992). Across time and cultures: Stylistic changes in the drawings of Dutch children. In D. Thistlewood, (Ed.), *Drawing: Research and development,* (pp. 75-88) Harlow, Essex, England: Longman.

Wilson, B. & Wilson, M. (1977). An iconoclastic view of the imagery sources in the drawings of young people. *Art Education,* 30(1),4-12.

Wilson, B. & Wilson, M. (1979a). Figure structure, figure action and framing in drawings of American and Egyptian children. *Studies in Art Education,* 21(1) 33-43.

Wilson, B. & Wilson, M. (1979b). Children's story drawings: Reinventing worlds. *School Arts,* 78(8), 6-11.

Wilson, B. & Wilson, M. (1979c). Drawing realities: The themes of children's story drawings. *School Arts,* 78(9), 12-17.

Wilson, B. & Wilson, M. (1981). The case of the disappearing two-eyed profile: Or how little children influence the drawings of little children. *Review of Research in Visual Arts Education,* (15)1-18.

Wilson, B. & Wilson, M. (1982a). Dimensions of meaning in children's story drawings: From theory to therapy. In *Art therapy: A bridge between worlds.* (pp. 69-80) The proceedings of the Twelfth Annual Conference of the American Art Therapy Association.

Wilson, B. & Wilson, M. (1982b). Strategies for a multi-dimensional cross-cultural analysis of children's graphic narratives. In *INSEA pre-conference on research into ideology, learning, evaluation and arts education.* (pp. 217-232). Enschede, The Netherlands: National Institute for Curriculum Development.

Wilson. B. & Wilson, M. (1983). Themes and structures in the graphic narratives of American, Australian. Egyptian and Finnish children: Tales from four cultures. *The Journal of Multi-Cultural and Cross-Cultural Research in Art Education,* 1(1),63-76.

Wilson, B. & Wilson, M. (1984a). A tale of four cultures: The story drawings of American, Australian, Egyptian and Finnish children. In R. Ott & A. Hurwitz (Eds.), *Art in education: International perspectives,* (pp. 31-38). University Park: The Pennsylvania State University Press.

Wilson, B. & Wilson, M. (1984b). Children's drawings in Egypt: Cultural style acquisition as graphic development. *Visual Arts Research,* 10(1), 13-26.

Wilson, B. & Wilson, M. (1987). Pictorial composition and narrative structure: Themes and the creation of meaning in the drawings of Egyptian and Japanese children *Visual Arts Research,* X(I) 10-21.

Wilson, M. & Wilson, B. (1982). *Teaching children to draw: A guide for teachers and parents*. Englewood Cliffs: Prentice-Hall.

Endnote

[1] Originally I had planned to do a more refined version on the computer. When I discovered, however, that I could not clearly show all of the interrelationships among my different projects and research studies, I decided merely to show the different classes of content, dates, places, studies, and creative work.

ARTICLE SELECTION

Duncum, P. (1997). Art Education for New Times. Studies in *Art Education*, 38(2), 69-79.

Sally McRorie

Senior Editor, 1995-1997

The world has changed so quickly in the intervening years, that Paul Duncum's (1997) article, *Art Education for New Times*, now may seem almost quaint. However, it remains a prescient look at the ongoing concerns of the field. The cultural developments that he discussed over a decade ago have come to characterize even more dramatically our own times: the treatment of culture as ordinary, material commodity; the proliferation of electronic visual images; and the multifaceted construction of individual identity.

Each development has become so increasingly prevalent in our lives and particularly those of our students, it may be hard to remember what the thinking in the field was like in 1997. Suffice it to say that we were still in the throes of wondering what would be the lasting impacts in art education practice of issues surrounding feminism, multiculturalism, the range of mental and physical abilities, sexual orientations, and the always simmering debate over which art works and artists students should study. We also were struggling to find a place for rapidly emerging technologies, then still a relatively new set of phenomena, especially in resource-starved art classrooms. We are hardly through with these debates, and although much of the terminology has changed, the passion has not (for example, read the polarized range of responses to the March 2008 issue of *Art Education*, which dealt with contemporary art).

Sally McRorie serves as Dean of the College of Visual Arts, Theatre, and Dance at Florida State University (FSU). She taught elementary and middle school art in the public schools and has served as Chair of Art Education at FSU, and Chair of Art and Design at Purdue University. She has published widely in the fields of art, art education, and aesthetics; has given over 100 lectures and presentations nationally and internationally; her recognitions include the Manuel Barkan Award, the Mary J. Rouse Award, and the Indiana and Florida Higher Education Art Educator of the Year Awards.

Remembering those 'new times,' I invite you to reread Duncum's article with our own times in mind. His call for an "inclusive conception of culture that can begin to address the proliferation of mass media images and their multiple readings by our multifaceted selves" (p. 77) continues to have implications for our work with today's students. They tend to have a personal relationship with technology, process a wide range of information at once and almost randomly, and exhibit an almost startling need to stay connected with their peers. They are in many ways the products of the three cultural developments Duncum examined. As a prelude to Duncum's work to follow, and a complement to that of many of our most influential contemporary researchers in art education, this article deserves another look. Perhaps someone should adapt it as a graphic novel for our own new times!

Art Education for New Times

Paul Duncum

Although art educators believe in educating through art, students live through the mass media. Students negotiate with the media in as many, often contradictory, ways as students themselves are multifaceted. This is not a new situation, but what is genuinely new is the current proliferation of images. A rapid increase in imagery is a central feature of what many critics call *postmodernity* (Baudrillard, 1988; Bertens, 1995; Jameson, 1991; McRobbie, 1994) and others call *new times* (Hall & Jacques, 1991).

The concept of *new times* has two meanings. It is both an analysis of the momentous changes otherwise called postmodern and the generation of a progressive perspective for them. In the postmodern period, a sea change of fundamentally new forms of social, cultural, and economic arrangements have come to characterize life in the West. New times theorists seek to move beyond the nihilism and reactionary politics of some post-modernists to offer an effective engagement with the forces shaping our period.

In this paper, I focus primarily on a number of cultural developments which are seen as linked to social and economic life. I address only three facets of new times, although each is close to the concerns of art educators: the treatment of culture as an ordinary, material commodity; the proliferation of electronic visual images; and, the multifaceted construction of individual identity. Each issue interpenetrates but, to simplify: to regard culture as ordinary relates to the subject matter of art education; electronic imagery relates to modes of learning; and multifaceted individual identity relates to the students we teach as well as ourselves as teachers. I also consider the choices open to us in responding to new times and offer an example of desirable classroom practice.

Culture as Ordinary

It is necessary to start from first principles to address the challenge of new times.

Most art educational theory and practice are based upon a high culture definition of culture (Pearson, 1995), whereas new times theorists base their observations on a semiotic view of culture (Featherstone, 1991; Hall & Jacques, 1991), where the most ordinary commodities are considered worthy of study (Sebeok, 1994). Most art education appears to be based on the idea that there is something qualitatively special about the fine arts. The fine arts are said to put us in contact with the most original, creative, subtle, intense, humane, honest, and inspiring aspects of ourselves and society. By contrast, the images through which the great majority of people create meaning are seen as pandering to the worst in society: to be conformist, violent, sentimental, and manufactured only with dollar signs in mind (Gans, 1974).

Many studies have explored and exploded this distinction (Duncum, 1990; Gans, 1974; Gowans, 1981). There are too many similarities of function and too many crossovers for any distinction of quality to be meaningful. It is possible to make distinctions of kind between high and popular culture, but not of value. Not only has high culture been exposed as functioning as a commodity as much as any other (Williams, 1983), but mass culture has been shown to offer the same range of pleasures and insights as high culture. For theorists of new times, the distinction between high and popular culture is effaced (Featherstone, 1991; Hall, 1991; Jameson, 1991).

In consideration of this new theoretical landscape, the operations of the institutions which continue to profit from the idea of high culture need to be made problematic. Bracey and Taylor (1988) saw critical interrogation of the operations of high culture institutions, including education in high culture, as the principal task for art education today. However, in itself such action seems hardly commensurate with the issues we face as a society. More pressing concerns appear to lie in the way the great majority of people position themselves in relation to mass media. As commonly observed, from both the left and the right of the educational spectrum (Bloom, 1987; Gannaway; 1994; Giroux, 1994), it is from popular culture that most people weave their identities and establish their relationships with others and the environment. Mass media images saturate our lives, structuring much of what we know beyond personal experience. We live through visual images as much as we do language.

Although images are regarded as a constitutive part of society, society is viewed-to use the spatial metaphor of the sociologists-as asymmetrical, as inherently unfair and unjust. Imagery, like language, serves particular social, political, and economic struggles. Imagery is a battleground of meaning, a site of ideological struggle, where competing interests co-opt meanings, censor, recontextualize, appropriate, and otherwise manipulate meanings to serve their ends. Before imagery is aesthetically pleasing or insightful, it is, like language (Williams, 1977), a weapon in the armory of competing groups in their quest for influence and power. Always, images tell us more about the interests of those who make images than the subjects represented (Willis, 1993).

As to what direction this critique leads art education, Pearson (1995) wrote:
... the object of concern for art education is constituted by the social fields in which images are produced, distributed and used. On this view, art education takes the form of investigation into the practices which constitute the field. (p. 11)

I would add that there are many fields. On Pearson's reading, the central issue for art education is the position of images in the social world. Meaning does not reside in images themselves, but in the way they are used by people in different situations. Central to Pearson's concern with the position of images in people's lives is the way "people dominate other people" (p. 12), and he argued that on analysis we will often find that it is ourselves who are dominated. Pearson concluded:
... what they [students] will also see, is how people go about the business of domination and that, at least, is the minimum requirement for students if they are to be empowered to challenge the use of symbolic power which denies their, and others, reality of social existence and social worth. (p. 12)

This means giving priority to the visual representational practices by which most people are positioned, position themselves, and position others. For a long time, many art educators have advocated an inclusive view of the visual arts (Chapman, 1978; Lanier, 1982; McFee & Degge, 1980), but usually the popular arts are simply added on, and, moreover, viewed from a fine art perspective. The popular is incorporated insofar as it influences fine art, but it is neither given priority nor viewed in its own terms. What art education needs is a paradigm shift that both acknowledges the hegemony of the mass media and approaches the media with appropriate conceptual tools.

If cultural theorists can no longer defend a distinction between high and popular culture, how long can art educators remain unaffected? Art education in this century has been founded on a high culture/popular culture distinction (Efland, 1990). The traditional disciplinary boundary that has maintained art as part of the curriculum has crumbled, and art education is left without a defensible rationale. To survive in the future in some form, it must find a new theoretical foundation. A semiotic view of culture offers a foundation wherein visual images are regarded as ordinary material commodities, which are as common as everyday speech, and as significant as the way the great majority of students construct their view of themselves and the world.

Thus, an education commensurate with new times would be broadened beyond the fine arts to include all visual images. A new times approach would not exclude high art from education, but only give it the prominence it has in society as a whole. Popular mass media would achieve prominence in proportion with its dominance within society.

The Proliferation of Electronic Imagery

The urgency of remaking art education is dramatically highlighted by the proliferation of mass media imagery through both existing and emerging technologies. Globally produced images circulate in an electronic informational hyperspace, and interactive multi-media is set to become the basis of a new information economy. The kaleidoscope of electronic imagery, however elevated or educational it can be, is mobilized to ensure the smooth operation of an economy which depends upon ever increasing consumption, including imagery consumption (Harvey, 1989; Jameson, 1991). The turnover of imagery is now very fast indeed; it can be like the "twinkling of an eye" which Marx saw as optimal from the standpoint of capital circulation (Harvey, 1989, p. 288).

New times theorists characterize contemporary consciousness as impacted by the proliferation of images with a pervasive sense of unreality, depthlessness, historical amnesia, and, even, meaninglessness (Featherstone, 1991; Harvey, 1989). A sense of dislocation and disorientation pervades because life, like schizophrenia, is experienced as a series of perpetual, present moments (Jameson, 1991). In place of the disinterested gaze and the transcendental, there has emerged an aesthetics of a consumer society, an aesthetics of desire, sensuousness, and immediacy (McRobbie, 1994). Instead of a delayed satisfaction via careful scrutiny, the aesthetics of the everyday involves an immediate impact, an economy of pleasure. Rather than viewing images in a state of contemplation, images are more likely to be viewed in a state of distraction.

The prevalence and self-referential character of mass media imagery raises doubt about what can be reasonably considered to have some basis in fact and what is illusion.

Baudrillard (1988) argued that the density and seamlessness of images means that any distinction between reality and its images has been effaced. All that now exists is representation, with its ability to seduce, overwhelm, intoxicate, and deliver us into a state of hyperreality. Everyday life has become aestheticized, enveloped in an aesthetics of the surface where discrimination has been replaced by revelry.

More cautiously, Harvey (1989) wrote that our current difficulties may lie not with the proliferation of imagery but our lack of psychological preparedness. He argued that most of us may not possess the perceptual habits required of new times. He suggested that a new times consciousness may prove simply to be qualitatively different, not necessarily better or worse, than the habitual ways of thinking of most mature adults today. Perhaps a proliferation of electronic imagery is leading—if it has not already done so, especially for the young-not to deficient modes of thought, but to different modes of communication and cognition.

It is now commonly held that the age of the image marks a change no less momentous than the invention of writing and the printing press (Gannaway, 1994; Spender, 1994), and it is useful to note that not everyone welcomed the invention of writing. Socrates, for example, refused to write down his thoughts; for, among other reasons, fear of them becoming ossified. He argued that human thought and communication were fluid and dynamic, and that understanding was based on constant interchange between people that writing denied. Writing, he argued, forced you to follow an argument rather than engage in one (Spender, 1994). Socrates' models were conversation and the oral tradition. Because some of the new technologies are immediate and highly ephemeral they are said to be more like oracy than literacy (Spender, 1994). New technologies may represent a return to Socrates' models.

Thus, the argument that we are living in an age of surface appearance may represent only the disorientation experienced by those without the perceptual habits necessary for the new technologies. New times, then, do not necessarily herald the deterioration of cognition or communication. The death of communication itself, as predicted by such observers as Baudrillard, seems to have been greatly exaggerated. However, it is crucial for art education to acknowledge that while visual communication survives, it has changed its form. Imagery is now infinitely more plentiful, pervasive, immediate, and ephemeral than ever before. And proponents of the information highway promise a high level of interactivity.

Individuals as Multifaceted

The meaning of imagery must also now be considered as site specific. Not only is our society more fragmented than before, it is important to consider individuals as sites of numerous intersections (Giroux, 1994). As individuals we are said to be increasingly positioned within and across a variety of identities, needs, and lifestyles. Increasingly, we appear to be aware of ourselves not as singular entities, but as beings comprised of multiple identities which are often contradictory. We find ourselves torn between the various antagonisms and struggles that characterize our society, but also characterize our own individual identities. This is why new times theorists talk of an absence of a unified self and, instead, of fragmented identities and a de-centered self (Giroux, 1992; Hall, 1991).

Many of us are members of marginalized groups, whether, for example, of ethnicity, age, class, gender, sexual preference, religious affiliation, political persuasion, education, or mental and physical ability. So many interests now are acknowledged as marginalized that marginalized "others" now take up the position of the dominant, if fragmented, center (Giroux, 1992; Hall, 1991). Art educators have begun to deal seriously with marginalized groups, especially ethnic and indigenous others (Congdon, 1991; Garber, 1995; Stokrocki, 1994; Neperud & Stuhr, 1993) but also, for example, people with alternative sexual orientation (Honeychurch, 1995), mental and physical disabilities (Blandy, 1993; Guay, 1994), and those with fundamentalist religious beliefs (Blair, 1995). However, this focus on the "other" almost invariably fails to address the fact that no matter what minority or combination of minorities a person may belong to, he or she engages as part of everyday, ordinary experience with popular mass culture.

Different life experiences, expectations, and emotional attachments lead to different kinds of negotiation with, and resistance to, mass media. In short, what mass media has to offer is employed in association with all the other locations of the self. However powerful other influences might be, no one's personal identity nowadays is created without negotiation with or resistance to popular media (Giroux, 1994). Students should be viewed as constructing meaning within the complex intertextuality of images (Freedman, 1994). We need to view students as free floating agents who create meaning out of the bits and pieces of stories, images, and objects that envelop them.

Educational Responses

How should art educators respond to new times? Harvey (1989) identified four basic responses to new times, although I will argue that only the fourth is viable for art educators.

The first response is withdrawal into a kind of shell-shocked, exhausted silence.

Suffering from sensory overload and feeling that new times are beyond anyone's control, one response is to acquiesce. Withdrawal is always a personal option, but it is not an option for educators charged with a public responsibility.

A second response is to try to ride out the storm by trying to keep abreast of change and so bring change under control. An example of this response, identified by Feldman (1994), is to be found in the rush by some educators to keep up with the very latest technological advances. While lacking a clear educational goal, they assume that the possession of the new technology alone will somehow lead students to master it.

A third response is to deny both the complexity and challenge of new times, and to offer simple solutions. Old fashioned values and ways of doing things are offered as virtues. Standards that were established in a pre-electronic image age are presented as the cure for our ills. This response has had a dramatic impact on education through the back-to-basics movement. Bloom (1987) and other conservatives have proposed a return to what they consider a literate culture, one founded on the skills of reading and writing and a knowledge of the alleged great works of literature. They see an educational site, to quote from Giroux (1992), as "a warehouse built on the pillars of an unproblematic and revered tradition" (p. 93). Similarly, Greer's (1984) formulation of DBAE, Smith's (1994) espousal of excellence, and Abbs's (1995) belief in the intrinsic qualities of fine art, ignore the plurality of practices from which most people derive meaning in ordinary, everyday life. This response to new times represents a closed-off, often defensive, minority view of visual culture. High art is celebrated at the expense of the plurality of production and use of images within society.

The fourth response is to acknowledge the importance of new media, and to devise curricula in partnership with students' use of it. Gannaway (1994) argues that the purpose of education is no longer to distribute information but to teach how to handle the vast amount that is readily available. Similarly, Giroux (1992; 1994) argues that we need to recognize sites apart from schools that actively shape student experiences and through which students define and construct their sense of identity, politics, and culture. A critical study of mass media would investigate how it situates us, what pleasures we derive from it, and how it forms part of the larger social, political, and economic agenda of others.

What is needed is a remapping of the areas between school and home, between traditional curriculum offerings and students' own knowledge of the world. Some educators have acknowledged the need for such border crossings in art education (Freedman, 1994; Hamblen, 1990).

New Times in the Classroom

How a new times art education might operate in the classroom can be glimpsed by examining current practice in media education. Media education is informed by a semiotic critique of contemporary cultural forms. Moreover, media education has long been centrally concerned with the representation of marginal groups, especially in relation to gender, race, and class (Buckingham & Sefton-Green, 1994). It attempts to offer strategies for broadening the art curriculum to incorporate social, economic, and political issues in ways which students can relate to their lived experience.

Media education commonly is comprised of four overlapping areas: production, values, audiences, and the media industry (Queensland Education Department, 1993). *Production* requires a knowledge of the codes and conventions with which media products are created, and involves students in creating their own media products. It also involves expression and aesthetic judgment. *Values* involve semiotic readings of the meanings of media products, especially of how apparent realities are created for their audiences and how these realities relate to social values and beliefs. A central concept is the selective representation of people, events, ideas, feelings, and objects. Students are taught that no media product can show more than a selective reality, and as a result students learn to recognize and judge the selective constructions of others.

Production and *values* are similar to production and criticism of art in art education. The significant departure of media education from art education lies in the further two areas of media education. Media students study audiences; in particular, how different audiences respond, and how demographics influence budgetary considerations. Students also study the media as an industry, the various agents involved, and the influences and pressures affecting the economics of production and the legislature governing their actions. Both areas of study-audiences and industry-provide the means by which teachers embed their students' study of cultural production within social, economic, and political frameworks. The opportunity exists for students to become politically literate by studying cultural products in which they have a personal investment.

The following description of young adolescents studying a popular soap opera is intended to illuminate the above emphases. The unit is adapted from McMahon and Quin's (1993) materials for teachers and students studying the popular Australian soap *Home and Away.* This soap is aimed mostly at young adolescents, and it is programmed in most countries in the late afternoon. This is only an example of media education, and different topics, different students, even a different soap would require different activities. How art teachers might adapt a media education approach is, at present, an open question.

1. Students watch a short sequence. They make distinctions between visual codes such as facial expression, gestures, and costume; technical codes such as focus, framing and editing; and aural codes such as dialogue and sound effects. They discuss how these codes work together.

2. An excerpt from a typical script is studied, and students ask: If you were playing the characters, what codes would you use? The class act out the script, refining their interpretation with repeated attempts.

3. Students watch a video in which the producer of *Home and Away* describes the roles of story editors, script editors, and scriptwriters, including the tight deadlines to which each works. Information is offered about how and why soaps are the product of an assembly line.

4. The text of a scene breakdown of an episode is studied, and the settings, time of the day, and the characters in each scene are noted. The class watch this episode and discuss the differences between how they imagined the episode and its realization.

5. Students examine studio floor plans, including sets, and they discuss why sets are used. They ask whether sets would save money and how many sets would be required per episode.

6. With a soap set in their school in mind, students draw their own studio plan and sets, and they compile a list of necessary props.

7. The class watch a further video interview with the producer of *Home and Away.* He explains, for example, that because he considers there are too many restrictions on what can be shown about drugs in the late afternoon, he prefers not to deal with drugs at all. Students discuss what other issues are rarely dealt with at this time and how a soap set in their school could deal with difficult issues. This leads to a discussion on which groups

in society would be more likely to have social issues raised in soaps and which would be unlikely. Issues of race, class, and religious affiliation are canvassed.

8. Students examine the audience for *Home and Away* and similar soaps. They study how audience ratings are gathered and measured. Students compare rating statistics with their own survey of family and friends. They draw up profiles of typical target audiences and compare them with the products advertised during the screening of soaps. Students consider who buys for the target audiences, and if the buyers are not watching, how they find out about the products. Students discuss how they would change a soap to attract an older age group and whether they could retain the existing audience. Students consider whether the mainstay of soaps, fam-ily-based personal and emotional relationships, are better dealt with by women. They also consider the gendering of terms like soap *addict* and sports *fan*. They examine the possible effects on ratings of particular actors, guest stars, changes in seasons from winter to summer, and switches in time-slots.

9. Class members debate the issue: "Soap operas never deal with real problems faced in life." Students draw upon their knowledge of character types, storylines, audiences, advertisers, soaps as an assembly line, and their own experiences and pleasures.

10. Students move to the production of their own soap episode about their school, including a story outline, a script, a storyboard, a production schedule, and finally, shooting and editing. Class members take the role of actors, lighting crew, director and so on. The episode includes a number of stories, one of which involves a social issue like gender, drugs, or racism in the school.

At this point, the study of mass media becomes especially interesting because students frequently go beyond mere imitation of their models. Production is a creative process because students move within the space between media realities and their own experiences. Pleasure is found in oscillating between a close emotional engagement and a knowledge of the artificiality and implausibility of media products (Buckingham & Sefton-Green, 1994). In the classroom, the result is often parody. In recreating media products they will sometimes mock their teachers as much as the media. This further layering of meaning is crucial. Without a playful, mocking resistance, there is a danger that in being incorporated into the classroom, popular culture will lose its popular nature (Buckingham & Sefton-Green, 1994).

Some students resist examining issues of gender or race which impinge upon their own identity. For example, they may resist a critical study of media stereotypes in which they have a personal investment (Williamson, *1981-1982)*. Buckingham and Sefton-Green's (1994) studies indicate that teachers should not expect students completely to work through media stereotypes, or come to a clear critical conception of an issue. They warn, for example, that students will often offer their teachers a version of the official school and wider societal line on controversial issues rather than fully engage with their own beliefs and values. They indicate that what teachers can do is provide opportunities for critical engagement and hope for at least partial resolutions.

Media education suggests that when dealing with mass media art teachers should expect complications which do not arise when studying someone else's culture. Multiple and subtle resistances are essential to mass media use, and its study invariably will involve similar complexity.

Conclusion

For art education to have a healthy future, it must be remade. It requires a paradigm shift toward a socially leveled, semiotic conception of culture. An inclusive conception of culture could begin to address the proliferation of mass media images and their multiple readings by our multifaceted selves. I have offered only one glimpse of where this might lead. As the term new times implies, the future of an art education for *new times* is undecided, open ended; it is a project of discovery.

References

Abbs, P. (1995). *The new paradigm in arts education.* Unpublished paper. University of Sussex, England.

Baudrillard, J. (1988). *Jean Baudrillard: Selected writing.* M. Poster (Ed.). London: Polity Press.

Bertens, H. (1995). *The idea of the postmodern: A history.* London: Routledge.

Blair, L. (1995). *Religion, censorship, and art in public schools.* Unpublished manuscript. Concordia University, Montreal.

Blandy, D. (1993). Community-based lifelong learning in art for adults with mental retardation: A rationale, conceptual foundation, and supportive environments. *Studies in Art Education, 34*(3), 167-175.

Bloom, A. (1987). *The closing of the American mind: How higher education has failed democracy and impoverished the souls of today's students.* London: Penguin.

Bracey, T., & Taylor, B. (1988). The core curriculum and teaching art as politics. *Australian Art Education, 12*(2), 17-23.

Buckingham, D., & Sefton-Green, J. (1994). *Cultural studies goes to school. Reading and teaching popular media.* London: Taylor & Francis.

Chapman, L. (1978). *Approaches to art in education.* San Diego: Harcourt Brace Jovanovich.

Congdon, K. G. (1991). A folk art focus. *Journal of Multicultural and Crosscultural Research in Art Education, (9)*, 65-72.

Duncum, P. (1990). Clearing the decks for dominant culture: Toward a contemporary art education. *Studies in Art Education, 31*(4), 207-215.

Efland, A. (1990). *A history of art education: Intellectual and social currents in the teaching of visual arts.* New York: Teachers College Press.

Featherstone, M. (1991). *Consumer culture and postmodernism.* London: Sage. Feldman, (1994). Teaching art and so on. Reston, VA: NAEA.

Freedman, K. (1994). Interpreting gender and visual culture in art classrooms. *Studies in Art Education, 35*(3), 157-170.

Gannaway, M. (1994). *Transforming minds: A critical cognitive activity.* Westport, CT: Bergin & Garvey.

Gans, H. (1974). *Popular culture and high culture.* New York: Basic Books.

Garber, E. (1995). Teaching art in the context of culture: A study in the borderlands. *Studies in Art Education, 36*(4), 218-232.

Giroux, H. (1992). *Border crossings: Cultural workers and the politics of education.* New York: Routledge.

Giroux, H. (1994). *Disturbing pleasures.* New York: Routledge.

Gowans, A. (1981). *Learning to see: Historical perspectives on modern popular/commercial arts.* Bowling Green, OH: Bowling Green University Popular Press.

Greer, W. D. (1984). Discipline-based art education: Approaching art as a subject of study. *Studies in Art Education, 25*(4), 212-218.

Guay, D. M. (1994). Students with disabilities in the art classroom: How prepared are we? *Studies in Art Education, 36*(1), 44-56.

Hall, S. (1991). The meaning of new times. In S. Hall and M. Jacques (Eds). *New times: The changing face of politics in the J 990s* (pp. 116-133). London: Verso.

Hall, S., & Jacques, M. (Eds). (1991). *New times: The changing face of politics in the 1990s.* London: Verso.

Hamblen, K. A. (1990). Local knowledge of art as a school art alternative. *Australian Art Education, 14*(3), 22-28.

Harvey, D. (1989). *The condition of postmodernity.* Oxford: Basil Blackwell.

Honeychurch, K. G. (1995). Extending the dialogue of diversity: Sexual subjectivities and education in the visual arts. *Studies in Art Education, 36*(4), 210-217.

Jameson, F. (1991). *Postmodernism: or, The cultural logic of late capitalism.* Durham: Duke University Press.

Lanier, V. (1982). *The arts we see; A simplified introduction to the visual arts.* New York: Teachers College Press.

McFee, J. K., & Degge, R. M. (1980). *Art, culture, and environment: A catalyst for teaching.* Dubuque, IA: Kendall/Hunt.

McMahon, B., & Quin, R. (1993). *Understanding soaps: A student and teacher's guide to learning about television.* Mount Coot-tha, Australia: The Seven Network.

McRobbie, A. (1994). *Postmodernism and popular culture.* London: Routledge.

Neperud, R. W., & Stuhr, P. L. (1993). Cross-cultural valuing of Wisconsin Indian art by Indians and non-Indians. *Studies in Art Education, 34*(4), 244-253.

Pearson, P. (1995). Looking for culture: Implications of two forms of social theory for art education theory and practice. *Australian Art Education, 18*(3), 6-18.

Queensland Education Department (1994). *Constructing realities. Media curriculum guide for Years 1 to 10.* Brisbane: Queensland Education Department.

Sebeok, T. A. (1994). *Signs: An introduction to semiotics.* Toronto: University of Toronto Press.

Smith, R. (1994). *Excellence II: The continuing quest in art education.* Reston, VA: NAEA.

Spender, D. (1994). A history of information media. *Australian Journal of Computing, 9*(1), 11-16.

Stokrocki, M. (1994). Expanding the artworld of Navajo students. *Australian Art Education, 17*(3), 39-49.

Williams, R. (1977). *Marxism and literature.* Oxford: Oxford University Press.

Williams, R. (1983). *Keywords: A vocabulary of culture and society* (2nd ed.). London: Fontana.

Williamson, J. (1981-1982). How does girl number 20 understand ideology? *Screen Education, 40,* 80-87.

Willis, A. M. (1993). *Illusions of identity: The art of nation.* Sydney: Hale & Iremonger.

ARTICLE SELECTION

Irwin, R.L., Rogers, T., and Wan, Y. (1999). Making Connections Through Cultural Memory, Cultural Performance, and Cultural Translation. *Studies in Art Education*, 40(3), 198-212.

Graeme Sullivan

Senior Editor, 2001-2003

What is an effective indicator of scholarly influence? An institutional measure is citation, which the online indexing industry now tracks to death. At its worse, citation can be as intellectually empty as name-dropping. At its best, citation acknowledges authority and can be the cornerstone upon which knowledge structures are built. The research community uses strategies such as peer review to ensure that scholarly conventions are benchmarked according to accepted practice. But the purpose of standing on the shoulders of others is to take in the view and to look out, not down.

Graeme Sullivan is Professor of Art Education, Teachers College Columbia University. He received his Ph.D. from The Ohio State University, Columbus, Ohio in 1984, and taught at the University of New South Wales, Australia from 1988, before taking up the position at Teachers College in January 1999. He has published extensively. In 1990, he was awarded the Manuel Barkan Memorial Award for his scholarly writing by the National Art Education Association (NAEA), and in 2007 the Lowenfeld Award for significant contribution to the art education profession.

Another criterion used to assess the significance of scholarship is the capacity of research to influence practice. The uneasy relationship between theory and practice has been a recurring theme in *Studies in Art Education* since its inception 50 years ago. We have tried the top-down approach of theory-based practice, and the bottom-up development of practice-based theory. And all with a pragmatic view that theory without practice is empty rhetoric, and practice without theory is aimless action. For instance, the current rush to secure defensible data in the quest to fast-track educational outcomes quickly unravels amid the complex realities faced in our schools, communities and cultures. Yet what art educators do best is to question the myriad difficulties of the real world and this is grounded in a belief in the unlimited potential of human imaginative insight. The outcome is an investment in vision as much as fact, and this is a commitment to research that is long-term.

Therefore, what is necessary in assessing the impact of scholarship is to keep a broad view in sight. And this can take a long time to bring into focus. The article referenced here, "Making Connections through Cultural Memory, Cultural Performance, and Cultural Translation" (Irwin, Rogers & Wan, 1999), is an excellent example of research that sets in place clear-sighted conceptual footprints for researchers to follow. It is not the shaky shoulders of assumed authority the authors cling to. In fact, it is a distinctively different view of the cultural landscape they offer that is 'below and within.' Part of their claim is that securing a single vantage point only ever permits a view that peers out from a privileged center and this severely limits the capacity to look back. With this in mind, the authors anchor their collaborative and communal perspective in three indigenous sites at the same time: the South Australian landscape of the Adnyamathanha people, the wooded regions of the North West Pacific of the Sechelt people of Canada, and the forested mountain areas of southern Taiwan that is home of the Paiwan people. The voice of indigenous peoples is used as much as possible to track the cultural footprints pressed into discussion by the authors. These themes include the close ties between cultural memory and land, how culture is 'performed,' and the possibilities for translation across lifeworlds. These are paths that continue to offer direction many years later and by any accounts, this is a very real indicator of the influence of research.

Making Connections Through Cultural Memory, Cultural Performance, and Cultural Translation

Rita L. Irwin[1], Tony Rogers, and Yuh-Yao Wan

In an earlier paper (Irwin, Rogers, & Wan, 1997), we suggested that in order to understand many Aboriginal artists and their cultures one needs to understand the relationship between Aboriginal people and land. This is because the cultural (collective) memory of many Aboriginal groups is deeply connected to land. Understanding the relationship between land and culture is antecedent to understanding the implicit and explicit enactment and embodiment of culture through cultural performance. Rather than perceive art as a separate entity, cultural performance is a translated concept that attempts to interpret an integrated cultural point-of-view. Attempting to understand culture is itself an act of cultural translation. Although we are not of Aboriginal ancestry, our research with Aboriginal peoples has offered us a vehicle to come together and learn from one another. Translations can never offer a perfect fit between languages. However, an effort must be made, and in the act of doing so, individuals learn more about themselves and their beliefs. Having said this, the following discussion highlights three Aboriginal cultures, on three continents, in an effort to encourage art educators and students to engage in cultural translation in cultural contexts. Aboriginal peoples in Australia (Broome, 1982; Isaacs, 1989), Canada (Gerber 1993) and Taiwan (Hung 1993) are very different from each other not only across continents but within countries. Even so, there are some commonalities of beliefs, values and attitudes within countries and across continents. Recently, we shared an opportunity to compare and contrast three Aboriginal cultures from these three countries.[2] We must emphasize that our findings relate to the three specific peoples with whom we have been working. We hope that our research will lead to other researchers asking similar questions of the Aboriginal peoples with whom they work, but far more research must be done before common conclusions may be drawn. The three peoples with whom we work share certain commonalities but there are many differences too. For example, there are at least 256 language groups in Australia alone, so it would be fallacious to assume research findings from work with one Australian Aboriginal people could apply to other Australian cultures, let alone those in other countries. It ought not to be necessary to provide such a caution, but unfortunately much that has been written about Aboriginal cultures in the past has not sufficiently acknowledged fundamental differences between the nations.

The Adnyamathanha people of Australia belong to a land of gum trees, dry creek beds, and arid lands; the Sechelt people of Canada belong to a land of towering cedar trees, rivers, lakes, and the Pacific Ocean; and the Paiwan people of Taiwan belong to a land of Chinese fir, cypress, and pine tropical forests and mountains. All three Aboriginal peoples embrace a deep relationship with the land of their ancestors. Aboriginal peoples have always relied on land for survival and cultural meaning. It is only since the intrusion of colonial powers that this reliance has been threatened. While government legislation in Canada, Australia, and Taiwan now reflects greater awareness of diversity and difference in pluralistic societies, the fact is that the beliefs and practices of Aboriginal peoples are still marginalized. Such marginalization is not necessarily deliberate, but results when norms which are culturally specific to the dominant society are mistakenly thought to apply also to other societies. Devastating as this is for most Aboriginal peoples, they maintain relationships with their traditional lands and cultural practices that are uniquely different from those of Westerners or Chinese. In the following accounts, we detail how these cultures maintain their beliefs and values through their relationship with the land. We then go on to describe how this relationship with the land becomes the basis from which cultural performance is nurtured. Cultural performance is an important concept for art educators as it questions taken-for-granted perceptions of critical questions (see also Neperud & Stuhr, 1993) such as "what is art?" and "is there a comparable concept of art from one culture to another?" Once we have explored the cultural memory and cultural performance of these three cultures, we offer a view toward cultural translation in an effort to illustrate how knowing these cultures might be considered within an art education setting.

Cultural Memory: Connections with the Land

The responsibility for land is part of a cultural system which closely connects with personal and group cultural identity. The societies with which we work have been orally-based cultures. Today they are beginning to write down their cultural beliefs but they still rely heavily on their oral traditions. Clifford suggests that "oral tradition can be very precise, transmitting a relatively continuous, if rearticulated cultural substance over many generations. This is particularly true when there is a land base to organize recollection, as with Native American societies, Melanesians, or Aboriginals" (1997, pp. 44-45). These collective memories might be viewed as cultural memory. The cultural memory of the societies with which we are working is based upon notions of responsibility rather than upon notions of rights. Therefore, their relationship with land is one of connection. They are profoundly connected to the land in physical, spiritual, cultural, aesthetic and emotional ways. We suggest that their cultural memories are enacted along a continuum of belonging to the land, honoring the land, and inheriting a place. All of these memories conceptualize cultural lifeways which are different from mainstream cultures. In the dominant societies of these three countries, ownership of a piece of land implies the right to do with the land as the owner wishes. However, the Adnyamathanha, Paiwan and Sechelt Aboriginal peoples share a sense of responsibility toward the land. Their conceptions of this responsibility are based upon different relationships with land, but the notion of responsibility is paramount. For instance, *The Adnyamathanha people believe they belong to particular places and sacred sites.* These places embody their identity, their ancestral dreamtime stories, myths and beliefs, their past, present and future. Their beliefs are implicit and non-negotiable. The Paiwanese believe in the importance of place and particularly places having ancestral sacred meaning, yet they do not share the same attachment to the land. The Sechelt people feel a deep responsibility toward the land knowing that particular places hold great cultural significance; however, as tribes fought against one another in previous generations, winning tribes often acquired territory. Thus, tribal responsibility toward land was important but particular places were, and are, less important than that felt by the Adnyamathanha people.

The Sechelt people have many legends and myths (see for instance *Sechelt Legends,* n.d.) illustrating their ancestral beliefs about the land. These legends continue to deeply influence their lives and their relationship with the land. Sechelt legends are similar to Adnyamathanha dreamtime stories which speak to the formation of the land and the creation of life by ancestral beings (see for instance, Issacs 1989). These stories and legends are meant to be educative, teaching successive generations how to survive and live, while feeling deeply connected to their ancestors and the time in which the earth, sky and water were created. In essence, *the Sechelt people have a strong sense of honoring the land.*

The Paiwanese also feel strong connections with their land. They too tell stories, myths or legends about the land (Hsu & Ke, 1994). These stories of particular places are revered and are retold from generation to generation. The Paiwanese are scattered over the mountainous area of Southern Taiwan. Each tribe tells slightly different stories and legends about the origin of their ancestors. However, a commonality among these ancient tribal legends is that they all relate to Mount Da-Wu. At Kulalau village, the Paiwanese believe their ancestors were originally two pieces of clay at the top of Mount Da-Wu. It is believed that a dog and a cat involved in a fight broke the clay figures and with that, the ancestors of Kulalau were born. Community members treat Mount Da-Wu as a sacred place, a place deeply tied to their origin and cultural identity.

The legends and stories of these three peoples point to an inherent and deeply felt connection to land that enforces a sense of responsibility toward the land. Traditionally, these Aboriginal peoples never believed in ownership of land, and for that matter, they did not believe in ownership of ideas or even things. The individual, rather than having rights as mainstream society believes today, had responsibilities. Today, Adnyamathanha and Sechelt peoples are faced with political and economic realities that assume ownership of land leads to financial independence.[3]

Interfacing these mainstream beliefs with traditional beliefs has led to legal battles between Aboriginal peoples and governments at each attempt to obtain legal land settlements. Adnyamathanha, Sechelt, and other Aboriginal peoples in Australia and Canada, want the land to be honored as sacred. With their feelings of ancestral responsibility toward the land comes tremendous responsibility to ensure its future and thus, many Aboriginal people continue to fight for the land in an effort to honor land in sacred and cultural ways.

First through the rule of Taiwan by the Chinese dynasty, then the col-onization of Japanese, and then the Chinese Nationalist government, Taiwanese Aboriginal groups struggled to survive and continue their cultural beliefs. The Paiwan is one such group (Hung, 1993). *The Paiwan consider land a sacred inherited entity to be respected.* Particular places within the environment, the land, are honored as ancestral places of meaning, of inheritance. These places are so sacred, they believe their souls return to these places after they die.

Just as the Adnyamathanha and Sechelt peoples believe they cannot own land, the Paiwanese believe they cannot sell or give land away. Instead, land is inherited from ancestors and thus represents an inheritance of cultural identity. In Paiwanese society, a Chief builds a "Family House" on inherited land which is, in turn, used for rituals and represents the power and status of the Chiefs family. Commoners do not inherit land but are given permission by the Chief to use the land.[4] Through the inheritance of land, Paiwanese culture is sustained, ritualized, and honored. The relationship between people and land is similar to the Australian Aborigines in that Paiwanese elders believe their souls belong to ancestral lands. Therefore, if they are forced to leave their land, their lives are considered meaningless. This was put simply and clearly in an interview with one Paiwan potter, Mr. Hsu (Paiwanese name, Saguliu), when he said "the hearts of all elder villagers here are still at the old village of Kulalau deep in the mountains, where they know they really belong." There are several ways to show strong relationships between land and people. First, by building a "family house" on a piece of their ancestors' land, the status of a Paiwan chief was affirmed according to the name of that family house and his descendants and followers were therefore entitled to the land and the house as well. Second, the Paiwanese usually designated their ancestors' names for rivers, lakes, mountains, and specific trees to mark their land territory. This was a way for Paiwan tribes to identify each other's origin and territory. Third, the Paiwanese followed rules and taboos of land set by ancestors, and transmitted from generation to generation. Accordingly, it was through land that young people learned the way to be Paiwanese. Once away from their original land in an unfamiliar place, Paiwanese had little opportunity to trace their origins and cultural systems back to the ancient lands. Dramatic changes have been imposed upon the Paiwanese by political dominators since the Ching Dynasty in a similar way to those imposed upon the Aboriginal peoples of Australia and Canada. Later the Japanese and now the Chinese Nationalist government see ownership and control of land as a means to control people. All the land of the Paiwanese was claimed as property of the government. When the Chinese government implemented new land policies during the mid-20th century, all peoples could own land as personal property. Consequently, chiefs of tribes no longer had the right and responsibility to be in charge of Paiwanese ancient land and hunting grounds. Now every villager has legal land rights. Many believe the new land policy is culturally destructive to the Paiwanese cultural identity.

Though there are differences among these three Aboriginal cultures and their relationship with the land, there is a common theme: their per-sonal and cultural identities are deeply connected to the land. This is highly apparent in their communities as local craftspersons and artists create cultural artifacts using local materials to create tourist trade items such as baskets, canoes, wooden utensils, and knife sheaths (eg. Chen, 1961).

Some contemporary Aboriginal artists in these communities critique the dominant culture by painting images which challenge stereotypical views of Aboriginal peoples and the degradation of sacred sites of land. In each community, people talk often about the importance of place, where they come from and belong, and the responsibility they have toward sacred land. Their identities are grounded to the land.

Although these three Aboriginal peoples[5] feel a sense of belonging to place and honoring the land, it is the Adnyamathanha who hold the strongest beliefs about belonging to a place, and it is the Sechelt who hold the strongest beliefs which honor the land. And though all three peoples feel a certain attachment to places and believe that land is passed from generation to generation, it is the Paiwanese who most strongly hold a sense of inheriting a place. These relational shifts with the land may be directly tied to an influence by technology within each cultural group. Australian Aborigines have the most intimate relationships between land and language (Abram, 1996, p. 172) while the Sechelt have closer relations than the Paiwanese. Technological advances have artificially separated language and culture and in turn, artificially separated land and conceptions of living from culture and language.

Cultural Performance: Creating and Living Connections

For art educators, it is imperative that we attempt to understand the depth of these relationships with the land as we attempt to understand forms of cultural performance and production created within these societal groups. Neperud and Stuhr coined the phrase visual cultural produc-tion in recognition of the broad area of visual products that mayor may not be recognized as [Indian] art in the traditional Western sense" (1993, p.246). In our individual and combined studies (Irwin & Farrell, 1996; Irwin, Rogers & Farrell, 1997b; Rogers, 1994; Rogers & Irwin, 1995) we have also found this to be true with indigenous artists in Australia and Canada, and more recently in Taiwan. However, we suggest Neperud and Stuhr's definition may be extended to situate the understanding of visual cultural production more closely to the cultures with whom we have worked. We suggest the notion of *cultural performance* in which the visual aspects of culture are embedded in the performance of culture. Juane Quick-to-See Smith, a Flathead painter and curator states, "art was never a separate endeavour in any tribe. In fact, there is no word for art in any of our 3000 languages. Art and identity are linked in the process of living. Art is a celebration of life and a reaffirmation of identity" (College of Webster Art Museum, 1992, p. 12). From an Aboriginal perspective, art is a conceptual category created first in a non-Aboriginal ideology and subsequently superimposed or translated (poorly) onto Aboriginal beliefs. With any translation, it is important to recognize that some elements may be translated fairly while others will be unfairly represented, even misun-derstood (Rogers & Irwin, 1997). In our research, we have found that art as a concept cannot be translated and therefore, the cultural performance within Aboriginal societies cannot be fully appreciated. This is where cul-tural memory, and the connections with land, contextualize beliefs and help those involved in cultural translation with coming to understand themselves and one another.

The cultural performances of Aboriginal peoples are deeply grounded in their relationships to the land. Stuhr, Krug and Scott (1995) suggest that as cultural translators we need to understand different views of the land from mainstream society. In the dominant society, land is considered an economic resource waiting to be exploited. However another view is that land may be "represented as a place where life is experienced and his-tory is lived" (p. 37). Abram (1996) speaks of changing our relationships with the natural world and much of what he offers is similar to this notion and resonates with what we are learning from the Aboriginal peo-ples with whom we work. His work is helpful in understanding why indigenous cultures give so much importance to places:

To members of a non-writing culture, places are never just passive settings .... A particular place in the land is never, for an oral culture, just a passive or inert setting for the human events that occur there. It is an active participation in those occurrences. Indeed, by virtue of its under-lying and enveloping presence, the place may even be felt to be the source, the primary power that expresses itself through the various events that unfold there. (pp. 161-162)

To stress our point, it is important to look at notions of art and cultural performance from the perspective of Aboriginal peoples. Sharon Cruse, an Adnyamathanha academic who teaches Aboriginal Studies at an Australian university, is adept at understanding the conceptual processes of her own culture as well as those within the mainstream society. When asked whether the Western concept of art might be a concept found in her traditional culture she pointed out that such a concept did not exist and in fact, separating out the appearance of such a manifestation would be artificial. In essence, art was not a concept found in the Adnyamathanha culture and language. As an academic, she admits that an Adnyamathanha could discuss art, but only as an exercise for the benefit of non-Adnyamathanha people:

Certainly I see [art] as a part of communication, but also as a part of celebration … I think art encompasses dances, songs, storytelling too … but it's very central to the maintenance of a culture and, you know, could be seen as a means of celebrating … I see art as being part of a holistic approach [to life] as well. In order for Aboriginal cultures-well for any culture-to survive, they have to have mechanisms by which the transmission of that culture goes from generation to generation. In terms of Aboriginal cultures, art was a means of passing on to generations, passing on to children who, in turn, will pass it on to their children, in a nutshell, I suppose, the meaning of life … In fact, it's really hard to separate culture, or it's really difficult to separate art and language, story telling and dance, because they all serve the same purpose-to maintain the culture. (quoted in Rogers & Irwin, 1997, p. 29)

A Canadian scholar, Vastokas (1992), describes this disjuncture between Eurocentric thought and Aboriginal thought as one in which the former concentrates on art as an object, whereas the latter concentrates not only on the object but on the environmental context and especially, the participation of creators and viewers with objects. She views "Native art as performance" (p. 40) because it is in the participation with objects that meaning is created and sustained. Given our translations of Aboriginal experience, with the guidance of our Aboriginal colleagues, cultural performance appears to be an intermediary phrase between art and life that attempts to convey an integrated experience of meaning-making. Yet, the distinction is critical. Without an attempt to understand the integration of experience, little has been learned about these Aboriginal cultures.

The coming together of sensory experiences within the everyday lifeworld of a community become ongoing, implicit, ordinary and extraordinary acts of cultural performance that are valued within a particular cultural context. Sensory cultural experiences maintain and nurture culture, give and receive meaning, create and re-create culture again and again from generation to generation. They are holistic integrated experiences situated in a complex web of meaning.

In all three of the Aboriginal cultures with whom we have worked, art as a concept (or as a word) could not be translated from English to the Aboriginal language. Elsewhere, we have gone into great detail about a series of interviews and conversations with Adnyamathanha and Sechelt people (Rogers & Irwin, 1997) in which we attempted to understand how our Aboriginal colleagues perceived their world and culture, and especially how they might integrate notions of art and creativity[6] with their own cultural understandings. In every case, translations were extremely difficult. Individuals were often physically uncomfortable and wondered if language had been lost or forgotten. With other individuals it became apparent that language was not lost, rather translations could not be made because the concepts never existed.

Molly Wilton, an Adnyamathanha elder, makes artifacts such as boomerangs and carved emu eggs. Her work is highly regarded within the community. Although her first language is Adnyamathanha, she was able to identify the word wandu as a translation for her work. Elsie Jackson, a cultural educator, also used the word wandu to describe art created by school children, and when asked to translate the word, she replied "that looks very good" (Rogers & Irwin, 1997, p. 24) with wandu meaning "that is good." On an occasion when one of us met with Molly Wilton during a rainstorm, and asked how she might respond to such an event from an aesthetic point of view, she recalled the actual events: '"we can hear the thunder coming,' 'rain coming,' 'there is a shower of rain on the hill.' Asked for words that would describe the beauty of the event, Molly Wilton used wandu (p. 25). Through these descriptions and others from Adnyamathanha people, it became apparent that there were no words in the Adnyamathanha language to talk about notions that are closely aligned to Western aesthetic notions of beauty and creativity. However, the Adnyamathanha people are able to translate (loosely) what they know and can speak of in one language to what they know and can speak of in another language. To those of us who are not fluent in both languages (and ideologies), we must be careful not to assume superiority of thought. To the Adnyamathanha people, art as a concept could not be separated from everyday living. Rather, visual experiences and expressions were an integral part of cultural life and thus it seems to us that it may be prefer-able to speak of cultural performance rather than art as we attempt to understand and translate conceptual relationships from one language to another.

The experience of the Adnyamathanha people is very similar to the experience of the Sechelt people in Canada. When asked if there was a way of translating art within the Sechelt language, many individuals said they were unable to identify a word or phrase. An elder, Mary Craigan, had the same difficulty but elaborated at length about notions of beauty, art, and creativity as they might be equated with respect, spiritual gifts, and harmony with mother earth.

> [My parents and grandparents] really depended upon mother earth ....They really respected mother earth. What they took out of mother earth they wanted to put back in some other way. So they, in order to make it look like, you say, beautiful- they had to do things like that. ... [My grandson, an artist, has] a gift, a skill that has been handed down. And that's the only way that I would think about it and describe it because it just comes to him in a vision and he puts it down ..... everyone has a gift some way or another. (quoted in Rogers & Irwin, 1997, p. 27)

Mary Craigan was attempting to teach us, to translate for us, the essence of her cultural beliefs. In the Sechelt culture, the land-mother earth-is the place from which they honor their lives and their spiritual source; it is a place to be honored, respected, cherished. Sechelt peoples are primarily interested in living in harmony with mother earth and with their spiritual source as they use the gifts granted each person.They are not concerned with separating particular concepts such as art, for that would disintegrate an integrated experience of their culture: it is culturally irrelevant to do so.

Our work with the Paiwanese people of Taiwan raises similar comparisons among the Adnyamathanha, Sechelt, and Paiwan cultures, and therefore, issues regarding language. However, our work also raises a heightened sensitivity toward a cultural translation of language and action. With the Adnyamathanha and Sechelt peoples, we were able to locate individuals who could speak English and their own Aboriginal language.Thus, the Aboriginal people themselves were translating the ideas, beliefs, and language from one culture to another while we attempted to understand the similarities and differences between cultures. In essence, they were acting as cultural translators and cultural pedagogues. In Taiwan, this was not possible. Few elder Paiwanese people speak Mandarin fluently and virtually none speak English. Since one of us speaks Mandarin, interviews were conducted with a Paiwan translator who could translate into Mandarin. From here, we tape-recorded English translations, recognizing that with two levels of language translation already in place, our attempts at cultural translation became more tenuous.

Some researchers might suggest that two levels of language translation severely limits what can be learned. However, we have come to believe that cultural translations like this happen continuously in our pluralistic society as immigrant families relocate. Attempting to understand another's culture through respect, interest, and participation in cultural events (Chalmers, 1996), allows us as cultural translators to actively engage with those with whom we would have never encountered previously.Together, we are able to learn from one another.

The Paiwan did not identify a word or phrase that might be translated to mean art or creativity. However, through long discussions about their culture, it is apparent that certain words[7] are used to describe activities with natural objects, or objects made from natural materials. For instance, *vinzig* is used to describe "being able to do (carving, embroidery, bead-work)." A thing of beauty might be called *nonwag or* if it is very beautiful, *nonwagwag*. Participating in some of the local events and activities, talk-ing with elders, chiefs, and shamans, one becomes aware that the culture is rich with carving and beadwork. Local people are very aware of what might be considered a Paiwanese style of imagery and use specific words to describe the work. For instance, *mamaopaiwan* means somewhat similar to Paiwan style, *sacizwainyan* means a style similar to the ancestral style, *sapaiwan* means very similar to Paiwan style, while *gacizwainyan* means exactly the same as the ancient ones. In describing Paiwanese work they may use words such as *nawagu* to describe costumes and carvings that are excellent, while *jarranonwnongan* is used to describe anything that is very good. When asked if they gave a name to the makers of such objects, they struggled to find the following words: *rraruvenzigan* meaning the one who carves often, and *rraruwalunya* meaning the one who weaves, beads or does cross-stitch very often. Any maker of cultural objects who uses his or her own inspiration (as opposed to continuing the exact same Paiwanese style over and over) to do something often is referred to as *rarrovakecan*. Paiwanese elders and those interested in main-taining the traditional beliefs also seek to maintain traditional designs. These designs are distinctively Paiwanese and emphasize snakes, eagles, men, and women. Chief headdresses include eagle feathers, tiger teeth, and deer tail. Traditional designs tell ancient stories of relationships among people(s), whether they are of ceremonies or tribal conflicts, passed from generation to generation. If the designs are considered truly ancient, they cannot be sold for fear of offending spirits. Paiwanese headdresses have various styles according to personal social status. No matter male or female, all Paiwanese wear eagle feathers and they distinguish each other's social status by different patterns on the feathers. For instance, Chief headdresses include specific eagle feathers from wings which are easily identified by triangular patterns. Hunters wear leopard teeth and tails as if to record personal hunting success. However, many Paiwanese today have adapted the Paiwan style for tourist trade items which do not possess cultural stories. These stories are always situated in the context of Paiwan land, beliefs, and values. Their cultural performance sustains the generational stories.

Understanding the complex relationships between Aboriginal peoples land and their cultural performance is a task for cultural translators. Muecke (1992), a linguist, cautions us not to superimpose European ways of understanding the world onto Aboriginal ways of understanding the world. This is a difficult task as we all come to view the world through our own lenses. However, if we enter the lifeworld of another person or another culture with the idea that each of us are cultural participants, cultural translators and cultural pedagogues, learning from and teaching one another, there is a greater chance of interpreting partial tales (Stuhr, Krug & Scott, 1995) which hold meaning for all involved.

The cultural performance of the three Aboriginal cultures and peoples introduced here are deeply situated in the context of culture. In each community, people hold a deep and abiding attachment to the land symbolically, spiritually, emotionally, physically, and aesthetically. Through the very partial tales told here, we have endeavored to briefly compare and contrast three Aboriginal cultures with the hope of illustrating the groundedness of their cultural identities with the land and their environment while attempting to describe the harmonious integration of their cultural performance within the language, daily life, and ideology of each group. It is very tempting to apply the word art to objects found in each community and to name certain people as artists. But those con-cepts do not exist in these communities, and if we are to respect the traditions of each community it behooves us to find ways of shifting our lenses so that we can begin to understand the importance of cultural complexity in understanding the cultural performance of each community.

Cultural Translation: Connections for Art Education

To understand a culture (as insider or outsider), one needs to immerse oneself in the lifeworld of a culture. Yet that is not possible for most of us as we attempt to understand and appreciate many cultures represented in a pluralistic society. It becomes even more difficult when our teaching and learning is defined, not by cultural studies but, by disciplines of art, music, drama, etc. If we are to reflect upon, learn about, and respect other cultures then we, as educators, must find ways to bridge the conceptual gulf which separates Western culture from those peoples such as the Sechelt, Paiwan, and Adnyamathanha. This presents a great challenge.

An entry point for many art educators into cultural experience requires them to bring a disciplinary frame to a cultural (integrated) frame. This is an approach that may provide one bridge. However, many Aboriginal peoples do not speak of art in their cultures and if they do, it is for the benefit of those with whom they are speaking. Some might even attempt to translate what they think non-Aboriginal people want to hear. So we really should not speak of art in such cases. The term *cultural performance* may be a better one to use. *Cultural performance* is a phrase that translates, as nearly as possible, "a coming together of cultures." Otherwise, in order to understand, respect and honor traditional Aboriginal beliefs today, educators should be working with Aboriginal elders in a cultural study experience: not from a purely discipline-based experience (see Cahon & Kocur, 1996). However, this is simply not possible. Our schools are teaching about the *art* of Aboriginal cultures. This being the case, it may be preferable to shift the teaching of *art* to the pedagogy of cultural performance through the act(s) of cultural translation.

Stuhr, Krug and Scott (1995) present cultural translation as a collaborative research method that forces researchers to move beyond research that seeks to perpetuate cultural transmission, cultural reproduction and cultural (re)production. Cultural translation is about researching *with* people rather than *on* or *about* people (Alcoff, 1991). They begin their cultural translation by situating their backgrounds, histories, and geo-graphical roots in an effort to share with readers their own diverse life experiences. They believe this to be necessary as all cultural translations are interpretations, set against personal experiences, and can never be complete translations, regardless of shared language. Therefore, one must understand why cultural translations are important, especially to art educators: "to translate is an effort to know more about ourselves and the world we live in" (Stuhr, Krug, & Scott, 1995, pp. 31-32). Participation in the world is enriched when we understand that the world and our lives are meant to be full of meaning-making and meaningful action. Researchers, educators, artists, and other interested individuals in cultural translation become active participants in an ongoing collaborative activity of coming to understand another's lifeworld, albeit through one's partial perceptions.

Krug states that "cultural translation is a way to study the contextual complexity of cultural identity—through a collaborative, ethnographic research method" (1997, p. 1). He goes on to suggest that teachers and students should use cultural translation as a way to learn more about people who make things in their own communities (see also, Stokrocki, 1995). As teachers and students learn to record personal experiences while collecting documentation of changes and continuities in a particular community at a particular time, they are able to construct "short stories of complex sets of lived events" (p. 1). These short stories or partial tales provide a basis for mutual understanding.

In this paper we have attempted to show how cautiously and reflectively cultural translators must proceed when there are dramatic language and ideological differences among cultures. However, this should not deter anyone of us from participating in cultural translation. Art educators named in this paper offer detailed information on theoretical and practical perspectives toward cultural translation. Their work should be reviewed before beginning. However, we would like to end with some suggestions for how art educators might begin to engage their students within a cultural paradigm emphasizing cultural translation and understanding cultural memory and cultural performance.

Rather than seeing the student-as-consumer, or student-as-artist, we suggest seeing the student-as-cultural translator. Goodman (1996, p. 19) discusses ways in which media educators might provide a paradigm for cultural education. Although we are not proposing an emphasis on media education, we acknowledge that cultural translation is about our ability to understand and interpret the world, essentially, to read and represent the world. To achieve this, educators may endeavour to: a) engage a student-as-cultural translator in a dialectical process of cultural performance and cultural reflection; b) nurture students-as-cultural translators within a community of cultural translators dedicated to open dialogue, collaboration, and participatory research; c) introduce students-as-cultural translators to alternate forms of expression and representation; and d) model the activity of cultural translation to students-as-cultural translators in an effort to develop an ability within individuals to experience the world from different points of view.

Making connections between notions of cultural memory and cultural performance are critical for cultural translators. It is especially important for art educators who wish to provide experiences for students-as-cultural translators within local Aboriginal communities if we are to encourage intercultural understanding, respect, and appreciation.

References

Abram, D. (1996). *The spell of the museum* New York: Vintage Books.

Alcoff, L. (1991). The problem of speaking for others. *Cultural Critique, 20*(4), 5-32.

Broome, R. (1982). *Aboriginal Australians.* Sydney: Allen & Unwin.

Cahan, S., & Kocur, Z. (Eds.). (1996). *Contemporary art and multicultural education.* New York: The New Museum of Contemporaty Art.

Chalmers, F.G. (1996). *Celebrating pluralism: Art, education, and cultural diversity.* Los Angeles, CA: The Getty Education Institute for the Arts.

Chen, Chi-Lu. (1961). *Woodcarving of the Paiwan group of Taiwan* (in Chinese). Taipei: Nan-Ten Publication.

Clifford, J. (1997). Routes: *Travel and translation in the Late twentieth century.* Cambridge, MA: Harvard University Press.

College of Webster Art Museum. (1992). *We, the human beings: 27 contemporary Native American artists.* Wooster, MA: College of Webster Art Museum.

Gerber, P. R. (1993). The political. economic, and sociocultural conditions of life for the Indians of Canada in the twentieth century. In the Canadian Museum of Civilization (Eds.), *In the shadow of the sun: Perspectives on contemporary Native art* (pp. 121-136). Hull, QC: Canadian Museum of Civilization.

Goodman, S. (1996). Media education: Culture and community in the classroom. In S. Cahan & Z. Kocur, (Eds.), *Contemporary art and multicultural education* (pp. 18-23). New York: The New Museum of Contemporary Art.

Hsu, Kung-Ming & Ke. Huei-1. (1994). *The ritual and culture of the Ku-Lou village of Paiwan* (in Chinese). Taipei: Dou-Hsiang Publication.

Hung, In-Sheng. (1993). *Taiwan early inhabitants' Footsteps* (in Chinese). Taipei: China Times Publishing.

Irwin. R. L., & Farrell, R. (1996). The framing of Aboriginal art. In D.A. Long & O. P. Dickason (Eds.), *Visiom of the heart: Canadian Aboriginal issues* (pp. 57-92). Harcourt Brace: Toronto.

Irwin. R. L., & Reynolds. J. K. (1992). Creativity in a cultural context. *Canadian Journal of Native Education* 1~1), 90-95.

Irwin, R. L.. & Reynolds, J. K. (1994). Ojibwa perceptions of creativity. *Journal of Multicultural and Cross-cultural Research in Art Education, 12*, 34-49.

Irwin, R.L., Rogers, T., & Farrell, R. (1997a). The Irrelevance of multiculturalism. *Kdurna Higher Education Journal, 6*, 43-48.

Irwin, R. L., Rogers, T., & Farrell, R. (in press). The Irrelevance of multiculturalism to the realities of Aboriginal artists. In R. Mason & D. Boughton (Eds.), *International perspectives on art education and cultural diversity.* New York: Teachers College Press.

Irwin, R. L., Rogers, T., & Farrell, R. (1997b). The politics of culture and the work of contemporaty Aboriginal artists. *Journal of the Canadian Society for Education through Art, 28*(I), 17-22.

Irwin, R. L., Rogers, T., & Wan, Y. (1997). Belonging to the land: Understanding Aboriginal art and culture. *Journal of Art and Design Education, 16*, 315-318.

Isaacs, J. (1989). Australian Aboriginal paintings. Sydney: Weldon.

Krug, D. H. (1997). Cultural translation and the study of cultural identity. *Arte Na Escola Journal* (Universidade Federal Do Rio Grande Do Sul, Brasil) 3(4), 37-50.

Muecke, S. (1992). *Textual spaces.* Sydney: New South Wales University Press.

Neperud, R. W., & Stuhr, P. L. (1993). Cross-cultural valuing of Wisconsin Indian art by Indians and Non-Indians. *Studies in Art Education, 34* (4), 244-253.

Rogers, T. (1994). Arc and Aboriginal cultures. *Journal of Art Education,* 17 (2), 12-20.

Rogers, T., & Irwin, R. L. (1995). A 3D view of art in global education: Difference, diversity and distance. *Journal of the Canadian Society for Education through Art,* 26 (I), 15-21.

Rogers, T., & Irwin, R. L. (1997). Language and indigenous cultures: A key to understanding. *Canadian Review of Art Education,* 24 (I), \9-32.

Sechelt Legends (nd.) *Sechelt kgends: sxwaxweyam.* No publisher listed.

Stokrocki, M. (1995). Oral histoty: Recording teaching folklore and folkways. In P. Smith (Ed.), *Art education historical methodology: An insiders guide to doing and using,* (pp. 16-25). Pasadena, CA: Seminar for Research in Art Education and Open Door Publications.

Stuhr, P. L., Krug, D. H., & Scott, A. P. (1995). Partial tales of three translators: An essay. *Studies in Art Education,* 37(1), 29-46.

Vastokas, M. (1992). *Beyond the artifact: Native art as peiformance.* North York, ON: Robarts Centre for Canadian Studies, York University.

Endnotes

¹ We welcome further discussion on related topics. Correspondence may be addressed to Rita L. Irwin, University of British Columbia, Department of Curriculum Studies, Art Education, 2125 Main Mall, Vancouver, BC, Canada, V6T IZ4, or Tony Rogers, School of Educational Studies, University of South Australia, Holbrooks Road, Underdale, South Australia, 5032, or Yuh-Yao Wan, National Dong-Hwa University, 1 See 2 Da-Hsueh Rd., Shou-Feng, 974 Hua-Lien, Taiwan, R.O.C.

² This research has been supported by a number of sources and would not have been possible without their financial assistance: The Social Sciences and Humanities Research Council of Canada. the International Council for Canadian Studies, the Association of Universities and Colleges of Canada and the Government of Taiwan, the National Art Education Foundation, The University of British Columbia, The University of South Australia, The National Dong-Hwa University, and the Pacific Cultural Foundation.

³ In Australia and Canada, Aboriginal people were colonized by the British among other Euro-western colonizers. As a result, the histories of settlement and subsequent governmental attempts at Aboriginal policy and multicultural policy in these countries have been similar (see Irwin, Rogers, & Farrell 1997a; in press). In particular, both countries have tried to isolate Aboriginal peoples more and more from their traditional hunting and sacred lands, which has inevitably led to great concern and debate.

⁴ In Paiwanese society, Chiefs inherit land and the Family House on that land is passed on from generation to generation regardless of the gender of the successive Chiefs who are entrusted with land for the people or on behalf of the people.

⁵ It is important to note here that the assertions made in this paper reflect the beliefs of the elders and community members with whom we spoke. It is possible that others in the community hold different beliefs.

⁶ See also Irwin and Reynolds (1992, 1994) for a discussion of creativity as a culturally irrelevant concept and possibly even in conflict with particular cultural beliefs and values. To Ojibwa peoples, creativity is responsibility, that is, the negotiation of feeling and lived experience culminating in a synthesis of meaning that must be ethically attended to within the context of the culture. This complex understanding has no direct translation from English to Ojibwa, or vice versa.

⁷ All of the Paiwanese words are phonetically spelled as they are said in the Paiwanese language. Linguists might disagree with our spellings or translations.

1960s
1970s
1980s
1990s

Selections from the 2000s

STUDIES
in Art Education

ARTICLE SELECTION

Chalmers, F. G. (2002). *Celebrating Pluralism* Six Years Later: Visual Transculture/s, Education, and Critical Multiculturalism. *Studies in Art Education*, 43(4), 293-306.

Kristin Congdon

Senior Editor, 2009-2011

I have several reasons for selecting this article for inclusion in this anthology. F. Graeme Chalmers is a leader in the field of art education and multicultural studies. He has given us decades of excellent *Studies* articles and other publications that have helped transform the field to be more diverse and inclusive. This article comes from his 2002 Invited *Studies* Lecture, and it reflects on a book he published in 1996 titled, *Celebrating Pluralism: Art, Education and Cultural Diversity.*

In this selected article, Chalmers begins by reflecting on a 1999 *Studies* review of his book by Pat Stuhr and her colleagues at The Ohio State University. He models a way to think about ideas as fluid, as he rethinks, re-establishes, and expands on his approach to teaching about art from varying cultures. This article is important not only because of what it says, but also because of the context of how the information is presented to us. As in any healthy field of study, its members dialogue with and critique each other. They draw on ideas from various disciplinary areas of study and build on previous research. Often new questions are posed or old ones are found to have increased validity in a current context.

Through this essay, the author reveals his understanding that art education must do more than simply "celebrate" the cultural lives of others. Recognizing that some members in the field thought *Celebrating Pluralism* was too meek in its tone and content, Chalmers questions the reaction. He digs deeper into the art educator's role and the position from which she can effectively speak, thereby moving into a new kind of dialogue about multicultural art education. He now claims that we need to do more than solely celebrate cultural pluralism.

Chalmers continues to value a theme-based approach to multicultural education. He poses important questions about how teachers can speak for cultures they do not belong to. He asks when someone can be considered inside or outside a culture, as the lines are

Kristin Congdon has taught art in a variety of settings, including public schools, correctional settings, treatment facilities, museums, and universities. She is Professor of Philosophy and Humanities at the University of Central Florida and Director of the Cultural Heritage Alliance. She has published extensively, including books on folk art, community arts, and feminism in an effort to celebrate artists and who have had little visibility in the art world. She has also been a World Congress Member for the International Society for Education Through Art and the president of the National Art Education Association's Women's Caucus.

often blurry and hybridity increasingly needs to be acknowledged. Furthermore, he asks, "How can and should the trauma of the oppressed affect the oppressor and the oppressor's descendents?" (p. 299). His conclusion addresses the importance of what we do at the present time and how we work together for joint liberation.

This is a timely article for deep reflection. The election of Barack Obama as president of the United States is a validation of the idea that our global health depends on understanding our connective past and present. It is only in working together that we will succeed in creating a better world. Like Obama, Chalmers works to reposition us.

Reference

Stuhr, P. (1999). Book review. Multiculturalism and the aesthetics of recognition. Celebrating pluralism: art, education, and cultural diversity. *Studies in Art Education, 40*(2), 180-191.

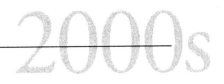

Celebrating Pluralism Six Years Later: Visual Transculture/s, Education, and Critical Multiculturalism

F. Graeme Chalmers

One of the longest book reviews, and I think the only "group-written" review to be published in *Studies in Art Education,* focused on my (Chalmers, 1996) *Celebrating Pluralism: Art, Education and Cultural Diversity.* In this review Patricia Stuhr (1999) and her faculty colleagues at The Ohio State University raised a number of points about the text. Kudos were given, but not as liberally as those conferred by James Scarborough (1998) whose laudatory review in Museum News concluded:

> In time the book will come to be recognized (if it hasn't already) as an invaluable primary source document as well as a manifesto for educational reform and social action. It is realistic enough to diagnose and confront rapidly escalating sociocultural realities head-on while retaining enough idealism to acknowledge the possibility that education can keep apace. Educators, school administrators, museum professionals (particularly curators and exhibition designers), students of all ages—in short anyone who cares for, is involved in, and will be affected by the material the book covers—will ignore *Celebrating Pluralism* at their peril. (p. 62)

Well, I'm not sure that it's quite that good. As some of you may know, Anita Silvers (1999), an aesthetician operating within a very different paradigm, and reviewing this same book in the *Journal of Aesthetic Education* was much more dismissive as she sought to defend the Western philosophical paradigm, which she perceived as unjustly and erroneously attacked.

But, to return to the OSU review, Stuhr commented that she thought that one measure of a book's "success" was the amount of discussion that it engenders and the thoughts that it generates beyond the text itself. Paraphrasing liberally, and without assigning particular objections to particular people, members of the Ohio State group seemed to question three things:

- The nature of multicultural education—what it is, and what it isn't—celebrating pluralism versus celebrating differences. Learning about art in a variety of cultures versus using art to make a difference.
- The book's seeming support for cultural relativism and lack of a clear statement supporting some universal moral values and decrying other more offensive belief systems and cultural practices. One member of the OSU group used the words "wishy-washy." In conversation with me recently, art education scholar Dipti Desai, who writes on the politics of representation, agreed with my own, present, more retrospective stance, that, although one can read between the lines, *Celebrating Pluralism* is really quite a "gentle" book.

- The OSU group also felt that by endorsing a discipline-based approach, I had made multicultural art education too tidy and too manageable by promoting "evolution" rather than "revolution?"

In order to address these and some related issues of possible interest to art educators, and especially to myself, I've taken a look at what has been happening in multicultural/transcultural education since the publication of *Celebrating Pluralism*.

I want to begin by considering three related books, published around the same time as *Celebrating Pluralism* that have challenged my thinking. At the times in which we were writing, none of us knew about each other's work. In the same year that *Celebrating Pluralism* was published, Sonia Nieto (1996) published the seemingly polar opposite, *Affirming Diversity*. Although we were not that "opposite," Nieto was more direct than I was in encompassing anti-racist education and critical pedagogy within a definition of multicultural education that entails a direct challenge to the societal power structure that has historically subordinated certain groups and rationalized the educational failure of these groups as being the result of their inherent deficiencies. Multicultural education as conceptualized [by Nieto and others]... challenges all educators to make the schools a force for social justice in our society. (p. xvi)

More recently Nieto (1999) identified six criteria that characterize what has become known as critical (or insurgent) multiculturalism. These should appeal to some of my Ohio State critics, and they increasingly appeal to me:

- Critical multicultural education affirms a student's culture [I would change this to constantly changing cultures] without trivializing the concept of culture.
- Critical multicultural education challenges hegemonic knowledge.
- Critical multicultural education complicates pedagogy.
- Critical multicultural education problematizes a simplistic focus on self-esteem.
- Critical multicultural education encourages "dangerous discourses."
- Critical multicultural education admits that multicultural education [in schools] cannot do it all.

Critical or insurgent multiculturalism, however, doesn't appeal to too many teachers. Teachers hang on to celebratory multiculturalism. Critical multiculturalism has been called an area "where teachers fear to tread" (Solomon, 1997).

Two years before *Celebrating Pluralism* appeared, Sneja Gunew and Fazal Rizvi (1994) (now both in North America, but then in Australia) published their edited text *Culture, Difference and the Arts*. As this book was not widely available in North America it was not until quite recently that I obtained a copy. *Culture, Difference and the Arts* is a compilation of work by 15 different authors, whose sometimes competing discourses remind us, as the OSU group demonstrated, that multiculturalism is politically controversial. "Contemporary debates surrounding cultural diversity and the arts have always been located within this contested terrain" (Gunew & Rizvi, 1994, p. xii). In searching for concepts against which to examine my own work, I was drawn to the chapters written by the editors themselves.

Gunew's chapter "Arts for a multicultural Australia: redefining the culture" foreshadows contemporary work on the arts, transculturalism, and diasporic experience. A clear statement at the beginning of her chapter reads, "responding creatively to multiculturalism often involves being out of step with prevailing orthodoxies," (p. 1) and throughout the chapter we are reminded that "something quite new develops as a result of transplanting to a new context and interacting with other groups. It can generate a new hybridized cross-cultural art" (p. 6). Art educators have been very slow to address hybridity, although newer approaches to visual culture education acknowledge the concept. Gunew emphasizes the tension between "where you're from" and "where you're at." She views multiculturalism as it then existed in Australia as too benign [she could be talking about "soft" multiculturalism as it is practiced in Canadian and U.S. schools] and concludes that "we should be exploring the local and global implications of the diasporic networks with their alertness to positionings and the many and varied elements which are in play within cultural production and its consumption" (p. 11).

Rizvi's chapter "The arts, education and the politics of education," is more directly related to education. It begins with an observation that "much of what goes on in [Australian] schools is based on a set of cultural assumptions that are antagonistic to diversity" (p. 55). He argues that although arts education rhetoric relates art and culture this is not well reflected in curriculum design and implementation. What has resulted, he states, is a

> version of multicultural education... [that] involves learning about 'other' cultures as a way of breaking down stereotypes and thus promoting greater tolerance of diversity in society. A major problem with this approach is that it does not define 'the other' in relational terms, in a way that might refer to the speaking position. Rather it naturalizes 'the other' in representations that are assumed to be objective. It obscures the issues of disadvantage and discrimination, and of the politics of ethnic formation. (p. 60)

Rizvi argues that this is the case because "the school is a site for containing the effects of marginalization and oppression by promoting a fiction of tolerance between social groups in order to produce a society in which a certain truce exists between ethnic groupings and classes" (p. 64). He is prescriptive in wanting educators "to teach for those forms of artistic imagination that problematize cultural formation and acknowledge that a politics of difference involves a dialogue with others who speak from different traditions, locations and experiences" and believes that "it is... essential for teachers, ethnic communities and... communities of artists to work together to unsettle the ideologies that sustain the practices of exclusion, marginalization and oppression" (pp. 66-67). And in this post September 11 world, this seems so very important. But like many writing for educators, he is "thin" on how to do this. If Rizvi's characterization of the nature of schooling is true (and it does parallel my observations of learning communities in Canadian public schools—incidentally, the most multicultural in the world) implementation of such notions require more than a general and rather vague statement that "school-based initiatives... link up with the struggle taking place on other sites" (p. 66). We are miles apart. It's true that well-meaning teachers value inclusiveness, that they try to avoid stereotyping, and that they strive not to "present" any group of people in ways that can be considered unflattering, demeaning, or limited, but, when I published *Celebrating Pluralism,* I believed that their so-called multicultural art programs tended to look like the outline shown in Figure 1.

A quick trip to most teachers' resource centers will show that they still largely look this way. Instead of this program, in *Celebrating Pluralism* (Chalmers, 1996) I directed attention to the big themes—themes that can address and incorporate transcultural hybridized experience. In exploring these themes, some of this art, studied and made, will strive to perpetuate established cultural values and will support continuity and stability in such aspects as religion and politics. Other art will urge and reflect change. Studio projects will encourage students to tell their own important stories. Technical skills and accomplishments will be admired and appreciated in objects from a variety of historical and transitory cultures. Students are asked to find similarities in "function" and to compare and contrast cross- and trans-cultural examples of art where the makers are, or have become, and where they themselves become ascribers of meaning, ascribers of status, catalysts of social change, enhancers and decorators, interpreters, magicians, mythmakers, propagandists, recorders of history, sociotherapists, storytellers, and teachers.

In contrast to some topics commonly used in multicultural education, these theme organizers are far from trite. They encourage us to see the multi- and trans-cultural common functions of art in a constantly changing world. Rather than view teachers as transmitters of huge bodies of hegemonic knowledge we should see them as leaders and

Figure 1: Multicultural Art Program

September:	Students make an African "harvest mask" from construction paper, dried grains, and beans.
Late October:	A moveable Mexican "Day of the Dead" skeleton with black cardboard and white paper.
November:	Red paper poppies.
December:	A "play dough" candelabra for Kwanzaa.
January:	Li See Chinese (lucky money) envelopes from red construction paper and gold paint.
February:	Mardi Gras masks from a variety of found materials and lots and lots of sequins
March:	Hammered shamrock leaf prints.
April:	Ukrainian "pysanky" from hard-boiled eggs decorated with glued-on colored tissue paper.
May:	A cardboard Chi Wara hat for a Mali planting festival.
June:	Brightly colored stuffed paper fish for Children's Day.

facilitators who are able to focus on the process and assist students in their investigation and understanding of commonalties in the functions and roles of art across transmogrifying cultures. When the focus is on the why of art, I said, and when teaching is viewed as facilitating, and learning is active, I still believe that the above themes offer much scope for learning about and making art. Such a perspective requires a questioning, problem-solving, and inquiry-based approach to instruction in a constantly changing world and may not be all that "gentle."

As a first step we can focus on why cultures need art and then hopefully go beyond this to challenge the political and cultural hegemonies of Eurocentrism and "School Art." Then, with other multicultural educators, (e.g. Mahalingam & McCarthy, 2000) we can begin to see that

> Multiculturalism should be seen as a paradigm for global education reform where bounded notions of culture, including the notion of "white," are constantly contested and challenged. We need to confront the ethnic absolutism now rampant in education and society with the complex historical record and the living experiences and realities of marginalized subjects. We need to generate critical pedagogical strategies that deeply articulate the embodied experiences of the marginalized. (pp. 5-6)

For many of us who teach, this presents a problem. Can we represent marginalized identities without sharing the burden of their historical past? Can we speak for the "other?" Now that I occupy the University of British Columbia's endowed "Chair" in multicultural education—and am the first "white guy" to do so—this has become a particularly personal issue. Steve Fuller (2000) identifies something that he calls "hyperculturalism" in which only natives of a culture are authorized to speak on its behalf. Others' voices are regarded as suspect because they have not immersed themselves in the life of that culture. Max Weber is an important target of this argument, as he set the pace for Western understandings of the sociology of India and China without having visited either country or mastered its language. Yet if Weber is excluded on those grounds, then what do we say about Aijaz Ahmad (1992) who performed the reciprocal function of diagnosing the Western fetish for "third world" and "postcolonial" cultural studies from a strategically detached vantage point in New Delhi? Indeed, can the hyperculturalist in good faith condone the activities [and recent flurry of post September the 11th writings] of Edward Said, a Palestinian Christian, whose academic training and practice has been in the United States but whose scholarship primarily concerns Europe's "orientalization" of Islam? (p. 17)

These are big issues, and I increasingly find myself wanting to tell my story—to share those aspects of my life that have shaped the person that I am still becoming today. I am more aware of my privileged position. Like many teachers I have never known what it is to be truly monitored, marked, and excluded. I have written elsewhere (Chalmers, 2001) about ancestral shame, which can be both problematic and productive, and how I have seen the lives of people of color, and of myself, through the smoke of historical illusion. Now, categorized as Manuwhiri (person from away) when I return to academic conferences in the land of my birth I can't participate in a powhiri (welcoming ceremony) without tears in my eyes. Am I inside or outside? How, through shame, may we come to a better understanding of each other? How can and should the trauma of the oppressed affect the oppressor and the oppressor's descendents? Especially we, who are white liberal multiculturalists, need to challenge our own privilege—to interrogate our own whiteness and the power we derive from it. I grew up in a Pakeha (White) world of self-deception, falsely believing, even as a beginning teacher in a school with a large Maori population, that there was lots of common ground and that New Zealand led the world in achieving a racial and cultural blending in which all people had equal opportunity. I am aware that we tend to reinvent our pasts based on our present; that "where we're at" colors historical memory. But it is true to say that in terms of common ground, I no longer believe such a myth. If you haven't seen the powerful movie Once Were Warriors, borrow it from the video store, and take a look at what I ignored in Aotearoa/New Zealand—it is set only a few miles from where I taught. Now my elder son works with immigrants. I have an Asian daughter-in-law, a wonderful little granddaughter—Jan Wai-Ming Chalmers. My family increasingly lives transculturally with all the tensions, contradictions, and opportunities that that involves.

Also in 1996, the same year as *Celebrating Pluralism* was published, Susan Cahan and Zoya Kocur (1996) edited Contemporary Art and Multi-cultural Education. This book focuses on utilizing vocal contemporary artists from shifting and diverse American subcultures whose work speaks about oppression, identity, and social change. Included are artists such as Guillermo Gómez-Peña who writes:

Today I wake up as a Mexican in U.S. territory. With my Mexican psyche, my Mexican heart, and my Mexican body, I have to make intelligible art for American audiences that know very little about my culture. This is my daily dilemma. I have to force myself to cross a border, and there is very little reciprocity from the people on the other side. I physically live between two cultures and two epochs. I have a little house in Mexico City, and one in New York… I am a Mexican part of the year, and a Chicano, the other part. I cross the border by foot, by car, and by airplane. My journey not only goes from South to North, but from the past to the future, from Spanish to English, and from one side of myself to another. (cited in Cahan & Kocur, 1996, p. 122)

And Polish-Canadian-American-sometimes French resident Krzystof Wodiczko who writes "I belong to those artists-in-transit who are critical and while crossing boundaries, change themselves, their art, and contribute to changing others' perceptions, imagination, and vision of the world. This is my culture: critical and mobile." (cited in Cahan & Kocur, 1996, p. 163)

Although discussion of such concepts seems to be increasingly common in art schools and universities, the impact of mobile cultures on schools has, I think, been minimal. I do, however, occasionally come across "transcultural" work, such as this piece by Yu Gu, then a Grade 12 student, who, through her work, speaks to younger Chinese Canadian Britney Spears "wanna-bes."

Hush, just stop. There's nothing you can do or say, baby I've had enough. I'm not your property as from today, baby. You might think that I wont make it on my own. But now I'm stronger than yesterday. Now it's nothing but my way. My loneliness ain't killing me no more. I'm stronger.

The swirling tornados in the air invite vomitting. I'm sitting through class and everything is a blur. No one knows what I'm thinking. I dream and imagine things, the prettiest, most perfect things, but they mean nothing. I struggle on this wind swept plane against an enemy inside my mind.

In June and July of last year the Vancouver Multicultural Society (Mercer, 2001) asked a number of key informants, myself among them, what "multiculturalism" meant to them. There were two common themes that emerged:

- Multiculturalism has evolved and social justice issues (human rights issues, antiracist pedagogy, programs that address systemic discrimination, equity, inclusion etc.) need to be firmly entrenched within the scope of multiculturalism.

- The "preservation" of culture is highly subjective due to the "fluid" nature of cultures and multicultural education efforts must recognize the realities of hybridity.

Within education, whether in the United States or Canada, multiculturalism as a positive dynamic force, a philosophy that should permeate all curricula is still far from a reality. We art educators have generally moved from a view of multiculturalism as "contamination" to thinking of multiculturalism as "celebration," (and I hope that I have played a small part in this). But we now need to move beyond. Many teachers, students, and parents appear to have limited understanding of multicultural education. For example, working in Vancouver, Samuel Adu-Poku (2002) found that this was a fairly typical Grade 7 student response: "Multicultural education involves the celebration of Black History Month, Chinese New Year, Halloween, First Nations' Potlach, and Multicultural Potluck Nights at the school." An astute African-Canadian parent added: "Multicultural education does not mean anything other than a human relations exercise. Cultural inequalities are not addressed in the curriculum."

Not only have we yet to put the "critical" in "critical multiculturalism." We have yet to put the "multi" in multiculturalism, the "trans" in trans-culturalism. Unfortunately what many well-meaning teachers do in the name of "multiculturalism" (what I have called the "totem poles out of toilet rolls" approach, and others the "food, song, and dance" "folkloric' focus) would, if they knew about it, be dismissed as agents of expressions of patronizing ignorance by members of the changing fluid cultures supposedly represented. Many schools have yet to truly be challenged by and respond to the changing cultural realities of North America and the world. But this is not surprising; few of our politicians offer very much vision in this regard. Too often xenophobia and white supremacy are embraced as not necessarily desirable, but nevertheless essential. We must not let September 11 provide an alibi for certain types of regressive racist behavior. Unfortunately it is still generally true that the lighter one's skin color, the easier one's life is going to be. A commitment to multiculturalism must mean more than "conditional" hospitality. As several of the Vancouver key informants in Mercer's (2001) study, and to which I just referred, stated: "To some multiculturalism is no longer an issue... there is a weakening sense of urgency...a shifting of focus." "I don't see multiculturalism being talked about as much... it is not at the forefront of our agenda." "Multiculturalism is no longer the flavor of the month." Within the schools "Apathy or indifference is increasing towards multiculturalism" state his informants (pp. 14-16). All this at a time "when affirmative action is in retreat; when poverty is a constant; when prisons [in both the United States and Canada] continue to be holding pens for minority men; when [North] American culture persists in reminding minorities, in ways large and small, that they are a problem" (Cotter, 2001, p. 28).

When, in education, action does take place it tends to be as the result of new demographic statistics, rather than it just being the right thing to do. But even if the impetus for change comes solely from numbers, we still need to increasingly acknowledge hybridity. A 1997 University of Michigan study (reported in Long, 1997) indicates that the rate of interracial marriage has at least quadrupled since the 1950s. According to Moss (2002), by the mid 1990s at least 1 in 300 children in Canada (where we don't have quite the same history of miscegenation laws), and 1 in 50 children in the United Kingdom was of mixed race. And it has been during this same time period that educators rejected the melting pot in favor of the mosaic. The melting pot was not a good metaphor, but neither is the mosaic. As used in education it also fails because the image implies that cultures and communities are static, self-contained, and impervious. As Patrick Dobel (1997) argues, a mosaic "enshrines a vision of individuals embedded in groups, perpetually strangers to outsiders, who are bound only by the forced cement of proximity. [Some transculturalists suggest a braid, but even this seems a little too tidy]. In real life people are thrown together. They work, mix, argue, love, fight, talk" (p. 12). Instead Dobel, who lives in Seattle, introduces two new metaphors: The Great Northwestern Halibut Taco, and The Big Muddy River. One presents an experimental concoction, an "impure" mixture of mingling but still identifiable flavors that may not be combined in exactly the same way next time; the other [the river] an image of something constantly forming and reforming by a concert of movement. We need to relate these images to art education. Néstor García Canclini (1995) could have been talking about the dilemma of secondary art teachers, and addressing those who want to re-make art education as visual culture studies, when he wrote, a year before *Celebrating Pluralism* appeared:

> How can we understand the presence of indigenous crafts and vanguard art catalogs on the same coffee table? What are painters looking for when, in the same painting, they cite pre-Columbian and colonial images along with those of the culture industry, and then re-elaborate them using computers and lasers? (p. 2)

García Canclini and others have called this "cultural re-conversion." In western cultures the co-mingling of various traditions in the visual arts has lagged behind what was happening in music. Edward Rothstein, (1991) *New York Times* music critic in the early 1990s (in Hanna, 1994, p. 68) wrote:

One reason for this cross-fertilization is that Western musical culture, far from condemning the Other to some netherworld of untouchable sound, has cultivated an impassioned interest in the music of different cultures. It has done so in order to gain a new perspective on its own music, and in order to explore the possibilities and the power of music itself. (p. 33)

Within Cultural Studies the notion of hybridity is rather old, but in school-based visual art education rarely, other than by perhaps looking at the influence of West African masks on Picasso, or the relationship between Van Gogh's work and Japanese prints, do students study such phenomena in schools. Physical borders may remain intact, but cultural borders have become much more porous. Rather than explore how a culture might be constantly (re)converting its "artmaking" to participate in a global market system, we tend to portray so-called "traditional" cultures as if they are fixed in an unsullied time-warp in an imagined homeland. This fairly dominant approach has been called the "food/festival/arts/quaint native garb" emphasis (Hanna, 1994, p. 74). It is critical that educators grasp the concept that cultures are both internally diverse and ever-changing. In schools, except in a few cases, it has seemed too messy to deal with new hybridized identities, forms, and cultural practices, so we have left them alone and instead reinterpreted, diluted, and exoticized selected cultures. Gunew (1994) could be describing the dominant form of multicultural education in schools when she states that such an approach

presupposes a kind of ethnic absolutism where the community [being studied] is both synonymous with a particular cultural formation and maintains its closed boundaries in terms of language and cultural traditions. The community is thus bracketed as an homogenized entity and frozen outside history and contemporary interactive relations. (p. 5)

Cultural theorists such as Homi Bhabha (1990) and others stress that identity is never fixed once and for all; that it never coheres into an absolute form. As Papastergiadis (2000) states, "identity always presupposes a sense of location and a relationship with others" (p. 193). But as well as teachers other cultural workers also have problems implementing this concept. On one hand, as Bhabha (n.d.) says in the documentary film Colors of Britain, even in the most politically sincere multicultural thinking which wants to say to a number of artists of migratory experience we respect you, we want to display you, we want to name you, but we want you to constitute a recognizable, quasi-national cultural identity, before we can really give you the recognition that you want.

And on the other hand, by focusing on art that is produced now and that is about issues of identity, race, difference, and power, we need to be careful not to again privilege those types of art and artists that are exhibited and performed in galleries and museums. We need to recognize that this new art is being produced, packaged, presented, and consumed in the West by an increasingly transcultural, but nevertheless rather small elitist group of artists, curators, critics, scholars and patrons. Traveling cultures, flexible citizenship are not available to all, but are unevenly distributed across class and gender. There is some danger that what the West used to call the minor arts or crafts—fibers, textiles, ceramics, body adornment, work by women, popular visual culture—all of which gained currency in liberal approaches to multicultural education, and, even if used in strange ways, have been the stuff of much multicultural art education in schools, could again be overshadowed by supposedly transcultural issues-based performance art, large paintings and installations. As stated over and over again in *Celebrating Pluralism*, we need to remember that everyone's art matters.

"Education is the sending and receiving of messages," wrote Judith Lynn Hanna, "often unintended messages are communicated resulting in unintended consequences" (1994, p.80). What is multicultural art education really doing? Some (e.g. Macedo & Bartolomé, 2000) argue that by making "tolerance" the focus of educational programs we mask the maintenance of class and race privilege, or, as Goodman (2001) states, we "reduce multi-culturalism to 'diversity management,' a kind of 'Benetton Multiculturalism' that does not threaten oppressive power but, rather, commodifies difference," (p. 29) Let me give an example from a picture book *All The Colors of the Earth* (Hamanaka, 1994) frequently read to primary age children and reminiscent of Rockwell's image that I showed you at the beginning of this lecture:

Figure 2: *All the Colors of the Earth* (Hamanaka, 1994)

Children come in all the colors of the earth–
The roaring browns of bears and soaring eagles,
The whispering golds of late summer grasses,
And crackling russets of fallen leaves,
The tinkling pinks of tiny seashells by the rumbling sea.
Children come with hair like bouncy baby lambs,
Or hair that flows like water,
Or hair that curls like sleeping cats in snoozy cat colors.
Children come in all the colors of love,
In endless shades of you and me,
For love comes in cinnamon, walnut and wheat,
Love is amber and ivory and gingers and sweet
Like caramel and chocolate, and the honey of bees.
Dark as leopard spots, light as sand,
Children buzz with laughter that kisses our land,
With sunlight like butterflies happy and free
Children come in all colors of the earth and sky and sea.

Henry Giroux elaborates:

This is not to suggest that caring and empathy, stalwarts of the liberal pedagogical model, are irrelevant. However, we have to be vigilant about pedagogical approaches that endorse notions of caring which either prevent the engagement of pertinent political issues at work in multicultural education or serve to produce other forms of "benevolent" oppression. Put differently, we need to mediate any notion of caring and empathy through the related issues of solidarity and politics. (cited in Macedo & Bartolomé, 2000, pp. 101-102)

There is often an uncritical missionizing, "helping," soft rather then critical aspect to many school-based "multicultural" programs, manifest for example, in such well-meaning action as signing on with the Heifer Project to purchase an animal for persons living in difficult circumstances. Some teachers have turned empathy into sympathy. And even with empathy, there is a problem. Educators need to realize that "we do not perceive and understand the Other thanks to some act of empathy; we do so by understanding what the Other is saying, thinking, and feeling, and through our ability to converse with the other" (Touraine, 2000, p. 279). Many who are white may not yet be ready to take out a subscription to *Race Traitor* and adopt the slogan "treason to whiteness is loyalty to humanity" but it is important that we heed the advice of Australian Aboriginal Lilla Watson, who said something like "if you have come to help me, don't bother, but if you have come because your liberation is tied up with mine, then let us work together." Many who teach are still a long way from this. It was a message implied in *Celebrating Pluralism*, but here it is more boldly stated.

And so, in conclusion, it's not where you're from, it's where you're at. I find that as a multiculturalist and art educator—to use Bennett's (2001) terms—I remain committed to curriculum reform. I stand behind what I wrote in *Celebrating Pluralism*. I continue to support what has been called "equity pedagogy," and I want each student and teacher to be multiculturally competent. But increasingly this is not enough, through novels, poetry, theatre, and music I can feel the unjustness of injustice. Through the visual arts too, all of our students, yes, even rich white kids, have this potential. Lilla's words increasingly haunt me: "if you have come to help me, don't bother, but if you have come because your liberation is tied up with mine, then let us work together."

References

Adu-Poku, S. (2002). *African-centered multicultural art education: an alternative curriculum and pedagogy.* Vancouver, BC: University of British Columbia, unpublished Ph.D. dissertation.

Ahmad, A. (1992). *In theory: Classes, nations, literatures.* London and New York: Verso.

Ang, I., & Goldman, M. (2001). *Parra: It's not where you're from, it's where you're at.* Sydney: Australian Centennial Fund.

Bennett, C. (2001). Genres of research in multicultural education. *Review of Educational Research,* 71(2), 171-217.

Bhabha, H. (Ed)., (1990). *Nation and narration.* London: Routledge.

Bhabha, H. (n.d). Commentary in *The colors of Britain.* (Video).

Cahan, S. & Kocur, Z. (Eds.). (1996). *Contemporary art and multicultural education.* New York: The New Museum of Contemorary Art and Routledge.

Chalmers, F.G. (1996). *Celebrating pluralism: art, education, and cultural diversity.* Los Angeles: Getty Education Institute for the Arts.

Chalmers, F.G. (1999). Cultural colonialism and art education: Eurocentric and racist roots of art education. In Boughton, D. and Mason R. (Eds.), *Beyond multicultural art education: International perspectives,* (pp. 173-183). New York: Waxman.

Chalmers, F. G. (2001). Knowing art through multiple lenses: In defence of purple haxe and grey areas. In P. Duncum and T. Bracey (Eds.), *On knowing art and visual culture,* pp. 86-98. Christchurch, N.Z.: Canterbury University Press,

Cotter, H. (2001, July 29). Beyond multiculturalism, freedom? *New York Times,* Section 2, 1 and 28.

Dobel, J.P. (1997). Kitchens and rivers. *Commonweal,* 124 (February 28), 11-12.

Fuller, S. (2000). Social epistemology as a critical philosophy of multiculturalism. In R. Mahalingam & C. McCarthy, (Eds.), *Multicultural curriculum: new directions for social theory, practice, and policy,* (pp. 70-83). New York: Routledge.

García Canclini, N. (1995). *Hybrid cultures: strategies for entering and leaving modernity.* Trans. C.L. Chiappari & S. López. Minneapolis: University of Minnesota Press.

Goodman, R.T. (2001). Review: Macedo, D. & Bartolomé, L. 2000. Dancing with bigotry: Beyond the politics of tolerance. New York: St. Martins, *Educational Researcher,* 30(6), 27-30.

Gunew, S. and Rizvi, F. (Eds.), 1994. *Culture, difference and the arts.* St. Leonard's, NSW Australia: Allen and Unwin.

Hamanaka, S. (1994). *All the colors of the earth.* New York: Morrow Junior Books.

Hanna, J.L. (1994). Issues in supporting school diversity: academics: social relations, and the arts, *Anthropology and Education Quarterly,* 25(1), 66-85.

Long, R.E. (ed.), (1997). *Multiculturalism.* New York: H.W. Wilson.

Macedo, D. & Bartolomé, L. (2000). *Dancing with bigotry: Beyond the politics of tolerance.* New York: St. Martins.

Mahalingam & C. McCarthy, (eds.). (2000). *Multicultural curriculum: new directions for social theory, practice, and policy.* New York: Routledge, 15-36.

Mercer, C. (2001). Vancouver Multicultural Society Operational Review Report #3. Garibaldi Highlands, BC: C.B. Mercer and Associates.

Moss, L. (2002). Theorizing métissage/hybridity. Conference presentation Cultural mingling: between, among, within cultures. Vancouver: University of British Columbia, February 23.

Nieto, S. (1996). *Affirming diversity: The socio-political context of multicultural education.* New York: Longman.

Nieto, S. (1999). Critical multicultural education and students' perspectives. In S. May (Ed.), *Critical multiculturalism: Rethinking multicultural and anti-racist education,* (pp. 191-215). London: Falmer.

Papastergiadis, N. (2000). *The turbulence of migration: globalization, deterritorialization, and hybridity.* Cambridge, UK: Polity Press.

Rothstein, E. (1991). Roll over Beethoven, *The New Republic,* (February 4), 29-34.

Scarborough, J. (1998). Class theory. *Museum News,* 77(1), 57-62.

Silvers, A. (1999). Essay review. Multiculturalism and the aesthetics of recognition: Reflections on Celebrating Pluralism. *Journal of Aesthetic Education,* 33(1), 95-103.

Solomon, P. (1997). *Beyond celebratory multiculturalism: Where teachers fear to tread.* Toronto: Faculty of Education, York University.

Stuhr, P. (1999). Book review. Chalmers, G. (1996). Celebrating pluralism: art, education, and cultural diversity. *Studies in Art Education,* 40(2), 180-191.

Touraine, A. (2000). *Can we live together? Equality and difference.* (Trans. D. Macey). Stanford, CA: Stanford University Press.

ARTICLE SELECTION

Lackey, L. M. (2003). Theorizing a Network Called Art Education: Re-envisioning and Extending the Field. *Studies in Art Education,* 44(2), 101-116.

Doug Blandy

Senior Editor, 2007-2009

Inspired by June King McFee's (1986) systemic description of Art Education as a network, Lara M. Lackey (2003) amplifies the premise in "Theorizing a Network Called Art Education: Re-envisioning and Extending the Field." Significant to Lackey's article is that it brings attention to antecedents in the field while simultaneously responding to the politics of the time in which it was written. The article also presages the appreciation that people working across the arts, culture, and heritage sectors have come to realize about the importance of coalitions and networks to advocacy and initiating change. Significant is Lackey's contribution to the research literature on a community-based focus for which there is little masked reviewed documentation.

While McFee's article was published in 1986, two decades earlier she had founded the Institute for Community Arts Studies at the University of Oregon. Associated with the institute was a "cultural services" graduate and undergraduate program in the Department of Art Education that prepared students to work in arts councils, museums, social service agencies, and community arts centers. This program was paired in the Department with an undergraduate art teacher training program and a master's degree program for teachers. Foundational to the Institute and Department's systemic conception of Art Education was Vytautas Kavolis' (1973) description of America's arts and cultural heritage as an extensive network through which children, youth, and adults could engage with art. This network included the schools as well as community arts centers, museums, churches, and health care facilities among many others. Continuing to the present this orientation has been explored and defined in academia as well as in public policy documents (Becker, 1984; The American Assembly, 2007; Ivey, 2007).

Douglas E. Blandy is Professor and Associate Dean for Academic Affairs in the School of Architecture and Allied Arts at the University of Oregon. His research and teaching attends to meeting the needs of all students with lifelong learning and to the relationships among art, education, community, and place. He has published in *Studies in Art Education, Art Education,* and *Visual Arts Research.* He has been associated with the editorship of five books. Dr. Blandy has received the Mary J. Rouse Award and the NAEA Manuel Barkan Research Award.

"Theorizing a Network Called Art Education: Re-envisioning and Extending the Field" brought the field of Art Education's (as represented by the community of scholars and practitioners associated with *Studies in Art Education*) attention anew to the broader conversation occurring across the arts, culture, and heritage sectors about the larger network in which Art Education occurs. Lackey advised participants in the network to avoid contentious and competitive relationships in favor of mutual support, critique, understanding, and appreciation. This wise counsel reinforces what policy makers and advocates have come to understand. That is that the health of the arts, culture, and heritage sectors depends upon the well being of all and that the overall health of the network can only be judged by the status of its most challenged members.

References

The American Assembly. (2007). The arts and the public purpose. Retrieved November 12, 2008 from http://www.americanassembly.org/programs.dir/prog_display_ind_pg.php?this_filename_prefix=arts_purpose&this_ind_prog_pg_filename=report.

Becker, H. (1984). *Art worlds.* Berkeley: University of California Press.

Ivey, B. (2007). America needs a new system for supporting the arts. The Curb Center for Art, Enterprise, and Public Policy. Retrieved December 28, 2007 from http://www.vanderbilt.edu/curbcenter/support.

Kavolis, V. (1973). The institutional structure of cultural services. *Journal of Aesthetic Education,* 7(4), 63-80.

McFee, J. K. (1986). Describing the field called art education / Decrire le reseau baptise education artistique. *Canadian Society for Education through Art Journal,* 17, 7-12.

Theorizing a Network Called Art Education: Re-envisioning and Extending the Field

Lara M. Lackey

Teaching and learning about art/visual culture occur within an array of formal, non-formal, and informal contexts with a variety of purposes: educational, religious, therapeutic, recreational, cultural, social, political, and commercial, among others. That art education takes place within many different social and economic arrangements means that the field as a whole is characterized by multiple practices and complex relationships among providers, making it difficult to conceptualize overall. My goal is to contribute to a conversation about how one might envision the field of art education in a way that embraces its multifaceted and sometimes unruly and fractious landscape. In addition, I consider ways in which macro and micro conditions frame educational contexts and therefore possibilities for practice. Arguments draw on sociological perspectives and empirical evidence.

I take the work of art educator June King McFee (1986) and her discussion of an art education "network" as a starting point and suggest that she both raises important issues about, and establishes a premise for, viewing our field with a wide lens. I then extend and embellish an understanding of such a network using, among others, the work of Pierre Bourdieu on the field of cultural production (1993) and Etienne Wenger (1998/1999) on communities of practice. Finally I use research from a study conducted in a non-formal setting, a community recreation center, to illustrate the extent to which internal and external conditions influence the nature of practice within a particular site. I suggest on one hand that there is much to be gained from taking a broad view of art education, and particularly from acknowledging the vast number of out-of-school domains for art learning. On the other, I assert that the diverse contexts of our field do not merely offer a selection of alternative locations for art experience, but rather they provide a set of unique orientations to practice in which art education takes on distinct meanings. These practices in turn delimit possibilities for learning.

McFee's Network

More than 15 years ago, McFee (1986) posed the question, "What is art education and what constitutes it as a field of inquiry and practice?" (p. 7). She suggested that the realm of art education could be construed as a kind of network composed of many sites, including but not limited to the institutions of schooling. Prior to McFee's article, "Describing the Network Called Art Education" (1986), the field's literature focused primarily on K-12 art education in public schools. McFee's conception, however, targeted art activity for all ages and included museums and galleries, community and recreation centers, and rehabilitation settings (such as prisons, nursing or seniors' homes, and sites of art therapy), as well as formal schooling. The list might also include informal and non-formal art educational

---

activities that occur through child care services; social groups and clubs; night schools; the media; private businesses; self-directed study; community-based programming generated by artists and artists' organizations; and those fostered by family members, mentors, etc. In any case, McFee charged art educators with the task of describing all aspects of this network and chastised us for getting caught up in insular and often competitive positions:

> Such describing needs to be continuous. The fact that we have done so little of it may be the reason we are having such a hard time defending the field today. We have spent too much time arguing from our different points of view, rather than identifying what we include. (McFee, p.7)

McFee notes six categories that need description: the operations we share, the common and distinct goals that characterize our work, the range of disciplines from which we draw, the methods and strategies we use, the agencies that frame our practice, and the social currents that influence operations. She argues that acknowledging this broader network and understanding the various institutional roles and social patterns that affect art education will ultimately strengthen our field.

Because I was an art educator practicing at the time in a non-school setting, McFee's assertion helped me feel validated rather than discounted and invisible within a field traditionally dominated by school-based educators. More significantly, however, I was and continue to be intrigued by the ideas expressed explicitly and implicitly within her work. First, although art has long struggled as a peripheral subject in schools, taking a bird's-eye view of the field permits seeing art education as a thriving practice that both pervades and is central to everyday life. This perspective depicts the field of art education not as marginal or inconsequential but as a vast, interesting, and complex arena ripe for new kinds of exploration.

Next, examining the nature of art education in its multiple forms is useful and important in terms of understanding practice and promoting the field. By exploring the ways that art education takes place in different contexts and social situations, we can see how each setting creates unique environments with which learners and teachers interact. Detailing these environments can help us reconsider taken-for-granted assumptions and practices within familiar workplaces, and facilitate understanding as we attempt collaboration across settings.

Finally, and I think most important, McFee acknowledges the tensions between and among the various providers of art education, but suggests that we need to examine the common "social and political forces that may affect us and the institutions through which we operate" (1986, p.7); these are forces that cut across all contexts but manifest in different ways within each setting. By better understanding the underlying causes of frictions, she suggests, we may clarify potential for collective action that will serve the interests of all.

McFee's work is important, therefore, because it re-envisions the field of art education in a way that does not reduce or confine it to the institutions and practices of schooling.

It acknowledges educational experience across formal, non-formal, and informal environments, and helps legitimize research in non-school contexts. It draws attention not only to the particularities that characterize the multiple sites of art education, but also to the broad structures and ideologies that establish rules of play for the field as a whole. Finally, McFee does not minimize the significance of frictions between school and non-school providers of art education, but rather reminds us that the tensions that seem to divide us are caused by essentially political circumstances that we share.

Fortunately, some of the descriptive work that McFee calls for has now begun. These efforts include grappling with the complexities of evaluating community arts centers (Congdon & Boughton, 1998), re-conceptualizing the nature of community-based administrative work (Blandy & Congdon, 2001), and relating current and historic examples of community and non-school based practices (Bolin, Blandy, & Congdon, 2000; Congdon, Blandy & Bolin, 2001; Irwin & Kindler, 1999). Stokrocki (2002) notes that the interconnection of "content and context" (n.p.) is an important theme in art education research. Nevertheless, the breadth and complexity of a field embracing so many contexts make it difficult to grasp overall. In the next sections, therefore, I explore some ways of thinking about an art education network as a whole, both in terms of relations between and among providers and with respect to the nature of individual contexts. Again I remind readers of the magnitude of this topic and the necessarily narrow and selected focus of this discussion.

Art Education as Relational

As a metaphor for the field of art education, the term "network" connotes a kind of web through which individual and even autonomous sites are linked. It implies an emphasis on interconnection, inter-reliance, and communication among members. Other applicable ideas include Wenger's (1998/1999) notion of a "constellation of practices" (p. 126), using the term "constellation" to refer to a cluster that, like the stars, appears related from our perspective on earth, but in fact may not be. Congdon (1998) suggests an ecological relationship among art education providers, emphasizing the importance of each contributor to the functioning of the greater system. This analogy to natural relationships insists on the necessity of all the various components but, like nature itself, it does not preclude potential for power struggles between and among players. I suggest that ignoring these tensions between providers is both naïve and unhelpful, as such a view circumvents a deeper understanding of underlying causes of friction and shared problems.

Bourdieu (1993) has proposed a tension-filled conception of the field in which art is produced–the field of cultural production—that I suggest is also useful for understanding art education. His model depicts the field of cultural production as nested within the field of economics, which is in turn nested within the field of power, or politics. Each arena is caught up in a kind of tug of war, pulled between the influences of cultural or symbolic capital or status and those of economic status. The art world is depicted as suspended between two poles, that of high art (founded on the pretense of rejecting economic concerns, but actually engaged in the pursuit of long-term economic gain) on one end, and artistic production devised to appeal to a mass audience (and more immediate economic return), on the other. The field itself is comprised of a myriad of producers along a scale, each involved in the taking of positions within a continually shifting hierarchy, and permeated by the influences of the two poles. As each new position is taken, all the others are affected and must adjust. Bourdieu's field of cultural production, therefore, is a dynamic territory that he describes as both a field of struggles and a field of forces.

I do not suggest that Bourdieu's model precisely replicates either the worlds of art or art education. McRobbie (1999), for example, charges that a growing global economy and the ongoing breakdown of boundaries between high and popular art means that Bourdieu's emphasis on just two poles is no longer appropriate. It is also important to reiterate that Bourdieu's model is based on the process of artistic production and distribution, or the essentially economic network in which artistic work is created, legitimated, and exchanged, and does not refer specifically to the field of education. I suggest nevertheless that this gurgling, shifting, tension-filled notion of a "field" is useful as we think about the field of art education, because it draws attention to the wider social currents with which all art education providers grapple.

The Fields of Art and Education

It is not possible to provide a full discussion here of the different purposes of the fields of art and education. Nevertheless, I wish to make the point that these differences are key sources of tension for the art education network. To reiterate Bourdieu's (1993) position, the field of art is primarily concerned with the production and distribution of artistic and cultural products that translate into capital, symbolic, and/or economic. Formal education, on the other hand, offers educational capital—which may sometimes be exchanged for social and economic rewards—and essentially "produces" workers and citizens. Each realm may use the other for its own ends. Artists, for example, may use education as a vehicle for gaining economic support and legitimacy, while educators may use art, artists, and their associated cultural capital in the service of education.

Bourdieu (1993) suggests that tensions between artists and educators are based in a struggle between the institutions of high art and those of high scholarship, and over what will count as legitimate artistic achievement. Although the world of high art relies on its own dealer-critic system to consecrate art and artists in the short term, educational domains ultimately authorize which art and artists are recorded and esteemed for posterity through university teaching and art history text books. This, he implies, irks the art world:

> [art] producers cannot fail to pay attention to the judgments of university institutions. They cannot ignore the fact that it is these who will have the last word, and that ultimate consecration can only be accorded them by an authority whose legitimacy is challenged by their entire practice, their entire professional ideology. There are plenty of attacks upon the university which bear witness to the fact that their authors recognize the legitimacy of its verdicts sufficiently to reproach it for not having recognized them. (Bourdieu, 1993, p.124)

The different purposes of these fields also mean that the work of artists and teachers is organized and experienced differently, and may foster different orientations to the world. In modern times, for example, many teachers are employed by the state and work within bureaucratic hierarchies, while artists are often self-employed and have been mythologized as "free," self-directed agents (Wolff, 1993). As such, individual actors in each camp may come to view themselves, their identities and social purposes, in different ways, and to engage in behaviors of "distinction" (Bourdieu, 1984) through which they define their associations with and against particular social groups.

Such explanations help make sense of perceived rivalries between departments of fine art and departments of education in universities; between certified teachers and artists-who-teach; and between organizations like museums and schools. Tensions are exacerbated by the low status of art in our society generally and limited sources of funding for all.

Social Equity and Democratic Access

A focal point for conflict in the literature of art education has been the issue of equal access to art knowledge and how best to distribute funding to achieve it. This debate may appear to be a battle between school and non-school providers. Chapman (1992), for example, delivers a careful and devastating case against the Federal bureaucracy responsible for arts education funding at that time. Specifically she argues that the National Endowment for the Arts and the U.S. Office of Education together practiced a policy of de-schooling art education, through the employment of "artists and other non-certified personnel to deliver arts services to children and youth within the schools" (p.120) and reduction of funding for school-based art education. Chapman's argument is about justice and fairness, democratic access to learning, and the veracity of knowledge and educational experience. She argues that arts organizations are interested in funding for artists, not education, and often permit the unreflective, romanticized, and elitist ideologies of artists to drive children's educational experiences.

In the past, arts organizations have downplayed their complicity in agendas of social inequity, charging school-based educators with territorialism (Fowler, 1984). Without question, however, problems of elitism in the art world and issues of access to art knowledge are of critical importance to our field. Arguably artists' organizations often have been self-serving, and artists may well be arrogant, uniformed, or naïve in assuming that they know best how to teach art when they have spent little time examining the complexities of educational transactions (Chapman, 1992). Schools are the institutions our society has imbued with formal authority for educating future generations. The mandatory status of public schools means in theory that all have access to school knowledge and to the social rewards that can be obtained through educational capital. Bourdieu's (1984) often-cited theory of cultural capital partly supports this claim. His argument implies that to the extent that 'high' art knowledge cannot be accessed in schools and is available only through informal experiences and socialization, it becomes rarified and takes on a kind of exchange value that can be used by dominant groups to maintain social status and privilege.

It is important, however, to avoid the perspective that support for a free public school system automatically assumes inferiority of art education originating outside school or that school-based programs are inherently good, pure, and always foster meaningful education and social equity. This, of course, is not the case. Chapman's (1978) powerful critique of tacit school art policies, for example, is still valid in many respects. Schools, like all institutions, can produce practices that have negative as well as positive effects. Colucci (2000) uses the notion of "negative pedagogy" to describe educational practice in which harm and inequity are perpetuated and learning is obstructed or limited by discipline, evaluation, and constraints of time and space in the name of efficiency and rational planning and an ethic that frowns on pleasure and therefore stifles passion and curiosity. It might be argued that because schools have so tenaciously kept art education in a peripheral place within the curriculum, they are a most important contributor in maintaining the insignificance of artistic practices within popular collective perception. Critical theorists argue that schools use a hidden curriculum to maintain the social status quo and subvert social mobility (Apple, 1990; Bowles and Gintis, 1976). Others argue that what schools "teach" has little to do with the formal curriculum and everything to do with fostering an acceptance of a market economy as normal and natural and our roles as consumers rather than producers (Illich, 1971). Bourdieu (1993) suggests that while schools are indeed the institutions with the most potential for redressing social inequity, this potential is often subverted to the extent that the overall agenda of schooling rewards privilege under the guise of merit and talent.

Critical pedagogues, however, suggest that social equity is neither the sole responsibility of schools, nor is it within the power of schools to "fix" broad social problems that are structurally embedded. They argue that fostering a more equitable world must be approached from many sites and that working from the margins, outside the spotlight of official schooling, provides an additional way of perforating hegemony (Giroux, 1992). It has become increasingly common for artists to view themselves as cultural workers and critical pedagogues who incorporate social action within their practices (Lacy, 1995; Trend 1992). Artists of this persuasion often view non-school settings as sites of possibility for creating a more equitable world.

On the other hand, to suggest that schools are "bad" and coercive and non-schools such as community centers are "good" and "free" is equally erroneous and unhelpful in resolving the problem. Liberal traditions of adult education and modernist traditions in leisure studies, for example, often present access to programs in community, recreation, or continuing education settings as based on self-directedness and free choice. Attendance in these institutions may be characterized as the opposite of obligatory attendance in schools. This assumption seriously misinterprets the nature of access to these settings by ignoring constraints to leisure participation based on economics, socialization and comfort (often related to class and ethnicity), time, and social responsibilities related to family and child care (often related to gender). Access to these sites is often more about privilege than free choice, and art education practice within such settings is both influenced and complicated by its position in leisure (Lackey, 1999).

Bolton (1993) argues that all public institutions struggle with tensions between fostering democracy and perpetuating the status quo whereby "institutions are often sites where consciousness and consent are negotiated, and institutions are usually built upon enough contradictions to make such negotiation possible" (p. 13). As such, the potential for movement toward greater equity is not exclusive to one institution, but depends on political and economic circumstances within and surrounding a site, as well as the actions of thoughtful people. Every institution will have both formal or overt and informal or tacit agendas. Every setting will contain both opportunities for and limits to democratic access and social equity related to art education. The relationship between each organization and the State, however, affects the extent to which a context is viewed as authoritative or legitimate as a venue of education.

Relations to the State, Authority, and Legitimacy

An important factor that influences and positions the contexts of art education within the field concerns the relationship to the state and the extent to which an educational practice is legitimized or made 'official' by government. Educational legitimacy is manifest in the capacity of an organization to provide students with credentials, such as degrees, that may be exchanged for social rewards, such as employment—although this exchange may not be direct or guaranteed. Bourdieu and Passeron (1990), for example, argue that educational capital may be used as a means of justifying a reward that is actually a matter of privilege. Obtaining employment in an art gallery, for instance, almost certainly requires cultural capital as well as educational capital, although it would be unlikely that such a qualification would be made explicit.

Hand-in-hand with credentialing is the notion of authority. Bourdieu and Passeron (1990) suggest that by virtue of state sanctioning of schools, schoolteachers' words and actions are imbued with a weight and authority not available to teachers in non-sanctioned settings. In this sense it is not simply the credentials that are recognized and legitimized but the whole set of overt and tacit curricular choices and organizational practices and omissions that are acknowledged as normal, natural, and appropriate. The arbitrary and socially fabricated nature of these choices is obscured.

Art education, however, is an interesting case in that even within school it is not counted as a fully 'legitimate' subject and is not required or assumed basic or essential for all students. In the struggle to gain greater legitimacy in schools, art education has often tried to align itself with popular and dominant educational and political discourses. The field has also been vulnerable to use by tacit in-school agendas, as in the role of re-creational respite noted by Efland (1976) and the soothing, nurturing, mother-like role noted by Collins (1995).

On the other hand, all institutions and social arrangements in which art education take place have some relationship to the state, even if it is the absence of sanctioning or sanctioning of something other than education. In museums and recreation centers, for example, 'education' is not the primary focus. Rather, in museums, selections of culture, art, and history are authorized while in recreation centers legitimacy is attached to particular forms of leisure. In each of these settings 'education' is positioned amid a larger and more dominant agenda, and participation in programs accrues some level of cultural rather than educational capital. These sites become important settings for studying art education in part because the possibilities for learning are filtered through these other agendas. Further, the lack of educational legitimacy and authority in non-school settings permeates and complicates educational practice in these environments, and grounds it in a pedagogy of negotiation and enticement (Lackey, 1999). In postmodern times, a key question concerns the extent to which the State will continue to be the primary authorizer of education and knowledge (Lyotard, 1983).

Art Education and Particular Contexts

In this section I introduce Wenger's (1998/1999) notion of "communities of practice" and apply it to a specific art educational setting, a community recreation center. Wenger's work is of interest because he illustrates the extent to which learning is not merely influenced by a particular environment but occurs in the context of negotiating meanings and building up practices in the everyday pursuit of a common enterprise. As such, he shows that each educational context, and the learning that occurs there, are necessarily unique to some extent.

On one hand, Wenger suggests, each community responds to its position within a wider social structure and history, including the kinds of conditions described in the previous section. On an internal level, however, he argues that practice takes place as an ongoing negotiation between "reification," or attempts to concretize and formalize ways to proceed, and "participation," or the interpretation of reifications in terms of their meanings and possibilities for day to day activity. His example considers gaps between formal training and official rules in a medical claims processing office, and the daily behaviors that claims processors have developed in order to do their jobs. These are the everyday practices that novice claims processors must learn in order to be considered competent. He traces the growing understanding of a new member of the workplace as she engages with these practices. An example extended to art education communities might include the multiple day-to-day coping and management strategies that schoolteachers must master in order to be able to do the work of teaching. This includes the knowledge required to negotiate and interpret a lesson plan in practice, the lesson plan being the reification, and the interpretation being the participation.

While Wenger makes a case for the need to understand and use everyday contexts as vehicles for training, especially for new members of a community, he simultaneously illustrates how such things as rules, guidelines, and standards intended to clarify and universalize practice are always negotiated, interpreted, and modified in ways that are specific to that setting. Each community defines what will count as knowledge, what will count as competence and skill, what must be attended to, what is valued, and what can be ignored or discounted. Wenger's notion assumes "doing" based on complex knowing that embraces aspects of the tacit and formal on many levels.

The concept of practice connotes doing, but not just doing in and of itself. It is doing in a historical and social context that gives structure and meaning to what we do. In this sense, practice is always social practice. Such a concept includes both the explicit and the tacit. It includes what is said and what is left unsaid; what is represented and what is assumed. It includes the language, tools, documents, images, symbols, well-defined roles, specified criteria, codified procedures, regulations, and contracts that various practices make explicit for a variety of purposes. But it also includes all the implicit relations, tacit conventions, subtle cues, untold rules of thumb, recognizable intuitions, specific perceptions, well-tuned sensitivities, embodied understandings, underlying assumptions, and shared world views. Most of these may never be articulated, yet they are unmistakable signs of membership in communities of practice and are crucial to the success of their enterprises. (Wenger, 1998/1999, p. 47)

In research dealing with art programming in community recreation centers (Lackey, 1997),[2] art educational practices are similarly constructed and shaped by the nature—both material and ideological—of the environment in which they take place. The example provided here is a common enough art educational activity, that of working with clay. The in-depth description, however, reveals something of the distinct meaning of art educational activity at the "East Side Center,"[3] a recreation center situated in a large urban setting on the Canadian West Coast. It was located in a community made up of families from many cultural backgrounds and characterized by lower than average incomes. The Free Family Art program there took place about once per month in what was called the Games Room. This room, equipped with pool and ping-pong tables, "foos" ball, and video games, was crowded with youth from the area on most week day evenings. Participants were primarily young males 12 to 18 years of age. They reflected the local community, comprised primarily of recent immigrants from Asia and established groups of Southern European and First Nations' heritage. Each night as the room filled with young people, it also filled with the loud, raucous noises of their voices, booming music, and other sounds of their play at the games. On a particular night, however, one of the ping pong tables had been covered with garbage bags in readiness for an art activity. Deborah, an artist-teacher, made preparations and would lead the activity. Chad, a young 'volunteer' of about 14 years of age, would assist. Although it was not common knowledge, Chad was actually completing community service in lieu of other forms of punishment for some legal misdemeanor. The staff at this recreation center was often called upon to supervise this kind of service, and I had observed several cases in which assisting with art activities fulfilled the requirement.

[Field notes, Lackey, 1997, pp. 206 - 207]

At 6 the room was opened and as usual filled almost immediately with "youth," who all went directly to the games. Simultaneously the music was turned on. The first people to arrive for the Family Art activity were a French-speaking woman and her two children, a girl about 9 and a boy about 7. She remarked on the music, which I found almost unbearably loud, and said that she hoped they would have the program in the small room next door instead, the room known as the "fitness testing" room, although it was simply a small carpeted room with no furniture or equipment in it. (Looking at the little family, I thought they seemed out of place. I would not have wanted to bring my own small children there. Besides the loud music, the environment was pretty rough, with the regular smoke breaks on the patio outside, and the rowdy play. Most of the kids who used the games room were much older than the children at the clay table. My reactions, I am sure, reflected my own middle class biases and lack of "fit" in the space.)

By the time the clay finally arrived there were 12 people around the table besides me, Deborah and Chad—a fairly good turn out. In addition to a Caucasian mother (whose first language was French) and her children, there was an Asian mother and her daughter, about 8, and three Asian girls (about 9, 9, and 11) who seemed to be on their own. A Caucasian woman (whose first language was English), wearing jeans and a white sweatshirt, came with a young child, perhaps 3 or 4 years, and two girls, about 5 and 7 respectively. Later two more boys and a girl came to join the group. It seemed as if the mothers were engaged in this activity with one or two children while others in their care were involved in other programs, as additional children later would arrive and some would leave, while the mothers stayed throughout.

Two of the little girls ran around the room chasing ping pong balls with paddles. Although Chad was officially there to help, he mainly made things himself with the clay. I asked him if he had worked with clay before and he told me, "Not for a long time." He worked quickly, rather frenetically I thought, trying to force together an ashtray. I tried to help him but I wasn't sure what he was trying to do. It was incredibly hard to hear—you had to get very close to people to hear what they were saying. I missed Deborah's demonstration because I had turned away briefly to talk with the room supervisor. I realized that my whole observation had occurred in that context—of not being actually able to hear what people were saying to each other at all. ...the effect was like watching TV with the sound off. I'm not sure how Deborah managed to explain to people what they were supposed to do, although apparently she had.

There were not enough chairs, and I had given mine up to one of the children. We were crowded into one corner of the room and it was difficult to move either along the outside edges of the chairs, down the narrow aisle between the clay table and the ping pong table or to squeeze between the chairs and the wall. Ping pong balls were continually flying into our area, and people took turns retrieving them and sending them back. (Deborah told me later that she felt like she needed to duck several times to avoid being hit in the head.) Standing back in the corner I kept having to move and began to feel like I was in the way and simply adding to the congestion. Eventually I moved out of the room and sat in the snack bar by the glass windows to watch. I felt relieved to be out of the crush and the din…

Everyone had started making coil pots. One of the small Asian girls was making a tiny one that was only about two inches in diameter. Chad scrapped the ashtray he was making and started building up coils, but had not made a base for his pot so there was a big hole in the middle. Later I saw him talking to Deborah, who gestured toward the hole, obviously wondering about it too. Soon after, I saw him out on the patio having a smoke. A young boy who had joined the woman in the white sweatshirt fashioned a long narrow clay form. He showed it to the woman and then to another boy who had just joined the group. Then he held it up with an outstretched arm, as if to show the whole room, the long object in front of the clenched fist of his other hand. I don't think it was a rocket ship.

Later I wrote in my journal that the two groups in the Games Room—those at the clay table and those at the games—seemed to be distinct in several ways—age and gender in particular.

In thinking about how art education was framed and influenced by this context, one might argue that in many ways this activity was not about making pots or art education at all. On one level, for example, this program was a demonstration of the East Side Center's attempt to comply with a new municipal mandate to incorporate more emphasis on art activity within leisure and recreation programs. The activity was 'free' in hopes of attracting participants from the surrounding area who might not have afforded it otherwise, or for whom art experience might be viewed as an unnecessary frill. Being free for participants, however, meant that costs must be recovered by the center, and there was little additional funding available. As such, the event was short-term, and the instructor's salary was quite low, lower than it would have been had she provided the same service in a center situated in a wealthier community across town.

The choice to hold the clay activity in the Games Room, however, was an attempt to attract some of the usual Games Room users, who were often reluctant to take part in activities in other parts of the center. It was deemed 'good' for these youth to diversify their leisure activity. I learned that the choice of location was also a statement by the center's administrators to the regular Games Room participants, that the room could be used for and by anyone, and that it was not only the domain of the male youth. There was a sense in which the center used this activity as a way of 'taking back' the room.

This event may be viewed as creating unique possibilities for art experience in some ways. It may well have attracted some participants who would not have attended under other circumstances, including a few of the regular games room participants who took part after the younger children were gone. Clearly, however, the setting was also a distraction for the young girls participating in the clay activity, and interfered with possibilities for teaching and learning due to the noise level and crowding in the room. Arguably, for Chad, this activity was actually a punishment and became a vehicle through which the center demonstrated its link to the state and its role in carrying out state authority. The choice of the space also inadvertently drew attention to the extent to which art experience may be associated with the feminine by highlighting the differences between the two groups in the room. At least one young boy seemed to sense this, and appeared compelled to demonstrate his male allegiance while participating.

The scene that I have shared is one example of many found in my research that suggested that art experiences in this site were negotiated with and permeated by the ideological and structural parameters of a particular recreation institution. Wenger (1998/1999) might argue that the program was in part a response to a reification—the new arts mandate—negotiated and interpreted in context. Fundamentally structured by economic issues and concerns, it also was used to support tacit agendas and underlying ideologies in the center. The excerpt spotlights traditional gender divisions within the organization as a whole, reflecting the history and traditions of managed recreation as preparation for the military and morally acceptable leisure activity for men (Rojek, 1993). It further reflects assumptions across Western society that associate leisure art with the feminine, and mirrors a tendency within the centers in which art is undervalued relative to overtly physical forms of leisure. In this setting, these ideas are all part of what can be learned about art—that it is acceptable to squeeze it temporarily into a facility that is built for something else, that it is appropriate for it to take place during an activity that will overwhelm it, and that it is something that requires little concentration. While activities like ping pong and foos ball can be practiced over and over in order to hone skill, clay work is something to try once. The 'teacher' here did not even have the authority to arrange the room in a way most conducive to participants' learning. In this one instance at least, clay work is just something different to do, an activity that is viewed as more appropriate than smoking on the patio or walking the streets and getting into trouble.

Still, there is a chance that a child might experience working with clay here for the first time, especially where space is not made for clay activity in schools. He or she might learn how to make a coil pot; find a sympathetic ear or mentor in an art instructor who does not have an obligation to evaluate one's progress; or share an important moment with a parent or sibling. Such settings do make choices possible for other ways to structure art experiences. Readers should be aware that this is just one rather negative example of art activity taking place in the setting. More in-depth and more positive experiences did sometimes take place, and both instructors and participants of these other activities cited numerous perceived benefits from art programming experiences in the centers. Like all educational contexts, this one provides both opportunities and constraints for art learning and teaching.

Importantly, however, while the activity of coil pot making is common across many art educational settings, this one is a manifestation of a complex and subtly distinct context. As such the knowledge and understandings through which actors justify and proceed with behaviors and practices can be very dissimilar to those in other settings. This is art education that is nested within a community of recreation practice and that is therefore unique on many levels. Moreover, I suggest that such distinctions occur to some extent within every environment in which art education takes place.

Conclusion

I have tried to articulate a vision of the field of art education as a complex network that embraces many particular contexts, each of which define themselves and proceed relative to each other and to wide social forces. I have argued the need both to recognize and comprehend tensions and competitions that exist among various art education providers. To the extent that each community providing art education is also distinct, no community of practice can be substituted for another. Changing the context for art education, it seems, does not merely change its location, but fundamentally alters possibilities for what can be learned and by whom. This means, for example, that it makes no sense to replace a school art education program with a non-formal one—nor vice versa. Each context creates both potential and constraints for art learning and experience.

Such a conception of the field is important because it acknowledges that some art educational providers may be more or less dominant, and more or less appropriate for certain forms of art experience, but it does not reduce the field to "schools" and "other." This perspective encourages us to move away from debates that cause schools and other art education providers to battle among themselves, but it does not preclude us from making value judgments related to what constitutes strong and weak art education. Instead, it implies that we need to ask the same questions of each and every site, schools and non-schools alike, and challenge each provider to engage with them. Such questions would include: What is the context—in all its complexity and on overt and tacit levels—that this setting provides for art education? What are all the things that this setting teaches? How do issues of economics and social hierarchy reveal themselves in this context? What is authorized and valued? What is the place of this organization relative to other providers and to the field of art? What is the relationship and is there a balance between reification and participation, between attempts to formalize practice and attempts to interpret it in everyday contexts (or settings)? How does this context provide possibilities and limitations for art experience and learning? These questions can open new ways of thinking about all forms of art education practice, allow us to learn from one another, and contribute to the ongoing tasks proposed by McFee (1986).

References

Apple, M.W. (1990). *Ideology and curriculum* (2nd ed.). New York: Routledge.

Blandy, D., & Congdon, K.G. (2001, March). Everyday life and arts administration. Presentation at the annual meeting of the National Art Education Association, New York.

Bolin, P.E., Blandy, D., & Congdon, K. G. (Eds.). (2000). *Remembering others: Making invisible histories of art education visible.* Reston, VA: National Art Education Association.

Bolton, R. (1993). Art as education. *New Art Examiner* 20(5), 12-16.

Bourdieu, P. (1984)). *Distinction: A social critique of the judgement of taste.* (R. Nice, Trans.). Cambridge, Massachusetts: Harvard University Press. (Original work published 1979).

Bourdieu , P. (1993). *The field of cultural production.* New York: Columbia University Press.

Boudieu, P., & Passeron, J. C. (1990). *Reproduction in education, society and culture* (2nd ed.). (R. Nice, Trans.). London: Sage. (Original work published 1977).

Bowles, S., & Gintis, H. (1976). *Schooling in capitalist America: Educational reform and the contradictions of economic life*. New York: Basic Books.

Chapman, L. (1978). *Instant art instant culture: The unspoken policy for American schools.* New York: Teachers College Press.

Chapman, L. (1992). Arts education as a political issue: The Federal legacy. In R.A. Smith & R. Berman (Eds.), *Public policy and the aesthetic interest: Critical essays on defining cultural and educational relations* (pp. 119-136). Urbana and Chicago. IL: University of Illinois Press.

Collins, G. (1995). Explanations owed my sister: A reconsideration of feminism in art education. *Studies in Art Education, 36*(2), 69-83.

Colucci, K. (2000). Negative pedagogy. In J. L. Paul & T. J. Smith (Eds.), *Stories out of school: Memories and reflections on care and cruelty in the classroom* (pp. 27-44). Stamford, CT: Ablex Publishing Corporation.

Congdon, K. (1998). Community arts programs: Definition and evaluation. In K. Congdon & D. Boughton, (Eds.), *Evaluating art education programs in community centers: International perspectives on problems of conception and practice* (pp. 175-183). Stamford, CT: JAI Press.

Congdon, K.G., Blandy, D., & Bolin, P.E. (Eds.). (2001). *Histories of community-based art education.* Reston, VA: National Art Education Association.

Congdon, K.G., & Boughton, D. (Eds.). (1998). *Evaluating art education programs in community centers: International perspectives on problems of conception and practice.* Stamford, CT: JAI Press.

Efland, A. (1976). The school art style: A functional analysis. *Studies in Art Education, 17*(2), 37-44.

Fowler, C. B. (1984). Who owns arts education? Some arts educators see the community as competition. *Design for Arts in Education, 86*(2), 4-7.

Giroux, H. A. (1992). *Border crossings: Cultural workers and the politics of education.* New York: Routledge.

Illich, I. (1971). *Deschooling society.* New York: Harper & Row.

Irwin, R. L., & Kindler, A. M. (Eds.). (1999). *Beyond the school: Community and institutional partnerships in art education.* Reston VA: National Art Education Association.

Lacy, S. (1995). *Mapping the terrain: New Genre public art.* Seattle, WA: Bay Press.

Lackey, L. (1997). Pedagogies of leisure: considering community recreation centres as contexts for art education and art experience. Unpublished doctoral dissertation, University of British Columbia, Vancouver, British Columbia.

Lackey, L. (1999). Art education wrapped/trapped in fun: The hope and plight of recreation centre art instructors. In R. Irwin & A. Kindler (Eds.), *Beyond the school: Community and institutional partnerships in art education* (pp 36-45). Reston, VA: National Art Education Association.

Lyotard, J-F. (1983). *The postmodern condition: a report on knowledge.* Minneapolis, MN: University of Minneapolis Press.

McFee, J.K. (1986). Describing the network called art education/Decrire le reseau baptise education artistique. *Canadian Society for Education through Art Journal, 17*, 7-12.

McRobbie, A. (1999). *In the culture society: Art, fashion & popular music.* London & New York: Routledge.

Rojek, C. (1993). *Ways of escape: Modern transformations in leisure and travel.* Houndsmills: MacMillan.

Trend, D. (1992). *Cultural pedagogy: Art/Education/Politics.* New York: Bergin & Garvey.

Stokrocki, M. (2002). Content & context: Participant observation research in art education since 1990. In M. Erickson (Ed.), *Translations: From theory to practice 11*(1), Summer 2002.

Wenger, E. (1998/1999). *Communities of practice: Learning, meaning, and identity.* New York: Cambridge University Press.

Wolff, J. (1993). *The social production of art* (2nd ed.). New York: New York University Press.

This article draws in part on a study completed for a dissertation (Lackey, 1997). I would like to thank and acknowledge Dr. Ellen Brantlinger and Dr. Enid Zimmerman, both of Indiana University, for their thorough and thoughtful editorial suggestions.

Endnotes

[1] This title is a reference to McFee, J. K. (1986). Describing the network called art education. *Canadian Society for Education Through Art Journal* 17, 7-12.

[2] The field notes presented in this article are excerpted from those collected for a qualitative study conducted between 1994-97 (Lackey, 1997). The study examined visual arts programming and art educational practices within the contexts of two community recreation centers situated within an urban Canadian West Coast Parks and Recreation Department. The research question guiding data collection and analysis was, "What is the context into which art programming in [these] community recreation centers is expected to fit and how does that context position and affect art teaching and art experience?" 250 hours of field work provided the opportunity to conduct extensive observations of numerous programs in the centers and to collect a wide range of documents and visual data that contributed to a description of the contexts. Open-ended interviews with center programming staff, art instructors, adult participants and parents of child participants focused on perceptions and experiences of art programming in the sites. Data were analyzed in order to generate themes relative to the research questions and to identify contradictions between formal and dominant organizational claims and alternative perspectives. Conclusions of the study argued that multiple tacit practices and agendas within the setting acted to interfere with intentions to implement a new arts policy within the settings. They further suggested that the practice of art educational activities took on particular meanings related to ideologies of leisure/managed recreation and were often understood in relation to and as distinct from schooling and education.

[3] In order to preserve anonymity, pseudonyms have been assigned to sites and individuals involved in this research.

ARTICLE SELECTION

Sweeny, R. W. (2004). Lines of Sight in the "Network Society": Simulation, Art Education, and a Digital Visual Culture. *Studies in Art Education,* 46(1), 74-87.

Doug Blandy

Senior Editor, 2007-2009

A primary purpose of education is to prepare young people to participate in democracy. As a consequence, it is necessary for art educators to engage with students as they develop as citizens. This includes assisting in their critical engagement with networked digital technologies such as those used for political purposes in 2008 by President Barack Hussein Obama's campaign. Significant also to Obama's election to the presidency was his campaign's strategic use of Web 2.0 capabilities. In part, young people persuaded to vote for Obama, were reached through the many social networking possibilities afforded by the Internet coupled with grassroots support networks on the ground. W. Lance Bennett (2008) would describe many of these voters as "actualizing" citizens favoring loose networks associated with interactive information technologies.

Robert W. Sweeny (2004) in his article "Lines of Sight in the 'Network Society': Simulation, Art Education, and a Digital Visual Culture" is among the first art educators to explore the terrain of Web 2.0 and offer insights on the ways in which art educators can assist their students to critically inhabit this network society. He does this by positing three theoretical "lines of sights" using metaphors from William Gibson (1984): cyborg, clone, and parasite. Sweeny also brings our attention to simulation and its use in artistic practice and its implications for art education. He brings these concepts together to begin to suggest a digital visual culture.

Douglas E. Blandy is Professor and Associate Dean for Academic Affairs in the School of Architecture and Allied Arts at the University of Oregon. His research and teaching attends to meeting the needs of all students with lifelong learning and to the relationships among art, education, community, and place. He has published in *Studies in Art Education, Art Education,* and *Visual Arts Research.* He has been associated with the editorship of five books. Dr. Blandy has received the Mary J. Rouse Award and the NAEA Manuel Barkan Research Award.

Over time, as digital technology becomes more multi-sensual, the visual culture orientation of this article will recede in importance. The multi-sensory examples of art used by Sweeny can be more fully addressed through approaches based in environmental aesthetics or material culture. However, his proposals for "tactically adapting spaces of flow" (p. 86) for art education practice will endure. Art educators will be using Sweeny's article as a point of departure for exploring the implications of Web 2.0+, the network society and as a means for considering and reassessing / re-imagining the role of

---

Chapter 17

technology in art education generally. For example, re-read and re-mix Vincent Lanier's (1973) conception of the uses of technology with Sweeny's appropriation of Castells' space of flows coupled with Gibson's cyborg/clone/parasite. Despite the 30 years that separate Lanier and Sweeny, each contributes to the understanding and appreciation of the other. Lanier's social purpose resonates with Sweeny, and it is fascinating to consider the space of flow being created by the students described by Lanier as they engaged in documentary and how their space of flow would be both the same and different today. Sweeny exemplifies the capability for research to ignite the imagination for public purpose.

References

Bennett, L. W. (2008). Digital natives as self-actualizing citizens. Retrieved November 13, 2008 from http://rebooting.personaldemocracy.com/node/79

Lanier, V. (1973). Art and the disadvantaged. In G. Battcock (Ed.). *New ideas in art education,* (pp. 181-202). New York: Dutton.

Lines of Sight in the "Network Society": Simulation, Art Education, and a Digital Visual Culture

Robert W. Sweeny

Cyberspace. A consensual hallucination experienced daily by billions of legitimate operators, in every nation, by children being taught mathematical concepts... A graphic representation of data abstracted from the banks of every computer in the human system. Unthinkable complexity. Lines of light ranged in the nonspace of the mind, clusters and constellations of data. Like city lights, receding... (Gibson, 1984, p. 51)

The social and technological networks that 'cyberpunk' science fiction author William Gibson (1984) has created serve as relevant forms of critique within our digital age. The Internet is possibly the most complex of these contemporary networks—connecting large portions of the world's population, allowing for new forms of communication and commerce, and the exploration of terrains previously unseen. This process of exploration represents both the exhilaration of newfound friendship and acquired knowledge, as well as the danger of power unchecked—the impulse to colonize these territories creating connections that constrain.

In *Neuromancer*, Gibson (1984) describes a future society that operates through various forms of simulation. Advancements in biomedical technology have allowed for rampant cloning and techno-human interfaces, allowing individuals to merge with the thoughts and actions of others through "simstim"—simulated stimulation. Individuals also have the ability to merge with computer systems in the vast geometries of cyberspace, the "simulation matrix" that combines aspects of the physical world with the virtual qualities of data.

Gibson's term "cyberspace" is now commonly used to describe the Internet—the contemporary networks of physical infrastructure and ephemeral interactions that include the text and image oriented webpages of the World Wide Web, the communication-based interactions of e-mail and Instant Messenger, and the recent diary-like weblog (blog) phenomenon. His descriptions of networked interactions have been equally influential in works of literature, popular movies, and video games. These highly influential fictions have had a direct impact on the language and perception of simulated interactions that take place on the Internet, affecting numerous aspects of contemporary lives lived within increasingly complex networks.

This article will explore the role that simulation plays in contemporary artistic practice, specifically looking at individuals and collectives that create and critique using tactics that are unique to our interconnected times. The simulation of visual information facilitated by networked digital computers challenges many Western art historical traditions and complicates the current discussion of visual culture and art educational practices.

This analysis of simulation will provide art educators with examples of critical practices that might then find application within the spaces of art education: practices that operate within the complex interconnections of the "network society."

The "network society" as described by Castells (1996) represents an interlinking of networked digital technologies with global trade and social interaction. As he suggests, there are no aspects of contemporary life that lie outside of complex social, cultural, and technological networks, no individual whose actions are not in some way interconnected with those of another. From the massive power outages that affected large portions of the northeastern United States in the summer of 2003 to the War on Terror, in which many nations are confronted by a dispersed web of terrorists, the notion of the decentralized network is of particular relevance in contemporary life. Addressing the role that art educators play within these complex networks—particularly those that make use of and reference digital forms of simulation—might lead to practices that are socially relevant and technologically critical, that help us to think through current moments of unthinkable complexity.

I will first describe the notion of simulation as it relates to the operations of contemporary computer systems. I will then discuss general network attributes, making connections between technological and pedagogical forms of interaction. Following this discussion I will describe artistic practices that operate within complex socio-technical networks. Finally, I will outline the possibilities for approaches to art education that respond to and participate within these networks, describing 'lines of sight' that intersect to form the matrix of a digital visual culture.[1]

Simulation and Art Education

Contemporary computer systems operate through processes based in simulation. From the early battle scenarios that helped to bring about the computer age, to video games such as SimCity that mirror and possibly mold contemporary life, simulation is essential to digital information processing (Manovich, 2001). The importance of networked computer systems within the lives of many has led sociologist Sherry Turkle (1995, p. 10), in *Life on the Screen*, to propose the existence of a "culture of simulation" that has profound influence within contemporary societies:

> We come to see ourselves differently as we catch sight of our images in the mirror of the machine.... A rapidly expanding system of networks, collectively known as the Internet, links millions of people in new spaces that are changing the way we think, the nature of our sexuality, the form of our communities, our very identities. (Turkle, 1995)

Turkle (1995) refers to the reflective nature of the computer screen, a visual metaphor that results in the doubling of the image of the individual computer user. She explores this process of multiplication through an analysis of online activities of computer users, and concludes that these 'simulated' virtual identities are not far from the roles that each of us plays in various daily situations. They do, however, lead to a notion of identity that is decentralized rather than unified, related to the operations of contemporary computer networks as well as much postmodernist theory (Turkle, 1995).

The primary focus of this article concerns interconnections between Internet-based art, art education, and digital technologies, informed by the concept of the decentralized network. Networked digital technologies function through the creation, manipulation, and transformation of data, a process best described as simulation. Unlike previous mechanical technologies that reproduced information from an original source, such as the photographic image derived from an actual event, contemporary computer systems operate by translating data into various forms, simulating rather than reproducing, calling the notion of originality into question (Nichols, 1996, Baudrillard, 1994). The complex interactions that take place within the decentralized structure of Internet reflect these processes; simulation should therefore be understood as a process that underlies many of the interactions within the network society. If art educational spaces were organized according to the decentralized structure of the Internet, then could such a model allow for a socially relevant, critically oriented approach to art education?

Various Internet-based approaches have been proposed within art educational literature. The Internet has been described as a tool for research (Dunn, 1996), a method for community building (Krug, 1997), a forum for interaction (Heise & Grandgenett, 1996). The possibilities for Internet-related aesthetic production, and how these technologies might involve new forms of creation and critique, are rarely discussed. It may be instructive to look at examples of these practices, as they may allow art educators to develop socially relevant approaches informed by attributes of networked digital technologies.

While general aspects of simulation and digital networks have been recently addressed by Krug (2002), much of the discussion of networked digital technologies in art education has emphasized issues related to the creation of hypertextual documents (Keifer-Boyd, 1997; Taylor & Carpenter, 2002, 2003; Tavin, 2002). Hypertext has the potential to illuminate connections between subject matter and modes of learning, particularly in regard to inquiry that draws upon a wide variety of visual cultural sources.

Arthur Efland (1995) offers a description of this type of decentralized curriculum. In *The Spiral and The Lattice: Changes in Cognitive Learning Theory with Implications for Art Education,* he describes the general relationship between educational content and methodology:

> It is assumed that certain arrangements of knowledge will enhance learning if, in some appropriate way, they are patterned after the structures of knowledge of the domain being taught, and that ultimately these structures enable learners to represent domain knowledge to themselves in flexible ways for effective application in relevant situations. (Efland, 1995, p. 135)

In order to challenge the dominance of traditional art educational curricular models, Efland compares the spiral model of cognition developed by Jerome Bruner in the 1960s to a lattice-like structure represented by the hypertext curriculum proposed by Spiro, Coulson, Feltovich, and Anderson in 1988. He suggests that a lattice type model for curriculum might better represent the learning that takes place in the "ill-structured domain" of art, based on Alexander's (1988) analysis of planned and unplanned cities.

Many similarities exist between the lattice-like structures described by Efland (1995) and the structure of the Internet: connections illuminated through Gibson's (1984) descriptions of cyberspace. Gibson's (1984) "constellations of data" resemble the geometric, grid-like structures common to Modernist architectural forms, and represent the monolithic institutional entities that attempt to maintain control within these virtual spaces (Bukatman, 2000). His protagonists typically hack into these structures through the adaptation of codes and the modification of passwords. Efland (1995) suggests a curricular model that is flexible, allowing for multiple forms of interpretation and implementation, and for students to individualize their art educational experiences.

If the centralized, spiral curricular structures common within art educational practice were instead based on the model of the decentralized network, a more complex version of Efland's lattice, then might the result be a pedagogy that is adaptive to changing social, educational, and technological conditions? The integration of digital technologies within educational programs that are organized according to socially dated modes of thought is problematic. It is, at the very least, quite challenging for art educators to address the complexities of the current personal, social and aesthetic shifts related to networked digital technologies through practices based in simplified geometries and analog technologies.

I will now present an overview of the concept of the "network society" as it relates to current discussions of visual culture in art educational literature, in order to explore the possibilities for pedagogical approaches influenced by decentralized networks such as the Internet.

Visual Culture and Everyday Life in the "Network Society"

As Gibson (1984) suggests, digital technologies are associated with multiple changes at many levels of society. A similar dynamic is described by Castells (1996) in *The Rise of the Network Society*. He states that much of the world's population is interconnected through contemporary networks of global trade, telecommunication, and commerce, including but not limited to digital technologies, and that these connections represent a new worldview. It is not so much that everyone is a member of the same society, but that multiple societies are interconnected, with the potential to develop new relationships, new communities, new societies. Castells's "network society" is not one in which each person on the planet has equal access to information, goods, or power. It represents the complex contemporary social connections that allow many to interact, while excluding many more.

While the "network society" reinforces many preexisting social inequities, Castells (1996) suggests that it also presents new possibilities for interaction, communication, and empowerment. The technologies that form the Internet best represent these possibilities:

People, institutions, companies, and society at large transform technology, any technology, by appropriating it, by modifying it, by experimenting with it. This is the fundamental lesson from the social history of technology, and this is even more so in the case of the Internet, a technology of communication... Since our practice is based on communication, and the Internet transforms the way in which we communicate, our lives are deeply affected by this new communication technology. On the other hand, by doing many things with the Internet, we transform the Internet itself. A new socio-technical pattern emerges from this interaction. (Castells, 1996, pp. 4-5)

Castells develops his theory of the "network society" through what he calls "spaces of flow" (p. 442). The first layer of flow is the physical basis for the network society: "The first layer, the first material support of the space of flows, is actually constituted by a circuit of electronic exchanges" (p. 442). These circuits are the technological infrastructure that allow for exchanges of information to take place, or exclude individuals, groups, or even societies from participation.

The second layer of flow is composed of the nodes and hubs that distribute information within the network.[2] Nodes and hubs are created by the idiosyncratic flows of information within networks, modifying the existing materiality through active exchange. While nodes and hubs are established according to preexisting hierarchies, Castells (1996) states that these aspects of the network are not static: "This hierarchy may shift depending on the evolution of activities processed through the network" (p. 440). He indicates that initial networks evolve through complex interactions between institutions and individuals.

The third layer of flow relates to the power of the individuals and organizations that use the network: "…the spatial organization of the managerial elite" (p. 445). This layer indicates the presence of institutional power within networks, often connected to the ownership of the material infrastructure. However, decentralized networks such as the Internet provide the opportunity for individuals to shift these power structures.

The relationship between the materiality of the Internet, its forms of interaction, and potential for various power arrangements leads to the possibility for new flows, for individuals to combine energies and redistribute power along alternate paths. The combination of a material infrastructure that is decentralized, layered with the ability for a vast range of users to actively modify the informational flows within the network has created an Internet that is almost impossible to manage. The interplay between top-down hierarchical forms of control such as passwords and firewalls and bottom-up, individualized redirections of power are crucial aspects of an Internet that exhibits potential for both oppression and empowerment.

The decentralized spaces of flow that comprise the "network society" help to describe the complexities of the structure of the Internet. They might also be informative for art educators who wish to gain a better understanding of the challenges related to increasingly complex visual networks, particularly those related to the notion of visual culture.

Visual culture is based upon the societal impulse to represent information in a visual manner, as Mirzoeff (1998) proposes:

Visual culture does not depend on pictures but on [the] modern tendency to picture or visualize existence…. One of the key tasks of visual culture is to understand how these complex pictures come together. They are not created from one medium or in one place, as the overly precise divisions of academia would have it. Visual culture directs our attention away from structured, formal viewings like the cinema and art gallery to the centrality of visual experience in everyday life. (p. 7)

Art educators have provided convincing arguments that acknowledge the relevance of these everyday aesthetic sources, such as professional wrestling (Duncum, 2002), television shows (Freedman and Schuler, 2002), and shopping centers (Stokrocki, 2002). The Internet certainly contributes to the increasing amount of visual information that comprises everyday experiences in the network society. What effect does the simulation of information central to the operations of the Internet have upon the impulse to visualize existence? What are the social implications of a digital visual culture?

Castells (1996) proposes that one of the products of the "network society" is a shift in traditional notions of space and time:

…the new communication systems radically transforms space and time, the fundamental dimensions of human life. Localities become disembodied from their cultural, historical, geographical meaning, and reintegrated into functional networks, or into image collages, inducing a space of flows that substitutes for the space of places. (Castells, 1996, p. 406)

These composite forms of experience relate to the notion of simulation as well as the previously discussed concept of a decentralized identity proposed by Turkle (1996). The image collage also emphasizes the role that vision plays within the network society, intertwining complex layers of institutional information, cultural interaction, and everyday experience, contributing to the complexity of digital visual culture.

The Internet represents not only a new form of communication, but also entirely new forms of visuality.[3] Information transmission and translation that flows through the Internet often takes visual form, but more often shifts between forms of visuality, textuality, and sound-based information, a unique process related to new media art that Manovich (2001) describes as transcoding. This transcoding can also be seen in everyday online interactions: "emoticons" are images formed through text character combinations that attempt to interject emotion, typically using facial expressions.

The ability for individuals to transcode digital information provides the opportunity for the creation of new forms of communication and vision. As de Certeau (1984) suggests, individuals have the power to create "openings of established technological networks," through tactics that modify existing institutional structures (The Practice of Everyday Life, p. 49). The network society that Castells (1996) describes is shaped through the interplay between individualized tactics and institutional strategies. The tactical activities of artists and collectives, described by de Certeau (1984) as representing an "aesthetics of tricks" (p. 26), may indicate the potential for further adpatation on the part of contemporary art educators.

In order to explore the challenges related to art education in the network society, it is necessary to inquire as to the cultural and social implications of these tactical network adaptations. The need for such inquiry is particularly necessary in art educational spaces, as the simplicity and the seductiveness of digital technologies may distract educators from questioning the potential for critical application and creative response. A critique of simulation as related to visuality is necessary for an art education that is socially responsible, culturally relevant, and critically oriented. Failure to do so might reinforce preexisting power structures, creating connections that restrict rather than instruct.

In order to explore these everyday transformations as they relate to networked art educational practices, I will identify three tactical forms of aesthetic trickery that operate through the modification of Castells's decentralized "spaces of flow." I will analyze these networked artworks in order to raise possibilities for art educational practices that address methods of critique that are actively formed in actual and virtual spaces—forms of communication that clarify and challenge previous notions of visuality. These three "lines of sight" represent forms of tactical adaptation related to simulation and vision within the network society, connecting individuals, objects, and institutions, forming the matrix of a digital visual culture.

Lines of Sight in a Digital Visual Culture

Gibson (1984) and Castells (1996) describe the complexities of social technological networks. The possibilities for tactics that critique these connections of individuals, objects and institutions may be better understood using metaphors drawn from Neuromancer: the cyborg, the clone, and the parasite. These are metaphors specific to complex networks that might help art educators to better understand the implications of artistic creation and critique within the network society.

Cyborg Vision. The first line of sight that I will discuss connects individuals and machines. The individual that interacts with others on the Internet begins to see aspects of identity simulated on the computer screen (Turkle, 1995). These reflections contribute to a culture of simulation, offering the potential for the 'real' user to critique his or her 'virtual' representation and question the boundaries between both. The combination of human and machine as cybernetic organism, or cyborg, represents the possibility for the critique of binary distinctions, as described by Haraway (2003). Garoian and Gaudelius (2001) have recently argued for the relevance of a cyborg pedagogy within art educational practice. Their discussion of the Australian performance artist Stelarc indicates the potential for embodied critique within the network society. I agree, and suggest that Stelarc also represents a valid critique of the contemporary networks that connect individuals and computers.

Stelarc has created numerous performance-based works that challenge the boundaries between human and machine. Works such as *Ping Body* (1993) involve intricate networks combining human interaction, machine augmentation, and Internet connections. Attaching electrodes to major muscle groups on his body, Stelarc allowed users from remote sites to send information into his server, which transcoded this information into sound and electrical impulse, moving his body outside of his control. Describing *Ping Body* in his essay From Psycho-body to Cyber-systems (2000), Stelarc states:

The usual relationship with the Internet is flipped—instead of the Internet being constructed by the input from people, the Internet constructs the activity of one

---

body. The body becomes a nexus for Internet activity—its activity a statistical construct for computer networks. (p. 571)

Establishing his body as a node within the Internet, Stelarc relinquishes partial control of his body, addressing the power that accompanies contemporary digital networks. The electrical impulses that make up the informational exchanges on the Internet are intertwined with the electrical impulses of the human nervous system, resulting in movements that simulate the autonomy of individual action, allowing for a critique of both systems. As Garoian and Gaudelius (2001) state: "Stelarc's body, and the constructed nature of our understandings of his body, is questioned just as this questioning also addresses the 'pure intelligence' of the Internet" (p. 341). Through this process, Stelarc reverses generally accepted characterizations of human and machine activity. The inverted relationship between machine network and operator, passive objects and active subject, creates a situation in which the human body is objectified, where the development of cybernetic feedback loops is resisted, and the body is dominated by electrical input. Stelarc performs the oppressive potential of life in the network society, adapting the materiality of his body, creating new forms of machine/human interaction that challenge his artistic authorship, his power as an autonomous individual.

The notion of "cyborg pedagogy" might be expanded to include a variety of transformations that accompany Internet use: the everyday cyborgs that develop through tactical e-mail communication, Instant Messenger interaction, and the digital dialogues that allow us to envision new perspectives within the network society. The simulation that Stelarc presents relates to a form of vision that is inextricably linked with digital technologies. These are technological networks that have the potential to both inhibit sight and to extend the range of human vision beyond biological boundaries, perhaps simultaneously. His work points to a distributed visuality that is unique within the network society: cyborg vision?

The metaphor of the cyborg raises issues related to contemporary everyday computer use. The networks that continue to develop between individuals and machines should be critically analyzed, as they have changed notions of identity and visuality. Art educators have the opportunity not only to discuss these issues as they relate to educational practice that is increasingly networked, but to construct responses that lead to further critique—to see the self reflected in the computer and the computer reflected in the self, within the network society.

Cloned (Ap)Perception. The second line of sight concerns networks of objects and their simulations. The individual that creates works of art on the Internet sees the potential for this object to multiply, challenging the notions of originality and authenticity that are central to Western aesthetics in the process. The simulated object created through digital processes, described by Jean Baudrillard (1994) as simulacra (a copy without an original) might offer educators the opportunity to analyze the aspects of their practice that are based in forms of simulation. Students that are socially linked through file sharing and multitasked machine interactions may be able to respond to these situations critically, and understand the relevance of the aesthetics of cloning within the network society.

Vuk Cosic is a Slovenian artist who uses the network structure of the Internet to critique similar issues. His works, which he calls "digital readymades," function as examples of cloned digital information that challenge issues of authenticity and originality, updating the iconoclastic activities of Marcel Duchamp in the early 20th century (Greene, 2000). His work consistently critiques new media art on the Internet, while pointing to the possibilities for accomplishing this critique in a playful, subversive manner. Some of his most notorious projects have treated portions of films as digital readymade, such as the infamous pornographic film *Deep Throat,* transforming them through the use of the outmoded computer code ASCII.

Logging on to www.ljudmila.org/ascii, the viewer sees a black screen with neon green characters covering the central rectangular portion. Depending on the speed of the Internet connection, the viewer then sees moving images represented by text-based ASCII characters. The grain of the original film is replaced by text characters that estimate the value of the individual bits, a process that, once again, relies upon the notion of transcoding. The once invisible grain of the film stock is now made visible through the program that translates the tonal range of the original film. Instead of a full color range, however, the film is now shown in various shades of green.

This translation is a playful, potentially offensive example of the simulation that is central to computer operations, and the accompanying shift in visuality brought about by cloned information. Through Cosic's code manipulation, the computer makes an approximation of the value of each grain of the original film, similar to a heavily pixilated digital image. The film plays as I watch the images move, yet I am constantly reminded of the transcoding that is taking place. I am also reminded, from time to time, that the simulated film is in fact pornographic. The graphic scenes play out probably much in the same way as early porn images were distributed on the Internet: grainy, pixellated, 'dirty.'

Cosic's cloned version of *Deep Throat,* copied from a copy of a copy, complicates Walter Benjamin's (1968) description of the relationship between developing technologies and related modes of viewing, which he relates to the "shock value" of film. Benjamin suggests that the technique of film montage created a state of apperception in the viewer, due to the continual distractions constructed by the filmmaker. The viewer eventually adapts to this state, but not before his or her method of perception is permanently altered, resulting in a new mode of (potentially revolutionary) social interaction that challenges the authenticity of the original work of art that is central to Western aesthetic models.

Cosic's ASCII films fluctuate between apperception and strained perception, as the film constantly shifts between code and image. Simulated pornographic images are made to 'flicker' between states—between reading and seeing—in a manner unique to digital information (Hayles, 1999). These flickering images lead to new forms of interaction, making visible the code that underlies the process, and challenging the power of the pornographic image to provide instant gratification. Cosic's project stands as a complex example of the challenges to traditional, fixed forms of vision that are inherent to digital information. *Deep Throat* is an appropriation based in a process of cloning that demonstrates radical possibilities for critical artistic production in a network society, made possible through the ease of digital simulation.

What are the connections between the work of Cosic and the spaces of art education? While viewing pornography would not be considered appropriate in most classrooms, art educators might benefit from an analysis of the everyday translations that accompany reproduced images central to many forms of instruction. Art educators who acknowledge the processes that allow for various reproductions used in practice—slides, posters, textbook images, not to mention the banners, advertisements, and consumer products that merge within educational spaces—might find the opportunity to critique these practices. A critical analysis of mechanically reproduced forms of visuality such as film or photography would lead to the much needed analysis of the changes in vision associated with digital information, and the challenges of an aesthetics of cloning within the network society.

Parasitic Double-Vision. The third line of sight consists of the networks created between individuals and institutions. Individuals are beginning to use the decentralized structure of the Internet to analyze and critique their positions within larger institutional structures. The network society offers new possibilities for critique within a visual culture that is increasingly formed of everyday images caught by videocameras, cell phone cameras, and visual surveillance technologies. These technologies represent a visual culture in which images equate with normalized behavior and questionable ethics—where images become layered with questions of social responsibility and civil liberty.

The Surveillance Camera Players (SCP) is a loosely defined collective made up of active members located around the world, who use simple means in order to confront public surveillance technologies. Their primary goal is to utilize existing surveillance camera networks in order to present short skits and plays, which often have direct references to the politics of surveillance, civil liberties, and constitutional rights within the network society. Their performances are often spontaneous, and are rarely seen by a public beyond those in the vicinity of the camera.

The SCP utilizes a number of complex networks in their activities. They have taken advantage of the Internet through events such as World Surveillance Day, which utilized the global network in order to organize and synchronize performances related to surveillance technologies. They also create a network of grass-roots style activism through the use of a variety of media: photocopied flyers, news broadcasts, and the surveillance images themselves. Using the materiality of existing media in order to create new forms of interaction, the SCP connect with a decentralized network of political activism and aesthetic tactics that can inform a pedagogy critical of the panoptic gaze in operation within most educational spaces (Sweeny, 2004).

The individual that connects with others through the Internet might begin to see the potential for collective action and tactical response, in the manner of the Surveillance Camera Players. Their ephemeral actions that operate within the gaze of the surveillance camera, as opposed to techniques of avoidance or aggression, might be described as parasitic: they drain power from the larger institutions without resulting in their demise

(Shaviro, 2003). When the informational flows that make up the network society include the images that can be read as representing suspicious behavior, it creates a situation in which vision is politicized. Through a doubling of the functions of the surveillance cameras, a tactic related to the Situationist practice of detournement (Baumgaertel, 2001), the SCP critique the social functions of these technologies without an attempt to suppress their original intent.

Art educators might find opportunities for similar forms of critique within educational spaces that often reinforce privileged form of visuality. The 'double vision' represented by the performative tactics of the SCP allows for multiple interpretations to exist simultaneously, and might influence educational responses that simulate power relationships in order that they might be critiqued. The networks of vision that develop within art educational spaces, the eyes that each see from a different position, might be acknowledged through parasitic forms of critique; translating lines of sight into power, influencing and informing art educational practice in the network society.

'Like city lights, receding …'

These are the lines of sight related to simulated forms of visuality in the network society that, if addressed by art educators, might begin to form a digital visual culture pedagogy. Each example that I have discussed is based in a process of simulation, tactically adapting the spaces of flow described by Castells (1996). Art educational practice might be organized according to these flows, creating decentered scenarios that are adaptable, that accommodate multiple technological perspectives. The critique of the complex technological networks that connect the self and the 'other,' the object and the clone, and the individual and the institution may allow for new approaches within the field of art education, if these networks are continually viewed from new angles, and are connected with previous approaches and familiar forms of vision. The networks that result may lead to forms of pedagogy based on socially relevant forms of critique and creation—envisioning new lines of sight within the matrix of a digital visual culture.

References

Alexander, C. (1988) A city is not a tree. In J. Thakara (Ed.), *Design after modernism: Beyond the object* (p. 67-84). New York: Thames and Hudson.

Barabási, A. (2002). *Linked: The new science of networks*. Cambridge, MA: Perseus Books.

Baudrillard, J. (1994). *Simulacra and simulation*. (S. F. Glaser, Trans.). Ann Arbor, MI: University of Michigan. (Original work published 1981)

Baumgaertel, T. (2001). Interview with Bill Brown (surveillance camera players). (Available on-line at: www.rhizome.org. accessed 4/04)

Benjamin, W. (1968). The work of art in the age of mechanical reproduction. In H. Arendt (Ed.) *Illuminations* (H. Arendt, Trans.). New York: Schocken. (Original work published 1955).

Bukatman, S. (2000). Terminal penetration. In D. Bell & B. Kennedy (Eds.) *The Cybercultures Reader* (p. 149-174). New York: Routledge.

Castells, M. (1996). *The rise of the network society*. Malden, MA: Blackwell.

Clark, G.A., Day, M. D., & Greer, W. D. (1989). Discipline-based art education: Becoming students of art. In R. Smith (Ed.). *Discipline-based art education: Origins, meaning, and development.* (p. 129-193). Urbana: University of Illinois Press. (originally published 1987)

de Certeau, M. D. (1984). *The practice of everyday life.* (S. Rendall, Trans.) Berkeley, CA: University of California Press.

Dunn, P. (2001). More power: Integrated interactive technology and art education. *Art Education, 54*(6). 6-11.

Duncum, P. (2002). Wrestling with tv "rasslin." *The Journal for Social Theory in Art Education, 22,* 103-119.

Efland, A. (1995). The spiral and the lattice: Changes in cognitive learning theory with implications for art education. *Studies in Art Education, 36*(3). 134-153.

Freedman, K., & Schuler, K. (2002). Please stand by for this important message: Television in art education. *Visual Arts Research 28*(2), 16-26.

Garoian, C., & Gaudelius, Y. (2001). Cyborg pedagogy. Performing resistance in a digital age. *Studies in Art Education, 42*(4). 333-347.

Gibson, W. (1984) *Neuromancer.* New York: Ace Books.

Greene, R. (2000, May). Web work: A history of Internet art. *Artforum, 38,* 162-167, 190.

Hayles, N. (1999). *How we became posthuman: Virtual bodies in cybernetics, literature, and informatics.* Chicago: University of Chicago.

Haraway, D. (2003). A cyborg manifesto: Science, technology, and socialist-feminism in the late twentieth century. In A. Jones (Ed.), *The feminism and visual culture reader.* (pp. 475-496). New York: Routledge.

Heise, D., & Grandgenett, N. (2001). Perspectives on the use of Internet in art classrooms. *Art Education, 54*(6), 12-18.

Keifer-Boyd, K. (1996). Interfacing hypermedia and the Internet with critical inquiry in the arts: Preservice training. *Art Education, 49*(6), 33-41.

Keifer-Boyd, K. (1997). Interactive hyperdocuments: Implications for art criticism in a postmodern era. In J. Hutchens & M. Suggs (Eds.), *Art education: Content and practice in a postmodern era* (p. 122-131). Reston, VA: National Art Education Association.

Krug, D. (2002) Electronic media and everyday aesthetics of simulation. *Visual Arts Research, 28*(2), 27-37.

Krug, D. (1997) Electronic learning communitites in art education. *Arts and Learning Research, 14*(23).

Manovich, L. (2001). *The language of new media.* Cambridge, MA: MIT Press.

Mirzoeff, N. (1998). What is visual culture? In N. Mirzoeff (Ed.), *The visual culture reader* (pp. 3-13). New York: Routledge.

Nichols, B. (1996). The work of culture in the age of cybernetic systems. In T. Druckery (Ed.) *Electronic culture* (pp. 121-143). Cambridge, MA: MIT Press.

Prater, M. (2001). Constructivism and technology in art education. *Art Education, 54*(6), 43-48.

Shaviro, S. (2003). *Connected, or what it means to live in the network society.* Minneapolis: University of Minnesota.

Stelarc. (2000). From psycho-body to cyber-systems: Images as post-human entities. In D. Bell & B. Kennedy (Eds.), *The cybercultures reader* (p. 560-576). New York: Routledge.

2000s

Stokrocki, M. (2002). Shopping malls from preteen and teenage perspectives. *Visual Arts Research,* 28(2), 77-85.

Sweeny, R. (2004). Between devil and detournement? Situationist tactics as critical inquiry in educational spaces. *Journal of Surveillance and Society.* Available FTP: Hostname: surveillance-and-society.org.

Tavin, K. (2002). Engaging advertisements: Looking for meaning in and through art education. *Visual Arts Research,* 28(2), 38-47.

Taylor, P., & Carpenter, S. (2003, Fall). Racing thoughts: Altering our ways of knowing and being in art through computer hypertext. *Studies in Art Education,* 45(1). 40-55.

Taylor, P., & Carpenter, S. (2002). Inventively linking: Teaching and learning with computer hypertext. *Art Education,* 55(4), 6-12.

Tolva, J. (1996). Ut pictura hyperpoesis: Spatial form, visuality, and the digital word (on-line document available at: http://www.cs.unc.edu/~barman/HT96/P43/pictura.htm. accessed 7/04)

Turkle, S. (1995). *Life on the screen: Identity in the age of the Internet.* New York: Touchstone.

Endnotes

[1] I use the phrase "lines of sight" to emphasize the role that vision plays within contemporary digital networks, and to imply the possibility for multiple perspectives within these networks. The term "matrix" is drawn from both the popular film series and computer science: "The network of intersections between input and output leads in a computer, functioning as an encoder or a decoder" (source: dictionary.com, retrieved 7/2004).

[2] Nodes represent the intersection of lines of communication, while hubs are heavily-connected nodes that serve as distribution points. See Barab-si (2002) for a detailed account of network structures.

[3] I will use the term visuality to refer to the complex sociological and biological relationships between what we see (the visual image or object) and how we see (vision). As Tolva (1996) suggests, digital information in hypertext form complicates the distinctions between reading and seeing, shifting visuality in the process.

s

ARTICLE SELECTION

Garoian, C. R., and Yvonne M. Gaudelius, Y. M. (2004). The Spectacle of Visual Culture. *Studies in Art Education*, 45(4), 298-312.

Kristin Congdon

Senior Editor, 2009-2011

Since the demise of Discipline-Based Art Education, (DBAE), the field of art education has turned to visual culture studies as a focus. Recent articles in *Studies* have reflected this change, in the same manner that they have always reflected new movements. It therefore seems appropriate to select an article that discusses what seems to be the most important movement or approach to art education in the first decade of the 21st century. "The Spectacle of Visual Culture," is striking in its ability to give depth to the visual culture discussion.

Charles Garoian and Yvonne Gaudelius are two of art education's most forward thinking scholars. They have written together many times, both before and after "The Spectacle of Visual Culture" was published in 2004. This article is a precursor to their 2008 book *Spectacle Pedagogy: Art, Politics, and Visual Culture* (State University of New York Press), which further explores ideas raised in this article.

The authors recognize that we live in a culture that is defined largely by spectacle. Recent examples include the opening and closing ceremonies for the 2008 Beijing Olympics and the Democratic and Republican National Conventions. Beyond the scale of the images that are currently being produced in these and myriad other events, is the quantity of images that we are bombarded with in our lives. Indeed, as the authors tell us, we are consumed "*by* and *in* images" (p. 299).

I have selected this article to highlight in this anthology for a number of reasons. The authors have repeatedly drawn our attention to the spectacle of our postmodern culture, and they continue to provide us

Kristin Congdon has taught art in a variety of settings, including public schools, correctional settings, treatment facilities, museums, and universities. She is Professor of Philosophy and Humanities at the University of Central Florida and Director of the Cultural Heritage Alliance. She has published extensively, including books on folk art, community arts, and feminism in an effort to celebrate artists and who have had little visibility in the art world. She has also been a World Congress Member for the International Society for Education Through Art and the president of the National Art Education Association's Women's Caucus.

with ways to examine and address it. They draw their research from interdisciplinary sources that raise issues about embodiment, subjectivity, social and political context, technological change, and cultural narcissism. Giving depth to the study of visual culture studies (or material culture studies), an area of exploration that sorely needs it at this time in our history, they demonstrate how "the conceptual strategies of collage, montage,

---

assemblage, installation, and performance art " can be used to "expose, examine, and critique the spectacle of visual culture" (p. 298). The focus of the discussion is on how images function as mediators of social relationships among people as they teach us how to think, behave, and relate to the world around us. It is critical that we understand how this process works and how we can responsibly respond, especially as we activate ourselves against social injustice.

There are many critical issues facing our field and our lives in this rapidly changing world. Instead of retreating from these issues, Gaudelius and Garoian repeatedly ask us to face these issues while providing us with the skills and know-how to make a difference in the world. I strongly believe that if we can embrace this kind of work as our goal, then art education's future can be bright.

The Spectacle of Visual Culture

Charles R. Garoian and Yvonne M. Gaudelius

In a society dominated by the production and consumption of images, no part of life can remain immune from the invasion of spectacle.

—Christopher Lasch, 1991, p. 122

The spectacle is the acme of ideology, for in its full flower it exposes and manifests the essence of all ideological systems: the impoverishment, enslavement and negation of real life.

—Guy Debord, 1967/1994, p. 151

Given the pervasive domination of society by visual culture through television, the movies, the Internet, advertising, and other forms of corporate production, the field of art education is currently in the process of defining curricular and pedagogical practices that will enable students to expose, examine, and critique the essentialized and immutable codes of mass mediated delivery systems. Is the critique of visual culture by art educators a legitimized form of voyeurism? Does the desire to covet its pleasures represent a form of cultural narcissism? What distinguishes between pleasure and criticism in the study of visual culture in art education?

While such distinctions have been well established by scholars in the field (Chapman, 2003; Freedman, 2003; Kindler, 2003; Tavin, 2003; Wilson, 2003), in this article we will extend these arguments by conceptualizing visual culture as spectacle pedagogy. Spectacle, according to cultural critic Guy Debord (1967/1994), "is not a collection of images; rather, it is a social relationship between people that is mediated by images" (p. 12). Or, as critical theorist Douglas Crimp (Takemoto, 2003) explains it, "an image isn't simple negative or positive but rather is the product of social relations and produces contradictory social effects" (p. 85). As visual pronouncements, images are ideological, they teach us what and how to see and think. They influence our choices and how we interact with one another. Considering this influence, we internalize the spectacle pedagogy of visual culture as naturalized dispositions in the body. In doing so, we constitute our identities as "one dimensional," according to cultural critic Herbert Marcuse (1972). Bereft of criticality, one-dimensional thought is "populated by self-validating hypotheses which, incessantly and monopolistically repeated, become hypnotic definitions or dictations," (Marcuse, 1972, pp. 24-25).

We characterize the spectacle pedagogy of visual culture in two opposing ways in this article: first, as a ubiquitous form of representation, which constitutes the pedagogical objectives of mass-mediated culture and corporate capitalism to manufacture our desires and determine our choices; and second, as a democratic form of practice that enables a critical examination of visual cultural codes and ideologies to resist social injustice. As the former, spectacle pedagogy functions as an insidious, ever-present form of propaganda in the service of cultural imperialism; the latter represents critical citizenship, which aspires toward cultural democracy. To resist the monocular regime of spectacle seduction, historian Martin Jay (1988) suggests a plurality of vision to "wean ourselves from the fiction of a 'true' [dominant cultural] vision and revel instead in the possibilities opened up by the scopic regimes we have already invented and the ones, now so hard to envision, that are doubtless to come" (p. 20).

A plurality of vision provides a framework for an inclusive democracy that has the possibility of yielding multiple perspectives, discourses, and understandings about cultural life. Short of such plurality, we argue that the undeniable lure of cultural spectacle becomes a form of narcissistic pathology. The current rise in private and public forms of surveillance through mass mediation supports this understanding of our desires to be consumed by and in images. As cultural critic bell hooks (1996, p. 2) suggests, there are those of us who consume visual culture to be entertained and there are those who seek it out to learn something. While visual culture in both these cases functions pedagogically, we argue that it is in our desire to learn something from it as we are constituted as critical spectators.

The Manufacture of Spectacle

Cultural critic Siegfried Kracauer (1963/1995) conceptualized the spectacle of visual culture as "the mass ornament," a metaphor that he used to typify the ornamental patterns of the Tiller Girls, a synchronized dancing group in the 1920s, and corresponded their synchronized legs with workers' hands in a factory. By comparing the "capitalist production process" with that of "the mass ornament" he distinguished each of them as an "end in itself" (Kracauer, pp. 76, 78). While ignorant of the obvious gender stereotypes embedded in his choice of metaphor, Kracauer's comparison of the performers and spectators of the mass ornament to workers used like component parts in a mechanized division of labor in modern factories corresponded with the rational plan of Taylorism (p. 78). He states: "The ratio that gives rise to the ornament [spectacle] is strong enough to invoke the mass and to expunge all life from the figures constituting it … it is the rational and empty form of the cult, devoid of any explicit meaning, that appears in the mass ornament" (p. 84). Thus for Kracauer, as the insidious spectacle of visual culture constructs its constituent/component performers and spectators, it mutes their private, individual values, meanings, and desires for the good of the mass ornament.

While Kracauer and the cultural critics of the Frankfurt School, namely Walter Benjamin and Theodor Adorno, wrote about the mechanized body of the mass ornament in the 1920s, later theorists such as economist Kenneth E. Boulding in the mid-1950s, and the historian Daniel J. Boorstin and media theorist Marshall McLuhan in the early 1960s, described what they were experiencing as the growing social, political, and economic effects of mass mediated images. These scholars explained our propensity to conceptualize and represent the reality of cultural life in images as a disposition that is epistemologically grounded. For Boulding (1961), beginning with the invention of writing to contemporary forms of imaging, the dynamic of a society is predicated on the assumption that "the image [as a 'dissociated transcript'] not only makes society, society continually remakes the image" (pp. 64-65).

Boorstin describes the same dynamic as "pseudo-events spawn[ing] other pseudo-events in geometric progression" (1987, p. 33). "Pseudo-event" is Boorstin's designation for the spectacle of visual culture, which is the creation and dissemination of mass mediated images of cultural experience whose truths, realities, and meanings are complicated with ambiguity to arouse and captivate public interest (Boorstin, 1987, pp. 11, 35). Boorstin's notion of the pseudo-event corresponds with Adorno's earlier characterization of the "pseudo-personalization," which denotes the commodity fetishism created by the spectacle "culture industry" of capitalism (Adorno, 1991, p. 173). For McLuhan (1964), electronic media served as an organic extension of the body's nervous system, namely its instantaneous and simultaneous electric communications capability that manifests the body's "passive" rather than "active" experience (McLuhan, 1964, p. 219; Boorstin, 1987, p. 188). Thus, by extension, systems of electronic delivery such as the television, the computer, and the Internet are organically linked to the body, as McLuhan suggests, hence enabling an experience of their digitized visual culture that is paradoxically vicarious yet impelling, as its ever-present images construct and determine our bodies' choices and desires.

Given its mass appeal, the power of spectacle culture is in its pedagogical functioning. Its captivating visual stimulus overwhelms and arrests our bodies' attention and in doing so inscribes it with the self-validating ideology of commodity culture, a form of "titillation" that journalist Lawrence Weschler refers to as "Pavlovian" (Bernhard, 1998). With its persistent indoctrination and commodification of our bodies, spectacle culture continues to establish itself as a driving force in determining both private and public desires, which media critics Edward S. Herman and Noam Chomsky (1988) refer to as the "manufacture of consent." Significant about their characterization of the power of the media is its paradoxical pedagogy of "debate, criticism, and dissent," which unlike that of radical democratic practice enables and perpetuates the commodity culture of corporate capitalism (p. 302).

This "politics as spectacle," as cultural critic Christopher Lasch (1991) has labeled it, represents a form of propaganda that "create[s] in the public a chronic sense of crisis, which in turn justifies the expansion of executive power and the secrecy surrounding it" (p. 78). Political historian Timothy Mitchell (1998) claims that this dominant order of criticality represents the "world-as-exhibition" where citizens are "continually pressed into service as [complacent] spectators" (p. 298). As such the critique that yields the world-as-exhibition by Madison Avenue advertising and other forms of mass mediation manufactures our "narcissus fixation" with this cultural spectacle, which occludes our critical understanding of its content as commodity fetishism (McLuhan, 1964, p. 33; Marcuse, 1972, p. 25; Lasch, 1991, p. 47).

Art educator Neil C. M. Brown (2003) raises similar concerns about the paradox of "advocating" and "elevating" popular culture, "under the banner of Cultural Studies, to a state of 'seriousness' commensurable with the high arts" (p. 286). Such advocacy for visual

---

culture studies can very well replicate the authorized transgressions of corporate capitalism while ignoring the potential of visual culture to resist social injustice. The danger of focusing on the critical deconstruction of visual culture, as an end in itself is an immanent one that leads to an "ethical cynicism that provides no guarantees for social reconstruction in the practice of art education," argues Brown (p. 288).

In effect, what appears as transgressive pedagogy may not always be the case claims cultural historian Elizabeth Wilson (quoted in hooks, 1996).

We transgress in order to insist that we are, that we exist, and to place a distance between ourselves and the dominant culture. But we have to go further—we have to have an idea of how things could be different, otherwise transgression is mere [narcissistic] posturing. In other words, transgression on its own leads eventually to entropy, unless we carry within us some idea of transformation. It is therefore not transgression that should be our watchword, but transformation. (p. 26)

Given that contemporary cultural life is always already immersed in spectacle, we affirm the necessity for a broad and inclusive understanding of visual cultural studies through a "plurality of scopic regimes," which includes the transgressive and transformative power of artmaking. Indeed, for the purposes of art education curriculum and pedagogy, this inclusive understanding is imperative.

The Spectacle of Politics and the Politics of Spectacle

Well, you weren't surprised were you? Did you expect anything less spectacular from Mr. Universe-turned-Conan the Barbarian-turned-Terminator-turned-Kindergarten Cop-turned-movie star-turned-business man-turned-multi-millionaire-turned Governor? Muscle man Arnold Schwarzenegger has done it yet again, reinvented himself as he staged a last minute, all out campaign to recall and replace incumbent Governor Gray Davis in the circus-like climate of the California gubernatorial race in October 2003. With no previous experience in government, his only claim to the national political scene was having strategically married into the Kennedy clan. Only fate would have it that this union of the political right and left would yield a viable candidate in the future. In true Hollywood movie-making fashion, "Arnold" has always understood the visual hyperbole and power of the spectacle to turn people's heads, to fix their gaze, to command attention, to use his own vanity to mirror the public's narcissistic desires. As Boorstin (1987) suggests, as a human pseudo-event, a "celebrity [like Schwarzenegger] is a person who is known for his well-knownness" (p. 57).

Banking on Schwarzenegger's larger than life persona, the myth of his filmic characters, "his well-knownness," his highly publicized campaign influenced not only a large voter turn out, but he also won at the polls by an unexpected, overwhelming margin. Whether referring to his constituents as "viewers" during his campaign or being referred to by them as having the makings of a "strong governor" because of his body's behemoth bulk, he successfully marketed himself by using his star appeal to gain the support of the voters.

Backed by a team of wealthy, high-profile business, media, and political strategists, Schwarzenegger's campaign was quickly, albeit carefully orchestrated with just the right amount of words, the right amount of interviews, the right amount of debates, the right amount of commercial time in the media, and the right amount of dollars, all of which ironically correspond with cultural critic Susan Sontag's (1977, p. 180) polemical appeal for an "ecology of images"—not to mention an ecology of gubernatorial candidates given the field of 135 nominees—albeit with a capitalist twist. This campaign was a case where not knowing what to say, not wanting to say anything, not knowing how to debate ironically worked in the candidate's favor.

Apropos Schwarzenegger's awesome spectacle in the California political scene, literary critic Roland Barthes (1977) characterized the snare of the photographic image in the electoral myth-making process as follows. "Inasmuch as photography is an ellipse of language and a condensation of an 'ineffable' social whole, it constitutes an anti-intellectual weapon and tends to spirit away 'politics' (that is to say a body of problems and solutions) to the advantage of a 'manner of being', a socio-moral status" (p. 91). Indeed, Barthes, Boorstin (1987, p. 61), and literary critic Louis Menand (2004, p. 84) argue that the mirror of photography, which can also be attributed to television and visual culture in general, enables a narcissistic complicity whereby political candidates and their voters find likenesses in each other. As the candidate is exalted through her/his photogenic qualities, "the voter is at once expressed and heroized, he/[she] is invited to elect himself/ [herself], to weigh the mandate which he/[she] is about to give with a veritable physical transference" (Barthes, 1977, p. 92). Thus, similar to the objectifying gaze of psychoanalyst Jacques Lacan's mirror (1977, pp. 1-2), Schwarzenegger's constituency bestows him and is in turn bestowed with mythic power. This relinquishment of reality to myth "depoliticizes speech," argues Barthes, and in doing so, myth empties reality of its history and naturalizes its historical insignificance (1977, pp. 142-143). For philosopher Richard Rorty (1979), the philosophical idea of such a self-referential epistemology, which assumes that knowledge mirrors the world in the form of mythic representations, must be continually challenged with the critical pragmatism of cultural history and politics.

According to journalist Andrew Sullivan, Arnold represents a "new kind of politician." "In our political wars, he's a synthesis. In our culture wars, he's a truce," qualities that Sullivan attributes to Arnold's blend of fiscal conservatism and social liberalism (Sullivan, 2003, p. 88). "[Arnold] was one of the first major movie stars who winked at the audience, understanding that they too were intelligent enough to see through the pyrotechnics and absurd dialogue to be amused by the pure entertainment of the spectacle" (p. 88). Indeed, the 1993 film Last Action Hero corroborates the irony of Schwarzenegger's wink. A depiction of "blockbuster mentality and movie fan obsession…[the film] clearly plays to an ironically intertextual mode of address as the film within a film simultaneously plays to and satirizes the high-octane Schwarzenegger star vehicle," explains film critic Rebecca D. Feasey (n.d.). What Sullivan and Feasey have identified in Arnold is a shrewd man whose identity is constructed by and for the media.

Given his essentialized position within the culture, is Schwarzenegger's mixture of right and left politics trustworthy? Considering his clever use of irony in his films, does the parody of his "wink" serve as a critical gesture to entertain and perpetuate institutionalized and corporate politics, or does it serve as a genuine disruption to resist social injustice? Art educator jan jagodzinski (2003) believes it is the former. He asserts that while Hollywood's wink lets the audience "know that what they are watching is simply exaggerated artifice," it nonetheless creates the 'false consciousness' [in the Marxian sense] of the "capitalist subject" that outwardly resists corporate capitalism while believing in its myth on the inside (pp. 108-109). Likewise, literary critic Linda Hucheon (1985) suggests that the parody of the Hollywood wink, while appearing subversive, in actuality is an "authorized transgression" (p. 26), "authorized by the very norm it seeks to subvert. Even in mocking, parody reinforces; in formal terms, it inscribes the mocked conventions onto itself, thereby guaranteeing their continued existence" (p. 75).

Insofar as the mass media demands viewers' loyalty to the spectacle of visual culture, it constructs their identities as "fanatics," or in the more innocuous and acceptable use of the word as "fans." Sociologist Pierre Bourdieu (1990) explains that such objectification of everyday life

constitutes the social world as a spectacle offered to an observer who takes up a 'point of view' on the action and who, putting into the object the principles of his relation to the object, proceeds as if it were intended solely for knowledge and as if all the interactions within it were purely symbolic exchanges. (p. 52)

While poet, critic, and philosopher Samuel Taylor Coleridge (1817/1985) long ago suggested experiencing spectacular symbolic exchanges through "the willing suspension of disbelief for the moment that constitutes poetic faith," such willingness to surrender one's critical faculties leaves one vulnerable to being consumed and co-opted by the commodity motives of visual culture claims Debord (1967/1994). Debord's manifesto-like aphorisms in The Society of the Spectacle (1967/1994) were written "with the deliberate intention of doing harm to spectacular society" (p. 10). They represent his vigilant positioning to expose, examine, and critique the acculturation of socially and historically constructed symbolic representations and dispositions of spectacle culture, the habitus against which Bourdieu suggests one has to "situate oneself within 'real activity' …the preoccupied, active presence in the world through which the world imposes its presence, with its urgencies" (1990, p. 52).

Bourdieu's concept of the "real" is not that of "Reality TV" where fame seeking contestants are paid to perform bizarre, and often emotionally and physically dangerous feats on television shows like Survivor, Dog Eat Dog, Fear Factor, and The Bachelor to confront the reality of their individual fears. The trivialized notion of "challenge" on these shows represents an extreme example of commodity fetishism, an insatiable appetite for gazing at others, who, while serving as our surrogates, undertake ridiculous risks for our pleasure and our hope of attaining sublime levels of personal experience, albeit vicariously, while we sit complacently in the comfort and safety of our living rooms. For jagodzinski (2003) the desire for such vicarious thrills valorizes the "jouissance," the "pleasure of resistance" and in doing so creates the fertile conditions of late capitalism, by constituting "subversive and destabilized [multiple and fluid] identities who seek new modes of enjoyment through forms of romanticized resistances" (pp. 107, 115). For Bourdieu (1990), such pleasured, internalized dispositions and idealisms of the social world impelled by visual culture, habitus, represents a social reality that is consistent with Barthes's (1977) characterization of mythic power, which "depoliticizes critical speech."

Cultural critic Jean Baudrillard (1994) concurs as he explains that the unidirectional gaze of the Panopticon is no longer a fitting metaphor for television. Given that its simulations now precede reality, we "no longer watch TV, it is TV that watches [us] (live)" (p. 29). The paradoxical crisis of Reality TV, its enabling of "being there without being there," abolishes participatory citizenship as it blurs the distinction between viewers' passive and active involvement in society and, in doing so, purges society of its political dimension (pp. 22-30). To challenge such complacent dispositions, Barthes (1991, p. 119) calls for a response to images that probes beyond the conformity of the spectacle and into an "ecstatic," embodied depth of being where the self cannot be tamed. It is within such an embodied depth, we argue, that we can find a space for transformation.

In his prescient essay "Cult of Distraction," cultural critic Siegfried Kracauer (1963/1995) echoes Barthes's imperative for confronting the "empirical habits" of photographic spectacle. Kracauer makes a case for the importance of exposing, examining, and critiquing "the mass ornament" to resist the regressive politics of historicism, the assumption that history is coherently constructed. Insofar as "distraction" exposes the complex and contradictory circumstances of contemporary cultural life it ruptures and makes possible a critical turn in the apparent flow of history. Thus, the disclosure of the spectacle of visual culture is morally and ethically significant, according to Kracauer, as it enables a critique of its mass-mediated codes and delivery systems (p. 326). If the potential for its critique is not realized the distraction of spectacle culture becomes transgressive unto itself as it takes on a cult status that results in the self indulgent, voyeuristic culture of narcissism (p. 326).

Visual Culture and its Encounter with Art[1]

It is no mere coincidence that the mediums of collage, montage, assemblage, installation and performance—arguably five of the most significant contributions of the 20th century to the history of art—emerged during a century of mass mediated production. Visual artists beginning with the Cubists, Futurists, Dadaists, and Constructivists at the beginning of the century through to the performance and installation artists of the 1980s and 1990s understood the power of visual culture and the need to contextualize the allure of its spectacle within art in order to problematize the authority of its capitalist ideology. Such exploration and improvisation of new images, ideas, and utopian representations are critical for the survival of subjectivity in contemporary times. While the multicentric representations of artists who used these mediums suggested early signs of postmodernity during the first part of the 1900s, these artists nevertheless retained the political and aesthetic objectives of the Modernist patriarchy until the late 1960s and early 1970s. During the period of the Civil Rights Movement, The Feminist Movement, and the anti-war demonstrations of the Vietnam War, these modes of representation were fully re-constituted as agonistic strategies in the service of postmodern identity politics.

Since then, contemporary artists like Rachel Rosenthal, Barbara Krueger, Cindy Sherman, David Wojnarowicz, Guillermo Gómez-Peña, The Guerrilla Girls, and others have used these mediums' liminal, contingent, and ephemeral strategies to challenge social and political injustice. Given the Feminist slogan, "the personal is political," they focused on performances of subjectivity, through transgressive artistic acts constructed from private memory and cultural history that in the face of dominant politics of public, institutionalized culture represent social activism in the arts. Some of the most provocative of these performances are those that are "site-specific," occurring within the very public places of dominant culture. Krzysztof Wodiczko, a Polish born contemporary artist who spent the first half of his life in the Soviet Union and now resides in Canada and the United States, is one such contemporary artist whose public, site-specific, multi-media performances in international politically charged hot spots are aimed at enabling a public discourse on cultural oppression. Wodiczko explains, "Public space is a site of enactment. It belongs to no one, yet we all are a part of it and can bring meaning to it" (Phillips, 2003, p. 35). Having lived in a closed, oppressive society, Wodiczko's objective with public art is the attainment of cultural democracy through critical citizenship.

An artist who uses the strategies of collage, montage, assemblage, installation and performance art interchangeably, Wodiczko believes in intervening and challenging the oppressive cultural forces that determine our choices, desires, and uses of new and emerging technologies. His recent performance in the U.S., The Mouthpiece (2003), consisted of outfitting aliens, residents, non-residents, legal or illegal immigrants, with an electronic audio/video recording "instrument," worn over the mouth ironically like a gag, to speak out in public spaces where they are ordinarily silenced and perceived invisible. The wearer of the instrument is able to pre-record a video image and audio voice of his or her mouth in the act of speaking and to replay and re-perform it in a time and space of their choosing. Such work echoes poet Audre Lorde's (1984) call for the use of language to transform silence into action. Lorde recognizes that there are many reasons why we might stay silent, "fear of contempt, of censure, or some judgment, or recognition, of challenge, or annihilation. But most of all, I think, we fear the visibility without which we cannot truly live" (p. 42). What both Lorde and Wodiczko have realized is that without finding a means through which we can speak, transformation is impossible.

Considering the spectacles of racial profiling, "zero tolerance" at the U.S. borders, and the general hysteria over international terrorism, which have raised suspicions about and silenced the Other since the attacks of 9/11, this and other works by Wodiczko serve as poignant metaphors in speaking to, challenging, and resisting the mass media's globalization of xenophobia. For Wodiczko, The Mouthpiece serves as "democratic artifice," one that

> points to the absurdity of any attempt at depriving speech rights in a democratic society. It responds to the actual political process and experience of such deprivation,

while at the same time it helps to translate this disadvantage into a new advantage. In other words, it is an instrument whose function is to empower those who are deprived of power. (Wodiczko, n.d.)

Similar to his other public performances, Wodiczko situates the body in a "live, performance assemblage" composed of heterogeneous, independent remnants of visual, electronic culture. In the spirit of philosophers Gilles Deleuze and Felix Guattari (1987), the body in Wodiczko's work serves as a "desiring machine" as it "deterritorializes" stereotypical representations of mass mediated culture as component parts and "reterritorializes" them within the context of art in order to create new knowledge and unforeseen visual and conceptual machinations (pp. 54-55). By considering the body as a component part in this way, Wodiczko "grafts" its materiality with that of other remnants, electronic devices in the case of The Mouthpiece, each serving as a "prosthetic" to enable the body to perform its subjectivity against the grain of dominant cultural politics. Thus the contingent space of assemblage and performance art represents a public agonistic site for Wodiczko, where the oppressed can participate in cultural politics in active rather than passive ways by "step[ping] out of their communities, to engage in independent speech. When they return [to their communities] it is with a form of agency and insight" (Phillips, 2003, p. 42).

The underlying principles of collage, montage, assemblage, installation, and performance art are their disjunctive, segmented, and often-disparate representations of visual forms. As such, these mediums represent acts of perception as disjunctive associations between and among cultural experiences—dissociations, which enable spectators to participate in the creation of meaningful yet mutable conjunctions. The dissociations of these mediums assume that all human experience is disjunctive, a problematic epistemology that requires creative conjunctions to enable new and differentiated understandings. These mediums cite and site visual culture within the context of art and, in doing so, serve as powerful metaphors of how the phenomenon of visual culture is always already constituted as disjunctive within society.

The Undecidable Pedagogy of Artmaking

The potential of collage, montage, assemblage, installation, and performance art in the enactment of critical pedagogy for visual culture in art education lies in their dissonant spaces, at the contested borders that exist between their dissociative remnants. Such "in-between" spaces for media and education critic Elizabeth Ellsworth (1997) are conceptually and emotionally charged. Their "volatility" is caused by the "imperfect fits" among the remnants of mass mediated culture found in these art forms (pp. 38-39). Citing cultural critic Shoshanna Felman's (1987) writing about Freudian and Lacanian psychoanalytic pedagogy, Ellsworth argues that the slippage and indeterminacy of knowledge that occurs within these volatile spaces, creates an errant, "undecidable" condition where meaning is continually negotiated and teaching as a position of absolute authority is rendered "impossible."

Using the medium of film as a pedagogical metaphor, Ellsworth (1997) claims visual culture is constituted by its "mode of address," the means by which the mass media assumes to know who its audience is and what it desires. Based on these assumptions, the objectives of the mass media are to construct audience members' subject positions as consumers of visual culture. Nevertheless, Ellsworth argues that the imperfect fits between the mode of address in visual culture and viewers' responses make it "possible to see the address of a text [and/or image] as a powerful, yet paradoxical, event whose power comes from the difference [undecidability] between address and response" (p. 37). Concerning critical pedagogy, Ellsworth asks an important question about the undecidability that is enabled by the paradoxical mode of address of visual culture:

What might a teacher make of the eventful and volatile space of difference or 'misfit' between who a curriculum thinks its students are or should be [their subject positions] and how students should actually use a curriculum's [mode] of address to constitute themselves and to act on and within history? (p. 37)

Thus, given the misfits between students' and the teacher's curriculum, Ellsworth argues that the pedagogical challenge is not one of transgression but transformation.

Ellsworth's theory of impossibility is good news for critical art educators given that it opens a dialogic space within which to critique the spectacle apparatus of visual culture. Her concept of "imperfect fits" corresponds with the disjunctive, paradoxical association between academic school curricula and students' personal memories and cultural histories. Given that students are always already immersed in visual culture, their personal experiences and perspectives serve as "montage" remnants within the classroom, differing modes of address that provide opportunities for their critical intervention and transformation. As a pedagogical metaphor the undecidable conditions that are created by the imperfect mode of address of visual culture and students' performances of subjectivity enables them to learn about and challenge the commodity fetishism of the spectacle of visual culture.

The slippage and undecidability of meaning that occurs in Ellsworth's in-between spaces is consistent with cultural critic Michel Foucault's (1972) "enunciative function," a mutability that enables language to resist and transgress the boundaries of codified culture. According to Foucault, the enunciative function assures such slippage through the complexity and contradiction of language (p. 105). It is within the gaps that separate the specific, paradoxical, and multivocal conditions of the enunciative function that transgressive and transformative representations and interpretations are possible. As such, the infinite potential of the enunciative function of language represents for Foucault an "archaeology of knowledge," whereby socially and historically codified representations are "excavated," examined and critiqued (p. 206).

Using the strategies of collage, montage, assemblage, installation, and performance art, contemporary artists' create volatile spaces within their art works to evoke the enunciative function. In doing so, cultural critic Carol Becker (2002) claims artists' works assume the role of 'immanent critique,' in a dialectical sense, which is to say that instead of offering superficial solutions, they expose society's inherent contradictions; and instead of pursuing absolute truths, they offer complexity, ambivalence, and, at times, aggressive confrontations with the status quo. (p. 17)

The critical strategies enabled through collage, montage, assemblage, installation and performance art suggest that these mediums represent a significant means through which art students can learn to create immanent critiques of the spectacle of visual culture through artmaking.

To avoid misunderstanding, we are not limiting the concept of immanent critique merely to students' collage, montage, assemblage, installation, and performance art projects in the classroom. Rather, we are suggesting that these modes of address have broader implications for challenging the dominant codes of contemporary cultural life given their volatile in-between spaces, which are constituted by the disparate, dissociative remnants of mass-mediated culture. Considering that the postmodern condition is pervasively mediated by visual culture, our awareness of its dominating assumptions, and our ability to expose, examine, and critique its spectacle make the critical pedagogy of collage, montage, assemblage, installation, and performance art all the more imperative.

Hence, the specific use of these art mediums for student assignments notwithstanding, all creative activities be they in the art classroom, the school in general, or the culture at large, present the possibility for cultural resistance if understood as immanent critiques. Assuming that to be the case, these classroom artmaking activities immanently qualify as examples of Kracauer's concept of critical "distraction," Barthes's "photographic ecstasy," McLuhan's and Lasch's critique of "narcissus fixation," and Ellsworth's "pedagogy of volatile spaces" when students are presented with opportunities to understand the critical and paradoxical relationship between their artmaking activities and the academic dispositions, the habitus of institutionalized schooling, and between the images and ideas that they create through art and the sensationalized pedagogy of the spectacle of visual culture. Therein lies the potential of artmaking for transgressive and transformative experiences in visual culture.

References

Adorno, T. (1991). *The culture industry.* London: Routledge.

Barthes, R. (1977). *Mythologies.* New York: Hill and Wang.

Barthes, R. (1991). *Camera lucida: Reflections on photography.* New York: Hill and Wang.

Baudrillard, J. (1994). *Simulacra and simulation.* Ann Arbor: The University of Michigan.

Becker, C. (2002). *Surpassing the spectacle: Global transformations and the changing politics of art.* Lanham: Rowman & Littlefield.

Bernhard, B. (1998, June 26-July 2). Calamity of excellence: Lawrence Weschler laments the loss of journalism that asks for nothing but our attention. LA Weekly. Retrieved December 18, 2003 from <http://www.laweekly.com/ink/printme.php?eid=1565>

Boorstin, D. J. (1987). *The image: A guide to pseudo-events in America.* New York: Atheneum.

Boulding, K. E. (1961). *The image: Knowledge in life and society.* Ann Arbor: The University of Michigan.

Bourdieu, P. (1990). *The logic of practice.* Stanford: Stanford University.

Brown, N. C. M. (2003). Are we entering a post-critical age in visual arts education? *Studies in Art Education, 44*(3), 285-289.

Chapman, L. H. (2003). Studies of the mass arts. *Studies in Art Education, 44*(3), 230-245.

Coleridge, S. T. (1985). Biographia literaria. In J. Engell & W. J. Bate (Eds.), *The collected works of Samuel Taylor Coleridge,* Volume 7. Princeton: Princeton University. (First published 1817)

Debord, G. (1967/1994). *The society of the spectacle.* New York: Zone.

Deleuze, G., & Guattari, F. (1987). *A thousand plateaus: Capitalism and schizophrenia.* Minneapolis: University of Minnesota Press.

Ellsworth, E. (1997). *Teaching positions: Difference, pedagogy, and the power of address.* New York: Teachers College, Columbia University.

Feasey, R. D. (n.d.). Last action hero. Retrieved January 24, 2004 from <http://www.nottingham. ac.uk/film/journal/filmrev/last-action-hero.htm>

Felman, S. (1987). *Jacques Lacan and the adventure of insight: Psychoanalysis in contemporary culture.* Cambridge: Harvard University.

Foucault, M. (1972). *The archaeology of knowledge: And the discourse on language.* New York: Pantheon.

Freedman, K. (2003). *Teaching visual culture: Curriculum, aesthetics, and the social life of art.* New York: Teachers College Columbia University.

Herman, E. S., & Chomsky, N. (1988). *Manufacturing consent: The political economy of the mass media.* New York: Pantheon.

hooks, b. (1996). *Reel to real: Race, sex, and class at the movies.* New York: Routledge.

Hucheon, L. (1985). *The theory of parody: The teachings of twentieth-century art forms.* New York: Methuen.

jagodzinski, j. (2003). Unromancing the stone of "resistance": In defence [sic] of a continued radical politics in visual cultural studies. *The Journal of Social Theory in Art Education, 23,* 104-139.

Jay, M. (1988). Scopic regimes of modernity. In H. Foster (Ed.), *Vision and visuality* (pp. 3-23). Seattle: Bay Press.

Kindler, A. M. (2003). Visual culture, visual brain and (art) education. *Studies in Art Education, 44*(3), 290-295.

Kracauer, S. (1995). *The mass ornament: Weimar essays.* Cambridge, MA: Harvard University. (First published 1963)

Lacan, J. (1977). *Écrits: A selection* (A. Sheridan, Trans.). New York: W. W. Norton.

Lasch, C. (1991). *The culture of narcissism: American life in an age of diminishing expectations.* New York: W. W. Norton.

Lorde, A. (1984). The transformation of silence into language and action. In A. Lorde, *Sister outsider: Essays and speeches* (pp. 40-44). Trumansburg, NY: Crossing Press.

Marcuse, H. (1972). *One dimensional man.* London: Abacus.

McLuhan, M. (1964). *Understanding media: The extensions of man.* New York: Signet.

Menand, L. (2004, January 5). Masters of the matrix: Kennedy, Nixon, and the culture of the image. *The New Yorker,* 82-86.

Mitchell, T. (1998). Orientalism and the exhibitionary order. In N. Mirzoeff (Ed.), *The visual culture reader* (pp. 293-303). London: Routledge.

Phillips, P.C. (2003). Creating democracy: A dialogue with Krzysztof Wodiczko. *Art Journal, 63*(4), 32-49.

Rorty, R. (1979). *Philosophy and the mirror of nature*. Princeton: Princeton University Press.

Sontag, S. (1977). *On photography.* New York: Farrar, Straus & Giroux.

Sullivan, A. (2003, October 20). Pumping irony. *Time, 162*(16), 88.

Takemoto, T. (2003). The melancholia of AIDS: Interview with Douglas Crimp. *Art Journal, 62*(4), 80-91.

Tavin, K. (2003). Wrestling with angels, searching for ghosts: Toward a critical pedagogy of visual culture. *Studies in Art Education, 44*(3), 197-213.

Wilson, B. (2003). Of diagrams and rhizomes: Visual culture, contemporary art, and the impossibility of mapping the content of art education. *Studies in Art Education, 44*(3), 214-229.

Wodiczko, K. (n.d.). Krzysztof Wodiczko. Retrieved December 26, 2003 from <http://www.mit.edu:8001/afs/athena.mit.edu/course/4/4.395/www/krystof/krystof.html>

Conclusion: The Future of Research and Theory in Art Education

Kerry Freedman

It often seems as if the only people who read research in a field are graduate students and the professors who teach them. However, building a research agenda is important to all layers of an educational field. Part of a research agenda for a pragmatic field, such as art education, must be determined by the questions and problems of practitioners, policy makers, and other stakeholders who do not themselves conduct research. Fortunately, most researchers in art education have been K-12 or community educators and have a deep understanding of the problems and possibilities of practice. So, a research agenda for art education can be understood as being built on a foundation of both research and practice and determined by the ways in which new research and theory can move beyond that past. Research in art education can have a greater influence on policy makers, school administrators, researchers outside the field, and teachers not only through the collection of new information, but by innovative questions and creative methods used to construct new knowledge. *Studies in Art Education* can help to facilitate that influence.

If this influence by art educators is to occur, at least three changes to research in art education are required. First, more attention should be paid to common topics of research so that lines of inquiry are formed and continued over long periods of time. This means that groups of people must work together to determine what research should be done to answer particular research questions or respond to a set of problems. Research and theory needs to be based on previous research in and across lines of thought so that questions are not only answered, but extended. This does not mean that a single answer will suffice; in art education, many answers often work better than a single answer. But, it does mean that researchers and theorists conduct work that contributes to the field and that other scholars help them to continue and deepen lines of inquiry by critiquing and extending their work. Some examples of persistent themes referred to in this text are artistic development, multiculturalism, technological conditions and applications, and gender issues and identities. But, although some individual researchers have deepened their study of a topic over time (many of whom are the Senior Editors of *Studies in Art Education* and the article authors represented in this text), these vital themes and others have tended to be investigated in a sporadic manner considering the richness of possibility they suggest for supporting and improving art education. For example, these themes have rarely been addressed in ways that specifically relate to high school students.

As illustrated by the articles in this book, and by many others in *Studies in Art Education*, art educators have been very successful in when it comes to theorizing and making change in curriculum foundations; the transformations that have occurred in the late 20th- and early 21st century concerning visual culture in art education are evidence of this. However, we have been less successful with basic research and other lines of inquiry, such as those focusing on issues of policy, leadership, and learning. To sustain itself, the field must include research that focuses on complex questions, but we are also in dire need of basic research, such as demographic studies, which support the development of more complex lines of inquiry.

Second, we need to attend to gaps in theory and research and the ways these gaps break down larger arguments that support the field. For example, a review of the articles in this volume indicates that we could reasonably revisit several research topics that have lost favor in art education, such as the notion of creativity. Eisner's challenge to the term and its application reveal deep concerns for its use in art education. Most art education policy statements made in the early 21st century do not include the term "creativity," and few include any terms that suggest the ambiguous and multifarious character of the arts. The word "creativity" was not included in the early 2000s Illinois State art exams because the pyschometrician test developers claimed that it could not be assessed with pencil tests. Also, other reasons exist for a lack of attention to the idea of creativity in art education scholarship, such as its connection to forms of art education that do not fit in this historical moment. Issues concerning artistic production require continual reconsideration and the idea of creative practice is one of these. It is often the case that old ideas need to be left behind because they have been challenged and rejected or because some new ideas require breaks with the past, but revisiting the more powerful of these old ideas in a new light can strengthen the field by helping us to review, critique, and construct better arguments.

Third, increased rigor is required in both the development of questions and the selection and application of research methods. Issues concerning methods of research emerge in this volume, such those related to the role of empirical-analytical studies of art education. Empirical-analytic research is based on the assumption that people can quantify, control, and predict educational settings, processes, and outcomes within an acceptable range. The methods and procedures for this type of research may include, for example, developmental studies, surveys, correlational studies, experiments, and quasi-experiments. However, other types of empirical research exist that emerge from questions about the symbolic nature of experience, such as those that lead to case study and ethnographic methods and depend on procedures such as interviews, participant observation, and role-